Culture and Customs of Ethiopia

Culture and Customs of Ethiopia

SOLOMON ADDIS GETAHUN
AND WUDU TAFETE KASSU

Culture and Customs of Africa
Toyin Falola, Series Editor

GREENWOOD

AN IMPRINT OF ABC-CLIO, LLC
Santa Barbara, California • Denver, Colorado • Oxford, England

Library of Congress Cataloging-in-Publication Data

Getahun, Solomon Addis, author.
  Culture and customs of Ethiopia / Solomon Addis Getahun and Wudu Tafete Kassu.
    pages cm. — (Culture and customs of Africa)
  Includes bibliographical references and index.
    ISBN 978-0-313-33934-9 (hardcopy : alk. paper) — ISBN 978-0-313-08606-9 (e-book)
  1. Ethiopia—Civilization.   2. Ethiopia—Social life and customs.   I. Kassu, Wudu
Tafete, 1963–   II. Title.   III. Series: Culture and customs of Africa.
    DT379.5.G48   2014
    963—dc23   2013043195

ISBN: 978-0-313-33934-9
EISBN: 978-0-313-08606-9

18 17 16 15 14   1 2 3 4 5

This book is also available on the World Wide Web as an eBook.
Visit www.abc-clio.com for details.

Greenwood
An Imprint of ABC-CLIO, LLC

ABC-CLIO, LLC
130 Cremona Drive, P.O. Box 1911
Santa Barbara, California 93116-1911

This book is printed on acid-free paper ∞

Manufactured in the United States of America

Contents

CONTENTS

Series Foreword

Africa is a vast continent, the second largest, after Asia. It is four times the size of the United States, excluding Alaska. It is the cradle of human civilization. A diverse continent, Africa has more than 50 countries with a population of over 700 million people who speak over 1,000 languages. Ecological and cultural differences vary from one region to another. As an old continent, Africa is one of the richest in culture and customs, and its contributions to world civilization are impressive indeed.

Africans regard culture as essential to their lives and future development. Culture embodies their philosophy, worldview, behavior patterns, arts, and institutions. The books in this series intend to capture the comprehensiveness of African culture and customs, dwelling on such important aspects as religion, worldview, literature, media, art, housing, architecture, cuisine, traditional dress, gender, marriage, family, lifestyles, social customs, music, and dance.

The uses and definitions of "culture" vary, reflecting its prestigious association with civilization and social status, its restriction to attitude and behavior, its globalization, and the debates surrounding issues of tradition, modernity, and postmodernity. The participating authors have chosen a comprehensive meaning of culture while not ignoring the alternative uses of the term.

Each volume in the series focuses on a single country, and the format is uniform. The first chapter presents a historical overview, in addition to information on geography, economy, and politics. Each volume then proceeds to examine the various aspects of culture and customs. The series highlights the mechanisms for the transmission of tradition and culture across generations: the significance of orality, traditions, kinship rites, and family property distribution; the rise of print culture; and the impact of educational institutions. The series also explores the intersections between local, regional, national, and global bases for identity and social relations. While the volumes are organized nationally, they pay attention to ethnicity and language groups and the links between Africa and the wider world.

The books in the series capture the elements of continuity and change in culture and customs. Custom is represented not as static or as a museum artifact but as a dynamic phenomenon. Furthermore, the authors recognize the current challenges to traditional wisdom, which include gender relations, the negotiation of local identities in relation to the state, the significance of struggles for power at national and local levels and their impact on cultural traditions and community-based forms of authority, and the tensions between agrarian and industrial/manufacturing/oil-based economic modes of production.

Africa is a continent of great changes, instigated mainly by Africans but also through influences from other continents. The rise of youth culture, the penetration of the global media, and the challenges to generational stability are some of the components of modern changes explored in the series. The ways in which traditional (non-Western and nonimitative) African cultural forms continue to survive and thrive—that is, how they have taken advantage of the market system to enhance their influence and reproductions—also receive attention.

Through the books in this series, readers can see their own cultures in a different perspective, understand the habits of Africans, and educate themselves about the customs and cultures of other countries and people. The hope is that the readers will come to respect the cultures of others and see them not as inferior or superior to theirs but merely as different. Africa has always been important to Europe and the United States, essentially as a source of labor, raw materials, and markets. Blacks are in Europe and the Americas as part of the African Diaspora, a migration that took place primarily because of the slave trade. Recent African migrants increasingly swell their number and visibility. It is important to understand the history of the Diaspora and the newer migrants as well as the roots of the culture and customs of the places from where they come. It is equally important to understand others in order to be able to interact successfully in a world that keeps shrinking. The accessible nature of the books in this series will contribute to this understanding and enhance the quality of human interaction in a new millennium.

Toyin Falola
Frances Higginbotham Nalle Centennial Professor in History
The University of Texas at Austin

Acknowledgments

We would like to thank Professor Toyin Falola, the Culture and Customs series editor, for commencing this giant project and keenly watching it to its fruition. The project provided us the opportunity to write a relatively all-inclusive Ethiopian history. For this, too, we are grateful. Our heartfelt appreciation also goes to Ms. Kaitlin Ciarmiello for her patience, understanding, and meticulousness throughout the period of writing this volume. Also, our appreciation goes to individuals who provided us with photographs and kindly let us use them.

In addition, we would like to thank our respective institutions: Central Michigan University and the Addis Ababa University, for creating a conducive atmosphere for the completion of this project by providing all the necessary help we needed. To our students, colleagues, and librarians at Central Michigan University, the Institute of Ethiopian Studies of the Addis Ababa University, to mention a few, we thank you for your support.

Last but not least, we are indebted to our families for their understanding and cooperation during our long absence for our research. A special thanks goes to my daughter, Hilena Solomon, who read some of the chapters and served me as "unofficial editor" and "critic" despite the rigorous demands of her undergraduate studies at Johns Hopkins.

We assume both credit and shortcoming, if any, in this volume because we are responsible for the views, information, synthesis, and analysis, on the following pages. We hope readers will find this volume as compelling as others in the series.

Solomon Addis Getahun
and
Wudu Tafete Kassu

Chronology

1000 BC	South Arabian immigrants and laborers settle around the present day of Aksum.
975 BC	The Ethiopian queen, Makida also known as Sheba visits King Solomon of Israel. Upon her return, Makida gives birth to a baby boy, Menelik, from whom Ethiopian kings trace their descent.
AD 100	Aksum emerges as one of the most powerful states in the Red Sea littoral.
4th Century	Christianity is introduced from Egypt to Aksum by the Middle East/Syria.
4th Century	Aksumite King Ezana destroys the rival state of Meroe.
5th Century	Ethiopia (King Kaleb) invades and occupies South Arabia.
6th Century	The Nine Saints come to Ethiopia and introduce monasticism, translate the Bible into the Ethiopian language, Geez, and proselytize Christianity.
6th Century	During the reign of Atse Gebremeskiel, a clergyman named Yared establishes (invents) the three musical notations (Geez, Izel, and Ararray) for spiritual/religious chanting.

570	The prophet Mohammed is born. He later sends his followers (including one of his wives and his nephew) to seek refuge in Ethiopia. He and his followers were being persecuted by the Qurish tribes of Mecca.
1137	People of Agaw origin establish the Zagewe dynasty and come into power.
1140	Aksum declines.
1270	Yekonu Amlak restores the Solomonic dynasty, also known as the Shoa or Amhara dynasty (or also called the Christian Kingdom).
13th Century	Orthodox Christianity begins taking root in south and central Ethiopia under St. Tekele Haymanot.
1434–1468	(r.) King Dawit (1380–1412) establishes official contact with Europe.
16th Century	One of the vassal states, Adal (often known as Harar), revolts against the central government.
1512	Queen Mother, Elleni, sends a messenger seeking help from Christian Europe.
1529	Ahmad Gragn conquers much of Ethiopia, and destroys churches and much of the recorded history of Ethiopia.
1541	Christopher da Gamma, a close relative of the famous Portuguese explorer Vasco da Gamma, comes to Ethiopia with 400 musketeers to help Ethiopia fight Gragn and his allies, the Ottoman Turks.
1543	Gragn is defeated.
15th to the 19th Century	The Oromos, otherwise known as Galla, migrate and occupy much of the present-day Ethiopia.
1622	Susinyos becomes the first and only Catholic king of Ethiopia.
1630s	King Fasiledes, the son of Susinyos, expels the Jesuit missionaries and establishes Gondar as the permanent capital of Ethiopia. After the Zagwe dynasty, the country does not have permanent capital.
1700	King Iyasue I "the Great" accepts Louis the XIV's emissaries.
1755–1769	(r.) King Iyoas I, whose mother hailed from the Yejju Oromo, rules Ethiopia. During his reign and successive

reigns, Oromifaa is the language used in the palace. Since then, the Oromos continue to play a major, if not a dominant, role in the making and unmaking of the Ethiopian state.

1769	Ras Mikael Sihul of Tigray murders King Iyoas.
1769–1855	Period known as "the Era of Princes," between the death of Iyoas and the rise of King Tewodros to the Ethiopian throne. During these times, the King of Kings has little or no power and the Ethiopian state is at its weakest.
1813–1847	(r.) King Sahile Selassie of Showa expands his kingdom. He signs two agreements with Britain and France.
1855–1868	(r.) King Tewodros reunites Ethiopia by conquering Shoa, Gojjam, Tigre, Wollo, and Gondar.
1868	The British invade Ethiopia and defeat Tewodros's army at Meqidella. Tewodros commits suicide. After defeating Tewodros, the British loot the country's treasures, including its libraries and monastic centers.
1872	Dejazimach Kassa of Tigray becomes Yohannes IV (1872–1889), King of Kings of Ethiopia.
1875	Yohannes IV defeats an Egyptian invading force at Gundet.
1876	Yohannes again defeats an Egyptian army at Gura that is led by mercenaries from Europe and America.
1882	Italian Shipping company called Rubbatino purchases Assab from an individual and passes the territory to the Italian government.
1885	The Italians, with the tacit approval of the British, occupy the Ethiopian port of Massawa.
1889	Yohannes IV is killed while fighting Mahdist forces and is succeeded by the king of Shoa, who becomes Atse Menelik II.
1889	Menelik signs a bilateral friendship treaty with Italy at Wuchale, which Italy interprets as giving it a protectorate right over Ethiopia.
1889	Queen Taitu, the wife of King Menelik, establishes Addis Ababa as Ethiopia's capital.
1895	Italy invades Ethiopia.

1896	Menelik II defeats the Italians at the Battle of Adwa and guarantees Ethiopia's independence. However, Menelik also becomes the first Ethiopian monarch to give up Ethiopia's territory, Midre-Bahire, to the Italians, who had occupied it in 1890. They rename the territory "Eritrea" in 1900.
1913	Menelik dies and is succeeded by his grandson, Lij Iyasu.
1916	Lij Iyasu is deposed and is succeeded by Menelik's daughter, Zawditu, who rules through a regent, Ras Tafari Makonnen.
1923	Ethiopia joins the League of Nations as the only black African country.
1930	Zawditu dies and is succeeded by Ras Tafari Makonnen, who becomes Atse Haile Selassie I.
1935	Italy invades Ethiopia.
1936	Italians capture Addis Ababa, Haile Selassie flees to Britain, and the king of Italy is made emperor of Ethiopia. The colonial rulers join Ethiopia with Eritrea and Italian Somaliland and create Italian East Africa.
1936	Haile Selassie flees the country on the pretext of appealing to the League of Nations.
1937	General Rodolfo Graziani, the commander of the Italian army and governor of Italian East Africa (1935–1941), also known as the "butcher of Addis," massacres tens of thousands of Ethiopian civilians in Addis Ababa and the surrounding areas. His victims were educated Ethiopians, including more than 2,000 monks of the Debre Libanos monastery.
1941	The Ethiopian patriots (arbegnoch), with the help of the British Commonwealth troops, defeat Italy. Haile Selassie assumes power.
1945	Ethiopia becomes one of the few founding members of the UN.
1950–1953	Ethiopia sends the Qagnaw Battalion to help South Korea during the Korean War.
1952	United Nations federates Eritrea with Ethiopia.
1962	Haile Selassie, with the blessing of the Eritrean parliament, unites Eritrea with Ethiopia.

1963	First conference of the Organization of African Unity is held in Addis Ababa.
1973–1974	An estimated 200,000 people die in Wallo Province as a result of famine.
1974	Haile Selassie is overthrown by a military coup. General Aman-Mikael Andom and then General Teferi Benti become heads of state.
1975	Haile Selassie dies in mysterious circumstances while in custody.
1975, November	The military junta kills former government officials, including General Aman-Mikael Andom.
1977	General Benti, the leader of the military junta, is killed and replaced by Colonel Mengistu Haile Mariam.
1977–1979	Thousands of government opponents die in "Red Terror" orchestrated by Mengistu; collectivization of agriculture begins; Tigrayan People's Liberation Front launches war for secession from Ethiopia.
1977	Somalia invades Ethiopia's Ogaden region.
1978	Somali forces are defeated with massive help from the Soviet Union and Cuba.
1985	Worst famine in a decade strikes; Western food aid sent; thousands forcibly resettled from Tegray and Wallo.
1987	Mengistu is elected president under a new constitution.
1988	Ethiopia and Somalia sign a peace treaty.
1991	Ethiopian People's Revolutionary Democratic Front captures Addis Ababa, forcing Mengistu to flee the country; Eritrea establishes its own provisional government pending a referendum on independence.
1993	Eritrea becomes independent following an Eritrean-only referendum.
1994	New constitution divides Ethiopia into ethnically based regions.
1995	Negasso Gidada becomes titular president; Meles Zenawi assumes the post of prime minister and commander in chief of the army.
1998	Eritrea invades Ethiopia and occupies Badme and the surrounding areas.

2000   Ethiopia defeats the invading Eritrean army, in a cam-
                                  paign dubbed "Operation Sunset," and forces Eritrea
                                  to sign a ceasefire agreement, which provides for a UN
                                  observer force to monitor the truce and supervise the
                                  withdrawal of Ethiopian troops from Eritrean territory.

2001, February 24   Ethiopia says it has completed its troop withdrawal
                                  from Eritrea in accordance with a UN-sponsored agree-
                                  ment.

2003, April   Independent boundary commission rules that the dis-
                                  puted town of Badme lies in Eritrea. Ethiopia says the
                                  ruling is unacceptable.

2004, January–February   Nearly 200 are killed in ethnic clashes in the isolated
                                  western region of Gambella. Tens of thousands leave
                                  the area.

2004, March   Start of resettlement program to move more than two
                                  million people away from parched, overworked high-
                                  lands.

2005, April   First section of Aksum obelisk, looted by Italy in 1937,
                                  is returned to Ethiopia from Rome.

2005, May   Third multiparty elections are held. Protests over al-
                                  leged fraud precipitate into violent protests in which
                                  around 200 people are shot dead.

2005, September   With just one result left to declare, election authorities
                                  announce that the ruling party has won 360 seats and
                                  the opposition 175 seats in parliament.

2006–2009   Ethiopia, invited by the Transitional Government of
                                  Somalia, routs Muslim fundamentalists and occupies
                                  parts of Somalia.

2011   Ethiopia announces the commencement of the Grand
                                  Dam, also known as Hidasse (Renaissance) Dam, over
                                  the Nile River. The Hydroelectric dam, upon comple-
                                  tion in 2015, will be the largest in Africa with a capacity
                                  to generate 6,000 megawatt of electricity. The construc-
                                  tion of the dam will cost the country about $5 billion.

2012, August   Prime Minister Meles Zenaw, chairman of the ruling
                                  EPRDF party, passes away after a couple of months of
                                  illness on August 21, 2012.

1

Introduction

LAND

Geographical Setting, Landmass, and Climate

Ethiopia is located in the Horn of Africa. It is situated 3 and 18 degrees north latitude and between 33 and 48 degrees longitude. It shares a boundary with Eritrea to the north and northeast, Djibouti and Somalia to the east, Kenya to the south, South Sudan to the southwest, and Sudan to the northwest. The total size of the country is 1,127,127 square kilometers. Ethiopia's landmass, climate, and physical features are very diverse, and they include mountain ranges, rugged terrain, lakes, rift valleys, rivers, waterfalls, highlands, and lowland semi-desert plains.

The Ethiopian Rift Valley is part of the Rift Valley that stretches from the Middle East and passes through the Red Sea, Ethiopia, and Eastern Africa, and thence to Mozambique. The Rift Valley divides the Ethiopian highlands into two. The Ethiopian Rift valley is home to several volcanoes, several of which are still active. The Ertale area in the Afar region is an active volcanic area and is a destination to a sizable number of tourists. The Rift Valley area is prone to earthquakes. It also has several hot springs.

The Ethiopian Rift Valley has several lakes that are very interesting tourist destinations. These are the Langano, Zeway, Abiyata, Shala, Awassa, Abiyata, and Chamo. These lakes are home to rare birds, some of which are endemic to Ethiopia. To the north of the lakes region, in southern Ethiopia, flows the

Awash River. The Awash River emerges in western parts of Shewa and emp-
ties its water into Lake Abe, near the Djibouti republic. The Awash valley
area has several volcanic mountains; among them is Mt. Zequwala, south of
Addis Ababa, which has a beautiful crater lake.

Outside the Rift Valley lakes, Lake Tana is the largest lake. There is also
Lake Ashenge in southern Tegray. The Abay River passes over Lake Tana,
and one can see the muddy waters of the Abay River overflowing the waters
of the lake during the rainy season between June and September.

Ethiopia is a mountainous country and is often referred to as the "Swit-
zerland of Africa." The mountain ranges are located east and west of the
Ethiopian Rift Valley. The general elevation of most of these mountains is
about 4,000 meters above sea level. The highest mountain is located in the
northwest of the country; it is called Ras Dejen (popularly known as Ras
Dashen). The highest elevation in the Ras Dejen mountain range is about
4,304 to 4,543 meters above sea level. There are several other mountains in
the north. Among the southeastern highlands, the Batu Mountain in Bale is
4,303 meters above sea level, while that of Chilalo is 4,036 meters above sea
level.

To the east and west of these two mountain ranges are lowland regions
running north to south. In the western region of the country, the lowland
region stretches from Tegray in the north to the Kenyan border in the south.
It also includes the Ogaden desert that stretches to the Somali coast. The
other lowland region extends largely in the Rift Valley and east of the southern
mountains. The climate of the region is unbearably hot and inhospitable,
with daily temperature reaching more than 40 degrees centigrade (104 degrees Fahrenheit). The general elevation of most of these regions is between
500 and 1,000 meters above sea level. The lowest point, the Dallol depres-
sion, is located in the Afar region and is about 100 meters below sea level. It
is the hottest spot in the Afar region of Ethiopia.

Ethiopia is characterized as the "water tower of Africa." It has several rivers
that drain their water either into the Mediterranean Sea or into the Indian
Ocean. The largest river is the Abay River (also called the Blue Nile) that
emerges in the Lake Tana region of northwestern Ethiopia. Together with
other rivers such as the Takkazze, Baro, and others, and several other tributary rivers, it drains into the Mediterranean Sea. The Abay River joins the
White Nile River, which emerges from Lake Victoria in East Africa, in Khar-
toum, the capital city of the Sudan, and then it travels through the Sudan and
Egypt and drains to the Mediterranean Sea. There is a saying that Egypt is the
gift of the Nile. This is in reference to the soil that is washed away from the Ethiopian highlands and is a major source of Egyptian agricultural activity. Only
the Wabe-Shebelle River in eastern Ethiopia does not reach the sea but sinks

in the desert region of the Ogaden desert in eastern Ethiopia. However, the Genele River and its tributaries reach the Indian Ocean.

Ethiopia is located in the tropics and receives abundant sunshine almost throughout the year. There is no major difference in the length of the day and the night. The temperature of the day and the night is dependent on altitude. The highland regions have pleasant temperatures with breezy evenings, while the lowland regions are relatively hot. The main rainy season is during the summer (June to September), and there is a period of little rain between February and May.

Ethiopia has rare animals and birds that are found only in this country. There are about 26 different kinds of rare birds. The rarest Ethiopian wild animals are walia ibex, mountain nyala, the red fox, and gelada monkey. The walia ibex is found only in the Semien Mountains, while the mountain nyala is found in the Bale Mountain. The Semien National Park, the Awash National Park, and the Omo National Park are some of the parks that the country has. All of these are major tourist destinations.

PEOPLE

Languages

Ethiopia has more than 80 different ethnic groups, and thus, the country can be termed as a "museum" of ethnic groups. These groups speak different languages that are closely related to each other. These languages have evolved from a common parent origin. Some of Ethiopia's languages also have a closer affinity with the languages spoken in Eritrea, Somalia, the Sudan, and the Middle East. Ethiopian languages can be divided into four main major language groups. These are the Omotic, Cushitic, Nilo-Saharan, and Semitic.[1]

The Omotic languages are spoken in the Omo River valley in the Southern Nations, Nationalities, and People's Region. There are about 26 different Omotic languages. Some of these languages are spoken by a small number of people, even fewer than 500 people. Included as Omotic languages are Dorze, Yam, Majji, Walayeta, Kafficho, Ari, Gamo, Basketo, Kollo-Konta, and others.

The Cushitic languages of Ethiopia represent the largest number of the Ethiopian people. The Cushitic people inhabit a large geographical area, and their languages are spoken almost everywhere in the country. Some of these languages include Agaw, Afar, Oromifa, Somali, Hadya, Sidama, Kambata, Konso, and Burji.

The Semitic languages are also spoken all over the country. These languages of Ethiopia are similar to Semitic languages spoken in the Middle East. The Geez language has a script and was employed in writing during the early period of the Aksumite Empire. It is now used only in the Ethiopian Orthodox Church. Some of the Semitic languages include Tegre, Tegregna, Amharic, Gurage, Harari or Adari, Selti, and Argobba.

The Nilo-Saharan languages are spoken in the western lowland regions bordering Sudan. These include Anuak, Nuer, Gumuz, Kunama, Majanger, and Berta.

History

Aksumite State, First Century AD–1140

Before the emergence of Aksum as a political center, several smaller ancient states emerged and declined in Ethiopia. However, we do not know their names or their territorial extent. Some of the well-known ancient states of northern Ethiopia were the Land of Punt and the state of Damat. Our evidence of the Land of Punt comes from Egyptian hieroglyphic sources dating back to 2700 BC. It was located south of the Red Sea, covering an area from Eritrea to the Horn of Africa. Egyptian sources indicate that Queen Hatshepsut sent merchants to the Land of Punt to buy natural products such as incense and frankincense, and when the merchants arrived back in Egypt, they were asked to paint the merchandise they had brought. These paintings are available at Deir el-Bahri. Damat is the most well-known pre-Aksumite state for which we have authentic local inscriptions.

The state of Aksum emerged in the first century AD. In Greek literature, the word *Aksum* first appeared in a document known as the Periplus of the Erythrean Sea, which was written in the first century AD by a captain of a merchant ship who had a clear knowledge of the Red Sea region. The document was a manual for merchant ships sailing in the Red Sea region. It describes regions on both sides of the Red Sea from Egypt southward to the Horn of Africa. It discusses peoples of the region, their diet, the import-export of the region, and ports. It indicates that Adulis was the main port of Aksum. It also indicates three inland towns—Adulis, Colole, and Aksum. The name Aksum was also found in a Geez inscription found in an ancient church in the Aksum area. The document was written in the first century AD and never indicated that Aksum was a political center, but mentions the pagan god of Aksum.

Aksumite society was composed of the ruling classes. The ruling classes controlled all agricultural lands and owned slaves, and monopolized the domestic and external trade. Agricultural activity was the main source of the economy. Peasants cultivated the land and paid taxes to the ruling classes. There were skilled and unskilled workers who were employed in constructional activities. Slaves constituted the lowest section of the society, and they were obtained by slave raids and were prisoners of war. There were also traders who were agents of Aksumite kings.

Aksumite kings had power over all political affairs of the empire. All state officials were accountable to the king, maintained law and order, collected tributes and submitted to the court, and protected trade routes and markets. Aksumite kings were commanders of the army. Some of the Aksumite army units included Mahaza, Duaken, Hara, and others. The inscription of Atse Ezana of the fourth century AD lists the names of several army units.

Aksum society believed in traditional religion. South Arabian gods, such as Almaqah and Astar, were introduced into the state of Aksum. There are inscriptions that indicate that Greek gods, including Zeus and Ares, were also worshipped in Aksum. There were also indigenous Aksumite gods such as Mahram, Baher, and Meder. There is an indication that there was also a Judaic belief in northern Ethiopia, resulting in the tradition of a people known as the *Beta-Israel* (*Falasha*) people.

The introduction of Christianity into Ethiopia was the result of the commercial relationship with the Greco-Roman world. Christian merchants

The trilingual (Geez, Sabean and Greek) stone inscription of King Ezana. (A. Davey)

and envoys visited Aksum, and gradually Christianity was introduced in the fourth century AD during the period of Atse Ezana. The man who brought Christianity to Aksum was known as Frumentius. He and his friend were traveling with a philosopher of Tyre to India, and on their way back they anchored their ship on the coast of the Red Sea. It was attacked by pirates and all of the crew members were killed, but the two men survived. They were taken as slaves to the court of the Aksumite king. When Ezana became the king of Aksum, they were set free and allowed to go. Frumentius traveled to Alexandria to report the presence of Christians and asked the patriarch of Alexandria to appoint a bishop to Aksum.

The Alexandrian patriarch appointed Frumentius as the first bishop of Aksum in c. AD 340. Frumentius was happily received in Aksum and succeeded in converting King Ezana to Christianity. Frumentius is known in Ethiopia as Abba Selama (father of peace) and Kesate Berhan (revealer of light). He is canonized as a saint by the Ethiopian Orthodox, Roman, and Greek churches. There is a church dedicated to him in Temben, in southern Tegray.

The conversion of Ezana to Christianity is clear from his Christian inscription written in Geez language. Before this we have the pagan inscriptions of Ezana where he says that he was the son of Mahram. Ezana's Christian inscription starts with an invocation that says "In the name of the Father, the Son and the Holy Ghost." He also says that he was the son of Jesus Christ. Thus Ezana lived both as a pagan and as a Christian ruler. Traditionally it is believed that Abreha (Ezana) and Atsbeha (Sayzana) were co-regents and both of them are believed to have accepted Christianity. Both of them are canonized as saints by the Ethiopian Orthodox Church. This makes Ethiopia the first country where Christianity was planted as an official religion in the royal court. Thus Christians were not persecuted. The conversion of Ezana is also confirmed by the letters of the Alexandrian patriarch. Ezana also received a letter from the Roman emperor who asked him to accept the doctrine of Arianism. The coins of Ezana also bore the symbol of the cross.

Later, toward the fifth century AD, Christian missionaries known as the nine saints came into Ethiopia. They are credited with the expansion of Christianity, building of churches and monasteries, and conversion of the local population. They also translated most of the Bible into the Geez language. This is clear from the inscription erected in Yemen by Aksumite king Kaleb, in the sixth century AD. The inscription begins with a quote from Psalm 24:8: "The Lord is strong and mighty, the Lord is strong in battle." This quote clearly indicates the existence of a Geez version of the *Old Testament*.

The major economic source of the Aksumite state was the export trade. Trade was the monopoly of the kings and kings had trader agents. Exports from Aksum were valuable natural products, such as ivory, rhinoceros horn, tortoise shell, gold, myrrh, incense, frankincense, cinnamon, slaves, live animals, and animal skins. These products were exported to Egypt, the Middle East, India, and China. Imports to Aksum were quality cloth, linen, leather garments, ornaments, olive oil, and wine.

Land was the other main source of economy. Land was held on the basis of lineage, and peasants paid tribute to the state. State officials and the church had *gult* rights (usufruct right). They had the right to collect tribute but had no right on the land. The land remained in the hands of peasants. In the ninth century AD, an Arab traveler, al-Yaqubi, indicated that the Aksumite king had several vassals who paid him tribute. In the 10th century AD, al-Masudi confirmed that Muslims in Ethiopia were tributary to the king of kings.

Aksumites frequently minted coins between the third and the seventh century AD. Coins were minted from gold, silver, and bronze. Gold coins were meant for the international market. Aksumite coins had the effigy of the king and a religious symbol. Coins minted before the introduction of Christianity had a pagan symbol of a crescent and disk, and those minted after this period had the symbol of the cross. Aksumite coins also had legends engraved in Greek or Geez languages. They also indicated the names of kings and his tribe. Because of Aksumite trade relations, foreign coins such as Roman, Indian, and Egyptian coins were discovered in various places in northern Ethiopia.

In the pre-Aksumite period, inscriptions were written in the Sabean language. But later the Aksumites wrote inscriptions in Greek and Geez. They also developed a high level of building technology. They built palaces, temples, churches (including rock-hewn churches), tombs, and altars; erected monuments; and created pottery and different kinds of jewelry. The standing stele (monument) in Aksum is about 23 meters in height, and the fallen stele is about 27 meters. Another stele, standing at 21 meters in height, was taken to Rome by the invading Italian forces in 1936 and was recently brought back and erected in Aksum. Aksumite monuments are registered as world heritage sites by the United Nations Educational, Scientific, and Cultural Organization (UNESCO).

The Aksumite Empire was noted for its territorial expansion into the surrounding regions. Aksum established its domination in the south Arabian region and politically administered the region between the third and sixth century AD. The first ruler who invaded the South Arabian region was Gadar or Gadarat. In an inscription discovered in South Arabia, Gadar called himself king of Aksum, and he also styled himself as king of Saba and Himyar. Saba and Himyar were South Arabian regions. In the fourth century AD, Ezana, ruler of Aksum, also named himself as the ruler of Saba, Salhen, Himyar, and Raydan, ancient states in South Arabia. Another Aksumite ruler in the sixth century AD, Kaleb, also mobilized a larger army in AD 523 and 525 to suppress a rebellion. However, the Aksumite power gradually declined and Aksum lost control of the region after AD 570.

Despite Aksum's loss of its political and economic domination in South Arabia, it still maintained its economic domination in the Red Sea. Its power began to decline beginning in the eighth century AD. This was because of the rise of the Muslim Arab Empire and the resultant economic rivalry over the Red Sea trade. It is generally believed that the prophet Mohammad had instructed his followers not to attack Ethiopia as long as the Ethiopians did not attack the Arabian region. As we will see next, Ethiopia was the first country that gave asylum to Muslim refugees in the early period of Islam. But an economic rivalry began after Mohammad's death.

The commercial rivalry was between the ancient Aksumite port of Adulis and the new port of Jeddah in Arabia. The first attack against Aksumite ships occurred in AD 640. The port of Adulis was not destroyed and the Muslim army was repulsed. In AD 702, the Aksumite army invaded Jeddah and caused heavy damage. In return the Muslim army occupied the Dahlak Islands, now in Eritrea, but failed to destroy the Aksumite naval force. In AD 768, the Aksumites again attacked Jeddah, and as revenge, the Muslim army destroyed the port of Adulis. This brought an end to Aksumite economic dominance in the Red Sea. Aksumite relations with the outside world were cut. Their export trade declined and its economy eventually declined. There were also internal rebellion and the expansion of the Beja people southward that destroyed trade routes. With its economy shattered, the political center shifted southward and a new dynasty that called itself the Zagwe dynasty emerged in Lasta and Wag. It is generally believed that Aksum declined in c. 1140.

The Zagwe Dynasty, 1150–1270

The Zagwe dynasty was an Agaw dynasty. The Agaw people of Lasta and Wag had much in common with the Aksumite people. The Agaws were employed in the Aksumite army and had accompanied Aksumite gold merchants to the south of the Abay River. With the decline of Aksumite power and the southward shift of the political court of Aksum, the regions of Lasta and Wag benefited from the transfer of the court. The Agaws were attracted to the Aksumite army, and the Agaw local chiefs held key political and military positions. According to local traditions, the founder of the Zagwe dynasty was Merra-Takla-Haymanot, an Agaw from the region of Bugna. He was an army general in the court of the last Aksumite ruler, Del-Nead, and was also married to Del-Nead's daughter.

The main stronghold of the Zagwe dynasty was the region of Lasta and Wag. They controlled Tegray, the highland regions of the present-day Eritrea, Amharaland, Bagemder, and areas to the north of Lake Tana and northern Shewa. But South Arabia and the Red Sea were not under their control. Their political seat was at Adefa, also known as Roha or Lalibela, named after one of their rulers.

Christianity reached the regions of Lasta and Wag during the Aksumite period. There is a tradition that the Aksumite ruler Kaleb, and his son and successor, built several churches in the region. Some of these churches are rock-hewn. The Zagwe rulers gave continuity to Aksumite state structure, Christianity, and the use of the Geez language. Christianity also continued to be the state religion and expanded to other regions. The rulers continued to import Coptic bishops from Alexandria and maintained good relations with Egypt and the Holy Land. It was also during their period that Ethiopia bought churches in the Holy Land. Because of their religious contributions, four Zagwe rulers—Yemrehana-Krestos, Harbe, Lalibela, and Na'akuot-la'ab—are canonized by the Ethiopian Orthodox Church, and a church is dedicated to them.

The Zagwe rulers are remembered for the construction of several rock-hewn churches. The construction of rock-hewn churches started during the Aksumite period, and there are more than 200 churches all over northern Ethiopia. But the rock-hewn churches of Lalibela are beautiful and more refined than those built before them. These churches were built by local masons and indicate the continuation of building technology of the Aksumite tradition. Some argue that these churches were built by foreigners, but this assumption is baseless. Most of these churches were built in their capital city Lalibela. Lalibela built these churches to emulate the significance of the Holy Land. Thus, church names in Lalibela are named after church names in the Holy Land. Local tradition also indicates that those people who visit the churches of Lalibela are considered as undertaking a pilgrimage to the Holy Land. Thus, large numbers of Ethiopian pilgrims travel to the town of Lalibela on Ethiopian Christmas Day (January 7). Father F. Alvarez, a member of the Portuguese envoy in 1520–1526, indicates that about 70,000 people visited the town on Christmas Day. Now Lalibela is a celebrated tourist destination to a large number of travelers.

The Amharic language developed as a court language during the Zagwe period. Several books were also translated into the Geez language. There are also Geez engravings in the walls of the churches of Lalibela.

Historians agree that the Zagwe rulers ruled the country between AD 1150 and 1270. The power of the Zagwe dynasty declined due to the following reasons. There was a frequent power struggle among various contenders, which weakened the Zagwe's power. They also attracted others in their power struggle. One such person was Yekkuno-Amlak, chief of Amhara land, who actively participated in the internal power rivalry. He killed the last Zagwe ruler and heralded the emergence of the Solomonic dynasty in 1270. The Zagwe rulers also did not control the trade routes to the Red Sea or effectively exploit the new trade routes to the port of Zayla in the Indian Ocean. Once again the political court shifted further south into Amhara land and thence to Shewa.

The Solomonic Dynasty, 1270–1527

The period 1270–1527 is rich in documented history. There are local and foreign sources that have been found: royal chronicles, hagiographies, soldiers' songs, and *gult* (land) charters. Arabic and other foreign sources are also available.

The year 1270 was the downfall of the Zagwe dynasty and the emergence of the Solomonic dynasty. The major reason for these historical developments was the emergence of Zayla as the major outlet for Ethiopia's export trade. The year 1527 was the downfall of the medieval period in the wars of the 16th century led by the leader of the Sultanate of Adal, Ahmed Ibn Ibrahim al-Gazi (popularly known as Ahmed Gragn or "the left-handed").

The main political stronghold of the Solomonic dynasty was medieval Amhara land, the region of Lake Hayq, now southern Wallo. The Solomonic legend was based on a traditional church book, the *Kebra Nagast* (glory of kings). The book relates the visit of an Ethiopian queen, the Queen of Sheba, to the court of King Solomon of Israel. It indicates the birth of Menelik I as the son of the Queen of Sheba and King Solomon. Menelik is regarded as the first ruler of Ethiopia. The book also argues that the Zagwe rulers were illegitimate rulers who do not belong to the Solomonic line. The book declares that the Zagwe rulers were usurpers who had taken power by killing the last Aksumite ruler. However, Zagwe traditions share in this tradition not through the Queen Sheba but through her lady-in-waiting. They also claim that they were descendants of Adil, who was a grandson of King David of Israel and son of Yetraham. Adil together with Menelik I came and settled in Ethiopia. This counter-claim was intended to counter the Solomonic legend that claimed that the Zagwe rulers were illegitimate. The Solomonic tradition was exploited by Yekkuno-Amlak, who is regarded as the restorer of the Solomonic line.

During this period, there were two major centers of anti-Zagwe opposition. The monasteries of Aksum Seyon and Dabra-Damo in Tegray were centers of the movement. This was because these religious centers were not favored by the Zagwe dynasty. During the reign of the Zagwe dynasty, the monastery of Dabra-Libanos Shmzena, in Eritrea, was favored. Thus, the monasteries of Aksum Seyon and Dabra-Damo felt they were being neglected. The chief of Enterta, in Tegray, was the leader of the movement. The other anti-Zagwe center was in Amhara land. This rebellion was led by Yekkuno-Amlak, the restorer of the Solomonic dynasty, who indicated that he was a descendant of the last Aksumite ruler and Solomon of Israel. It was also Yekkuno-Amlak who took advantage of the Solomonic legend. He was supported by the other chiefs of Amhara and Shoa and the Muslim community of northern Shoa in his struggle against the Zagwe dynasty. The presence of Amhara soldiers in the Zagwe court helped Yekkuno-Amlak's movement. He was also supported by the church, which propagated the Solomonic legend. The church gave legitimacy to the Solomonic line as documented in the *Kebra-Nagast*. The church became the ideological arm of the state. Thus, the church and the state established strong relations, and the Solomonic rulers economically supported and protected the church.

The new dynasty was confronted with problems such as political succession among the sons of its founder. In less than five years, from 1294 to 1299, five successive rulers came to power, indicating an intense power struggle. To solve this problem, the new dynasty established the royal prison of Amba Geshen, northwestern South Wallo. (Amba-Geshen is a celebrated religious center where part of the True Cross on which Christ was crucified is found. It was brought to the country in the 15th century and deposited there.) On the death of a king the sons of the deceased king were rounded up and taken to Amba-Geshen, where they remained for the rest of their lives. The royal prison was inaccessible and had only one gate. The gate was guarded by a strong army, and it minimized the frequency of power struggle. The royal prison served its purpose until it was destroyed in the wars of the 16th century.

The medieval state gradually expanded southward and controlled the regions to the south of Amhara land. The region of Shoa became the center of the medieval state. It then expanded to Damot, south of the Abay River. It subjugated the Falasha (Beta-Israel) regions north of Lake Tana. After a short period of power struggle among the descendants of Yekkuno-Amlak, the expansion of the state started afresh. During this period, the state expanded and suppressed local rebellions in Tegray and controlled the Red Sea coastal regions. Moreover, its main direction of expansion was toward eastern and southern Ethiopia where the Muslims had recently settled. The main reason for such expansion was to control commodity-producing regions and the lucrative trade route and market centers leading to the port of Zayla in the Indian Ocean. In this struggle, the regions of Ifat, Fatagar, Dawaro, Bali, Hadya, Harar or Adal, and others were brought under control. These regions were the main commodity-producing regions that both the Christian and Muslim rulers wanted to control. Thus, the medieval state brought under its control different peoples and forced them to pay tribute to the central court. Those petty-states that submitted peacefully were made tributary states and their rulers recognized by the central state. Local rulers who resisted the central state were removed and their regions were put under the direct control of the central state. Some regions were simply integrated into the central state. Local rulers had to pay annual tribute, recognize the king as their overlord, protect trade routes and markets, and contribute soldiers in periods of national crisis.

The territorial size of the medieval state was not the same. Its size enlarged depending on the power of the king and his army, and its size contracted in periods of weak kings.

The medieval period witnessed more political confrontation throughout the 14th and 16th centuries. The Muslim Sultanate of Yifat and then Adal (or Harar) staged fierce resistance against the integration policy of the Christian kingdom. Particularly the leaders of the Sultanate of Adal were militant and refused to be integrated or become a tributary state. The Christian leaders led an army deep into the arid regions of Adal and fought several wars. The militant leaders of Adal also raided the fertile regions of eastern Ethiopia. In all these confrontations, the lives of the settled communities and trade were highly affected. Both warring parties looted cattle and property by force; houses and religious places were demolished and war captives taken as slaves. The absence of peace weakened the conduct of trade. There was also religious propaganda on both sides to attract supporters and mobilize them to the war front. But the main reason for the prolonged warfare was to ensure the control of territory, trade routes, market centers, and commodity-producing regions. It was to impose political and economic domination.

The confrontation between the Christian kingdom and the Muslim Sultanate of Adal reached its peak in the 16th century. The rise of *Imam* Ahmed Ibn-Ibrahim al-Gazi (popularly known as Ahmed Gragn, the left-handed), leader of Adal, had a number of reasons. It was to push into the more fertile central highland regions, get pasture and water for their cattle, not have to pay tribute to the central state, and to raid regions to get slaves. Another major reason was the population movement of the Somali and the Afar that put strong pressure on the people of Adal. The Somali pushed the lowland Adal, and the lowland Adal pastoral community in turn pushed the agricultural community of highland Harar. Imam Ahmed brought together the Somali, the Afar and the Adali, and mobilized them to control the fertile highland regions of central Ethiopia. The religious leaders also took it as a war of jihad (holy war) and gave support to the project.

The Christian kingdom was already weakened by the political power struggle for succession. These frequent power struggles had sapped the power of the kingdom. There were two periods of succession problems—1430–1434 and 1478–1497. The institution of the royal prison of Amba Geshen did not altogether solve these problems. These political problems weakened the power of the king and the army, and eventually, the kingdom was unable to defend itself from Adal.

In a series of engagements, the Christian kingdom lost the battle and Ahmed Gragn was able to control much of the country. The kingdom was defeated in 1529. The king was unpopular among his nobility because he imprisoned, flogged, and exiled his officials. Some of these disgruntled officials supported Adal. The war continued until the Adali forces were defeated and their leader killed in the Battle of Woina-Dega, in the Gondar region, in 1543. During the last phase of the war, the Christian kingdom received the support of Portuguese soldiers, while Adal got support from Yemen. At the end of the war, both the Christian state and Adal were weakened and unable to resist the movement of the Oromo people. Trade declined. With more pressure from the Oromo, and to participate in the newly established trade route between Dambya, north of Lake Tana, and the Funj kingdom in the Sudan, the Christian state moved its seat to the Lake Tana region, while the rulers of Adal shifted their seat to Awssa.

One main economic source of medieval Ethiopia was land. The *rest* (communal) of land was in the hands of the local people who belonged to a common ancestor or clan who had developed it. The farmers paid annual tribute to a local chief, who then submitted a share of the tax to the state.

The medieval rulers also gave *gult* lands to officials, army generals, soldiers, and the church. These officials had no right on the land but collected annual tribute (usufruct right) from the people who had settled on it. They benefited if they were appointed over a fertile and populated region. The people who had such a right were called *bala-gult* (people who had usufruct right). The *bala-gults* were also local governors. Their duties were to maintain peace in their region, hunt down criminals, collect tribute, and protect trade routes and market centers. The people also gave corvée labor to the local officials.

The Ethiopian Orthodox Church was one of the beneficiaries of the *gult* system. The clergy were also members of the peasantry and owned land. Major churches and monasteries received land from the state and owned large tracts of land. The church–state relationship was further strengthened in the medieval period. During the period of King of Kings Zera-Yaqob, the monastery of Dabra-Libanos, Shoa, received all the revenue collected in the region. Thus, there was a revolt against such a huge economic benefit.

The most important economic income was derived from the export trade. The Christian state thus monopolized the export trade and waged a relentless struggle to keep its economic hold. The expansion of the state was thus to control the trade, market centers, and trade routes where taxes were collected. It was also to control the commodity-producing regions. These commodities were slaves, gold, ivory, civet, and other items. Slave-raiding activities devastated regions and had a negative effect on the local population. Slaves were used in domestic work and were exported to Arabia, Egypt, India, and Persia. *Amole* (slat bar) was an important commodity and was used as currency. It was extracted in the Afar region and passed through Tegray, with a local governor responsible for the taxes. Along the trade routes, several markets emerged. One of the important markets in eastern Tegray was visited by Father F. Alvarez, a member of the Portuguese mission in 1520–1526. The market center was visited by merchants from the outside world. Local merchants received loans from the king and had to pay high interest to the court. There were also several ports along the Indian Ocean through which commodities were exported to the outside world.

The Christian kingdom had extensively expanded its territory to the point that it was difficult to administer it properly. The kingdom reorganized its administrative structure and created two groups of administrative officials: hereditary officials and royal appointees. The hereditary officials were those who had established closer relations with the court, those who had loyally served the king and those who were often members of the royal family. These officials could transfer their offices to their descendants. The royal appointees held their office by the goodwill of the king. Their office was dependent on the king. They were constantly transferred, flogged, imprisoned, or lost their offices when they lost the confidence of the king. The main duties of these officials were to maintain order in their region, protect the trade routes, contribute soldiers in times of national crisis, and collect annual tributes.

The royal court of medieval Ethiopia was mobile in nature and had a temporary character, unlike the old political centers of Aksum and Lalibela. Its mobility was to control coastal areas, suppress rebellions, and perform other administrative and political duties. But there were times when a few kings had established their court in some ancient towns. One such case was the town of Dabra-Berhan established by Zera-Yaqob. The population size of such courts increased during periods of tribute payment and appeals. During the rainy season, the population greatly declined. According to Father F. Alvarez, who was in Ethiopia between 1520 and 1525, the court had about 50,000 visitors on some occasions. The royal residence of the court was usually built on a hill to protect it from attack. It had 12 gates and different people were admitted on a certain gate on the order of the king. The central place was reserved for the royal family. It had several royal churches, and the residence of the bishop was in one of the central enclosures of the court. It had a market further from the court and a large number of merchants came to exchange their commodities. The mobility of the court inhibited the emergence of permanent political centers, and it was a burden to the local people as people were forced to provide every necessity to the court.

Army organization was not new to medieval state. The Aksumite state had organized its army for its political expansion. In medieval Ethiopia, the army organization had two different units: regional and central.

The regional army consisted of local militia mobilized from all the provinces. This army was under the regional governors and it was mobilized to suppress local rebellions or in periods of national crisis. After they accomplished their tasks, they traveled back to their farms. During peaceful times, they worked in their farms. The regional army kept their tribal, linguistic, and regional identity. Their unit carried regional names such as Hadya, Damot, Gojjam, Lasta, Gondar, Koram, and others. The presence of a strong regional army in the provinces tended to strengthen the power of the regional governor at the expense of the king, and the court tried to control such tendencies.

The central army was a striking force for special missions. They were trained and armed as the best combatants. These armies were under the king and the independent army units were commanded by loyal commanders. They were attached to the court. They had symbolic names and the regional governors were afraid of them. They never participated in agricultural activity (called the *Chewa*) and were stationed in strategic places for quick combat or in the newly conquered places. Their number was constantly checked and balanced.

The Muslim sultanates had their own army. However, the Muslim army was drawn from the nomadic community and was renowned for surprise attacks. They were active in the raiding activity and could quickly melt into the desert when the Christian army was mobilized. The raiding activity of the nomadic forces largely affected the life of the settled community and the conduct of trade. Property and houses of the settled community were sacked and they were sold as slaves. Both the Christian and Muslim armies had similar armaments because they had the same access to the outside world. These armaments were bows, arrows, spears, and swords. Firearms were not introduced into the country until the 16th century. But the Christian rulers had developed an interest to import firearms and military officers to train their army.

The medieval court established international contact with the outside world. It established religious relations with Egypt and the Holy Land. Europeans from the Italian city-states, Vatican, Syria, Portugal, and Spain visited the country. Ethiopians also traveled to the outside world, particularly to Egypt and the Holy Land. Most of the foreigners who visited the country were traders, envoys, secretaries, artisans, painters, and army officers. The relationship with Egypt was more religious because the Coptic Church was the head of the Ethiopian Orthodox Church and appointed Coptic bishops to the Ethiopian Church. However, the relationship with Egypt was not always cordial. This was because of religious minorities in both countries: Coptic Christians in Egypt and Muslims in Ethiopia. These minorities were persecuted in their countries and sought support from Egypt and Ethiopia. The Egyptian government was also intercepting Ethiopian bishops traveling to Europe to prevent Ethiopia's contact with the outside world.

Ethiopia's relationship with Europe was rather good. A close relationship was established with Portugal. A Portuguese mission arrived in the country in 1520 and stayed in the court until 1526. One of them was Father F. Alvarez. He wrote a very informative book about medieval Ethiopia. He lived in the court of King of Kings Lebna Dengel (1508–1540) and traveled with the court from place and place, writing his observations. He also wrote about religious places, the tribute payment system, the markets, regional governors, and other topics.

Alvarez's book is titled, *The Prester John of the Indies* (2 vols.). He titled his book as such because it was a celebrated legend in the Christian world. Prester John was believed to have been a powerful ruler with a strong army who had an interest in supporting the Crusaders against the Muslims. The legend became famous during the period of the Crusaders when the Crusaders wanted to get military power to liberate Jerusalem from the Muslims. The exact location of the country of Prester John was not known. It was believed that he was the king of India until his country was associated with Ethiopian Christian rulers who were waging a relentless war of expansion and economic rivalry against the Ethiopian Muslim states. Alvarez titled his book as such, although he knew that the Ethiopian king was neither a priest nor John.

The first European letter to an Ethiopian king came to the country in 1400. It was written by King Henry IV of England. The first Ethiopian official envoy to Europe was sent two years later. Ethiopian rulers were keen on the technical advancement of Europe. Thus, Ethiopia sent missions to Portugal, Spain, and the Vatican, and the Ethiopian demand was to get military experts to train an army and to import craftsmen. They were also interested in importing firearms. Nevertheless, firearms were not introduced to the country until as late as the 16th century. In the first quarter of the 16th century, Ethiopia had established a firm contact with Portugal. During the wars of Ahmed ibn Ibrahim Al-Gazi in the 16th century, Ethiopia sought the military support of Portugal against its rival, the Muslim Sultanate of Adal, in eastern Ethiopia. Thus, 400 Portuguese soldiers commanded by Christopher Da Gama, son of Vasco Da Gama, arrived in Ethiopia. The Portuguese commander lost his life in one of the battles. With the support of the Portuguese soldiers, the Christian kingdom defeated Adal in 1543, which was supported by Yemeni soldiers.

A Yemeni Muslim scholar also came and lived in the country. He converted to Christianity and later became the abbot of the monastery of Dabra-Libanos, one of the prominent monasteries in the kingdom. He eventually wrote a religious book, *Anqasa Amin*. Another Yemeni scholar, Chihab ad-Din Ben Abdel-Qader (also called Arab Faqih), came to the country and wrote the accounts of the wars of the Ahmed Gragn.

The Gondarine Period

Following the wars of the 16th century, both the Christian Kingdom and the Muslim Sultanate of Adal were weakened. The Christian court began to reorganize its administration but was confronted with several problems. The problem of Adal was not solved, as its rulers had reorganized themselves in Harar. The Ottoman Turks, who opposed Ethiopia's relations with Portugal, occupied the Red Sea port of Massawa in an attempt to block the arrival of the Portuguese to the Red Sea region. With the decline of trade, loss of gult lands, and decline of the political power of the state, the Christian army disintegrated. The court shifted its political center to the region of Dambeya, north of Lake Tana, because of the emergence of a new trade route into the Sudan.

Atse Gelawdewos (1540–1559) died in an attempt to suppress the resistance of Adal in 1559. At about the same time, a major population movement was sweeping the central highland regions. This was the movement of the Oromo people from southeastern Ethiopia. The court was unable to resist, and could not protect, the central highland regions from the Oromo. This was because the king had earlier sent part of his army to attack the Turks, who had occupied the port of Massawa, and part of the army was defeated in Adal in the battle of 1559 where the king died. There was also a power struggle in the court, and the army did not direct its attention to resist the Oromo. The shift of the court to Dambeya had also left the local people to resist the Oromo on their own. The kingdom of Adal was able to protect the city of Harar only by constructing a walled town. Even then, they could not resist the pressure from the Oromo and had to shift their seat to Awassa, further north in the Afar region.

The original homeland of the Oromo people was east of the Rift Valley lakes in Bale and Sidama Provinces. Their movement became strong and noticeable after the wars of Ahmed Gragn. This idea is contested by recent publications, which indicate the presence of the Oromo people in the area even before this period. The Oromo were divided into two groups: the Baryatuma and Borana. The first group moved in eastern and northern directions, while the latter moved to the southwest. This happened between the 1550s and 1580s.

During their movement, the Oromo were both agriculturalists and pastoralists. They believed in Waqa, supreme god. They were also organized under the age-grade system (*gada*), whereby every eight years a group of people moved from one *gada* to another. The responsibility of the third *gada* was expansion. The fifth *gada* was responsible for administering the community. All men shared equal rights and responsibilities. They were all mobilized to do raids and this helped them defeat the less resistant regions. They also adopted the defeated people and made them members of their society through a *gudifecha* (adoption) system.

In their movement, the Oromo did not only fight against the people who had earlier settled or the various states established earlier but also fought among themselves to possess fertile regions. The people of Gafat, Semitic people who lived in northwestern Shoa, dispersed northward because of pressure from the Oromo and attacks from the Christian ruler.

Gradually, the Oromo settled and founded several kingdoms in the Gibe region in the beginning of the 19th century. These were the kingdoms of Limmu-Enaraya, Jimma, Gomma, Guma, and Gera. These states had their own kings and were commodity-producing regions, producing goods such as coffee. Their markets were connected to the market centers of northern and eastern Ethiopia.

The movement of the Christian court from Shoa to Dambeya was during the period of Atse Minas (1559–1563). Minas and his successor were confronted by pretenders and rebellious governors, and they fought desperate wars to suppress their resistance. In the transfer of the court to the region of Dambeya, few court sites were established until Gondar was founded as a permanent seat by Fasiladas (1632–1667). Before this, the country experienced a religious civil war over the issue of Catholicism.

It is to be remembered that Portuguese soldiers participated in the wars of the 16th century against Ahmed Gragn, the ruler of Adal. Atse Lebna-Dengel (1508–1541) requested military support against Adal. He sent a Portuguese man, Bermudez, with a letter to Portugal, and 400 soldiers came and fought on the side of Ethiopia. Bermudez claimed that he was appointed as a Catholic bishop of Ethiopia. In 1557 Jesuit missionaries arrived in Ethiopia with the aim of serving the remaining Portuguese soldiers and their descendants, and to convert the country to Catholicism. But Gelawdewos, the son and successor of Lebna-Denegel, refused to be converted to Catholicism. Later the

Catholics won the favor of Susenyous (1607–1632). Susenyous had a problem with suppressing the resistance of the nobility and the clergy, who opposed his power. He was attracted by the order and discipline of the Catholic missionaries, and hoped that a new ideology would provide stability to his kingdom. Thus he was converted to Catholicism in 1622 and declared Catholicism as the official religion of the country.

This action brought about major rebellion against his kingdom and his religious doctrine, Catholicism. The rebellion spread everywhere and peasants rose in rebellion in support of Orthodoxy. Susenyous was unable to pacify the country and dragged it into a bloody civil war. He won all engagements but was unable to bring political stability. The major area of the rebellion was the regions of Lasta, Wag, and Tegray. Thus in June 1632, he won his last battle, killing 8,000 peasants in one battlefield alone. He abdicated in favor of his son, Fasiladas, and died a Catholic in September 1632. Fasiladas restored the Orthodox Church and expelled the Catholics. He closed the country's doors to Europeans and established new relationship with the neighboring Muslim countries.

Atse Fasiladas founded Gondar in 1636. The town was once a major market center and was connected with the trade routes of the coast of the Red Sea, and Mattama in the west, on the Sudanese side. Fasiladas and his

Fasilades Castle in Gondar, Ethiopia. (Dmitry Kuznetsov/Dreamstime.com)

successors built castles and several beautiful churches. The castles were built by the *Falasha* (Beta-Israel) people and Indians. The city had weekly and daily markets, and its population was about 70,000. Gondar had established different living quarters to Muslims (an area now known as Addis Alem) and to the *Falasha*. The city had attracted foreign residents (Indians, Greeks, and Armenians). The ruling classes led a luxurious life, often going on hunting trips. Political intrigue was rampant in the court.

The *Zemene Masafent* (Era of the Princes)

The political assassinations in the court of Gondar resulted in a period of political instability and a gradual decline of the power of the monarchy. Atse Bakkaffa (1721–1730) was married to an ambitious woman, Etege Mentew-wab from the region of Qwara. When Bakkaffa died in 1730, his young son, Iyyassu II (1730–1755) came to power. Since the new king was very young, his mother began to control politics. She was also supported by her brother, who held an important political post in the kingdom. When King Iyyassu II died, they again brought his young son Iyo'as (1755–1769) to the throne. Iyo'as was married to an Oromo woman from Wallo. His relatives on his mother's side came to Gondar with their army hoping to get important political offices.

The nobility opposed Mentewwab's and her brother's power, and equally opposed the rise of the Wallo Oromo in the politics of Gondar. When her brother died, Mentewwab invited *Ras* Mikael Sehul, governor of Tegray, to help her suppress her opponents. Mikael used heavy force against the opposition and steadily grew in his power. The Amhara and the Oromo nobility did not like his political actions, nor did King Iyo'as, who plotted against Mikael. When the young king began to control politics, Mikael discovered his plans, and ended up assassinating him first, and installing another king and eventually killing him as well. This political event ushered in the period of the *Zemene Masafent* (Era of the Princes), 1769–1855. The Amhara and Oromo nobility allied together against Mikael's growing power. In 1771 he was defeated by the allied forces of the nobility of Gojjam, Wallo, Amhara, and Lasta. He was imprisoned for a few months in Lasta and later sent back to his region.

Then the nobility fought against each other to become kingmakers and to dominate the kings from the Solomonic dynasty. The kingmakers put kings on the throne and removed them on their own will. After Mikael Sehul, the nobility of Lasta and the Yajju Oromo lords assumed the office of the king-maker. Despite the strong rivalry and wars that they encountered, the Yajju Oromo lords (also called the Warra-Sheik dynasty) managed to dominate the politics of Gondar between 1786 and 1853.

The main feature of the *Zemene Masafent* was the decline of monarchical power. The Solomonic kings were puppet or weak kings, with no political and economic power. They were simply at the mercy of the kingmakers. They led poor and meager lives. The war lords collected taxes and used it to their own advantage, while the puppet kings did not raise any taxes. The annual revenue of the puppet kings in the 1840s was about 300 *Maria Theresa Thalers* (MTT). The annual revenue of King Shale-Selassie of Shoa was 85,000 MTT. The annual revenue of *Ras* Walde-Sellassie, governor of Tegray, was 75,000 MTT.

The Solomonic kings, though puppet kings, were recognized as the supreme power of the country. The kingmakers neither dared to crown themselves nor claimed descent from the Solomonic dynasty. The important thing for them was to put someone from the family of the Solomonic kings that they could crown or remove from power.

The kingmakers manipulated the puppet kings. They brought them to power and removed them as they wished. The kingmakers and provincial governors were in constant rivalry to annex other regions and to control the symbolic seat of the court. All regional governors of northern Ethiopia contested among themselves to assume the office of the kingmaker and to dominate the politics of the court. They were politically, economically, and militarily dominant. They formed alliances on a regular basis, but such alliances did not last for long. Alliances were simply formed and then quickly dissolved. It would also be a mistake to take these conflicts as a conflict of ethnicity or religion. The Yajju Oromo lords, who had Oromo descent, were opposed by other regional governors. Though they had a Muslim background, they were Christians and donated land to churches. The founder of the Yajju dynasty was buried in one of the churches of Lalibela.

The *Zemene Masafent* was generally a period of prolonged political rivalry and conflict. There was constant mobilization of an army from region to region. Soldiers were quartered in peasant households and all their maintenance was provided by peasants. There was also requisition of food as the army did not carry its own provisions to the battle field. Soldiers looted, burned down houses, raped women, and put all kinds of demands on peasants. They also flogged and mistreated peasants. The peasants usually served two chiefs, the *shifta* (bandit) who came at night and the local chief who bothered them in broad day light. Thus, the peasants led a miserable life. They either fled from their areas and moved to the periphery or joined bandit forces. The period witnessed a great deal of social banditry and lawlessness.

Merchants were heavily taxed, having to pay taxes on every tollgate along the trade routes. Trade routes were insecure and merchants lost their property. Conduct of trade was negatively affected. In the 19th century, the

Maria Theresa Thaler was the main currency, and in minor local markets, salt bar (amole) was used as a currency.

The Ethiopian Orthodox Church was divided over doctrinal issues over the nature of Christ. It thus failed to play its traditional role of supporting the Solomonic rulers.

Modern Ethiopia

The modern period of Ethiopia roughly begins in the 19th century. During the second half of the 19th century, the country was coming out of the *Zemene Masafent* period. The man who fought to end the period of lawlessness and bring about political stability was Kassa Haylu, who later became Atse Tewodros (1855–1868). Kassa himself was a product of the *Zemene Masafent,* but he had a sense of mission to carry out. As a self-made man, he started his career as a bandit and rose to be an Atse.

Kassa fought and defeated several regional governors one by one. He was married to a woman from the family of the Yajju dynasty, and his wife was very much committed to his political success. He removed the Yajju Oromo lords and brought to an end the period of the *Zemene Masafent* in 1853. In February 1855, he was crowned as Tewodros II. He took up the throne name because of the prophecy of the *Fekare Iyyassus,* a millenarian tradition about the coming to power of a just ruler who would bring about a period of equity, peace, and political stability.

After his coronation, Tewodros mobilized his forces against the regional governors and extended his power to Wallo, Shoa, Gojjam, and northern Ethiopia. He united the country with an iron fist and mercilessly suppressed his opponents. When the regional governors rebelled, he was forced to mobilize an army every now and then. He was not able to pacify the country but instead dragged it into a bloody conflict.

Tewodros tried to implement several reforms to modernize the country. But he lacked consistency and a method with which to implement them. His appointment policy was a departure from the old ways. He removed local dynasties that were against him and replaced them by his appointees. His appointees were to serve his program. He also tried an experiment of centralized state by appointing his loyal officials. He provided salary to his employees and soldiers, and tried to end the quartering and requisition system. He strictly warned his officials and soldiers not to loot the property of the peasantry. But his program lacked consistency, as he sometimes allowed his solders to loot.

Tewodros tried to establish a modern army. He wanted to replace the regional armies of the *Zemene Masafent* by a national army loyal to him. He wanted his army to be disciplined, organized, and well armed. For this he established the Gafat gun foundry and ordered the imprisoned missionaries to manufacture firearms. He did not want to import firearms but was determined to manufacture them in the country. He trained the army and introduced military titles. He cut the size of his army by avoiding the noncombatants from traveling together with his army, and thus, the army gained greater mobility. He also established the first documented arsenal.

Tewodros also tried to end the slave trade. He once allowed a large number of slaves to go freely when he saw them in one of the markets in Gojjam. The evolution of Amharic language reached a good point in his period. He had the first Amharic chronicler, which has a poetic elegance. His official chronicler was *Dabtara* Zeneb. There are also two other chronicles.

As Tewodros was determined to strengthen monarchical power and unify the country, he was interested in implementing good moral behavior. His chronicler indicates his moral virtues as compared to the decadence of the regional governors and the clergy of the period. He led a simple life and disliked luxury and pomp.

Tewodros tried to bring about religious unity as a means to bring political unity. He promised to enforce the Tewahedo (unionist) doctrine. He wanted to be the head of the church and the state. He also expelled the Catholic missionaries who tried to support his enemies. But he was a friend of the Protestants because of his friendship with two British men. He suppressed the Muslim revolt in Wallo, who had also led a strong resistance against his power. When Tewodros wanted to raise more revenue to pay his soldiers, the church refused to give him the extra land it owned. The clergy spread rumors, and he quarreled with the Coptic bishop. He imprisoned the bishop, who died in prison.

Tewodros wanted to control the Red Sea ports to establish relations with Europe, import artisans and craftsmen, and introduce Western technological development. He aspired to liberate Jerusalem. He also wanted to get European assistance in his war against the Egyptians, who had inherited the port of Massawa from the Turks. When he did not get a good response to his letters to European rulers, he imprisoned Protestant missionaries, including the British consul and later the British envoy to his court. He forced these prisoners to manufacture firearms at his gun foundry. The issue snowballed into a crisis as Tewodros refused to release the prisoners. The British sent an army led by General Napier from India.

When the British force arrived in the country, Tewodros had already lost its control. He had a much reduced army than he had previously. His trusted people and army generals had deserted him. His army was defeated. After releasing his prisoners, Tewodros committed suicide in defiance of the British. It was the internal political problem that brought down the power of

Tewodros than the British. The army looted a large number of manuscripts from his library, and took with them his son, who died a few years later, and left the country.

The next powerful ruler who came after Tewodros was Yohannes IV (1872–1889). Yohannes came to power by defeating his brother-in-law, Tekle-Giyorgis (1868–1871) of Wag and Lasta. Tekle-Giyorgis was in rebellion against Tewodros, who had killed his father.

A few years after Yohannes came to power, the Egyptians invaded northern Ethiopia and the region of Harar, eastern Ethiopia. This was part of their plan to colonize the whole region of the Nile Basin. They were eager to profit from the rich resources of the region to pay their European debt. They also did not allow the import of firearms to Ethiopia and prohibited the travel of Ethiopian envoys to the outside world. In two engagements, Yohannes defeated the Egyptian army, which was also led by mercenary commanders from America and Denmark, at the battles of Gundet and Gura in November 1875 and March 1876, respectively. But the Egyptians did not acknowledge their defeat and did not evacuate the region.

When Yohannes sent an envoy to Egypt, his envoy was imprisoned. The Egyptians sent an envoy, who was a British man, to Ethiopia. The envoy recommended that the Egyptians remain in the occupied regions and that the Italians should occupy the port of Massawa in the Red Sea region. In their entire endeavor, the Egyptians were supported by the British.

But the emergence of a Mahdist revivalist movement in the Sudan since 1881 facilitated the withdrawal of the Egyptian forces from Ethiopia. The Egyptians had colonized the Sudan since 1821 and the Mahdist rebellion was to liberate the country. The Egyptian forces in the Sudan were trapped, and the only way out was through northern Ethiopia and the port of Massawa. The British sent their naval commander to negotiate peace with Yohannes. Thus, the Hewett or Adwa Treaty was signed on June 3, 1884, which gave free access to Egyptian forces to withdraw. Yohannes facilitated Egyptian withdrawal and bought the enmity of the Mahdist forces for supporting Egypt. The Egyptians did not keep their promise and did not hand over the port to Ethiopia. But on British advice, it was transferred to the Italians. Ethiopia fought a number of wars with the Mahdist forces and Yohannes himself lost his life fighting the Mahdist forces in 1889.

Like Tewodros before him, Yohannes followed a policy of unification. He chose a federal policy and appointed two kings under him, Takla-Haymanot of Gojjam and Menelik of Shoa. His major rival was Menelik of Shoa. Menelik submitted in 1878, and promised to pay an annual tribute. Menelik was interested in controlling the region of Kaffa and southern Ethiopia to control the commodity-producing regions. Menelik defeated Takla-Haymanot of

Gojjam, who was earlier appointed for Kaffa, and gained control of Kaffa. Menelik was also supported by the Italians.

Starting in 1868, the Italians were in the port of Assab, and later in February 1885, they occupied Massawa. In their expansion to northern Ethiopia, they met stiff resistance and their force was defeated at Dogali in January 1887. The Italians were also supported by the British, who sent an envoy to mediate. But the terms of the negotiation were not acceptable to Ethiopia. The Italians also tried to attract the nobility, such as Menelik, to their side to destabilize the power of the king of kings.

In the last period of his reign, Atse Yohannes faced a series of problems. His forces fought several wars against the Mahdists, whose forces invaded the region of Gondar, looted the town, burned down churches, and took the people as slaves. The Italians were gradually encroaching inland. Yohannes mobilized his forces against them but the invaders stayed in their forts and were not ready to fight in the open field. There was an epidemic disease and lack of provision forced the army to travel back to their region. Moreover, his vassals rebelled against him and so Yohannes was forced to travel back to punish them. He devastated the region of Gojjam and did not attempt to cross the Abay River to punish Menelik because he knew that the Italians would benefit from the internal rivalry. Instead, Yohannes chose to travel to Mattamma to fight the Mahdists who had devastated Gondar region. The Battle of Mattamma was in March 1889. At first, the Ethiopians defeated the Mahdists. But the king was wounded and the Ethiopian army was in disarray. The Mahdists beheaded Yohannes and also pursued and attacked the Ethiopian army. With the political vacuum created in the north, the Italians advanced to the highland areas and occupied Asmara, declaring Eritrea as their colony. Menelik acceded to the throne and the political center shifted southward to central Ethiopia.

Menelik was the king of Shoa between 1865 and 1889 and king of kings of Ethiopia between 1889 and 1913. The present-day territorial boundary of Ethiopia was built under his unification process. The direction of his expansion was mainly directed into southern Ethiopia to control the commodity-producing regions and the trade routes. The economic benefit of the south expended to buy firearms and build an army to achieve the imperial throne.

Menelik's expansion had three phases. In the first phase—1865–1889—while he was the king of Shoa, Menelik expanded as far as the Awash Valley, which included the Gurage, Arsi, Harar, Leqa-Naqamte, Leqa-Qellem, Jimma, and the Gibe states. Some of these states were conquered and the others submitted to him peacefully. In the second phase—1889–1896—the regions of Walayeta and others were brought under his control. In this period his expansion was affected by the Great Famine of Ethiopia, 1889–1892. In the third phase, the post-Adwa period, the peripheral regions of Kaffa, the Ogaden, Beni-Shangul, Asossa, Borana, and others were incorporated. We have to bear in mind that before an army was mobilized a letter was sent to local chiefs requesting them to submit. If regions submitted peacefully, local rulers were maintained. If the offer of submission was turned down, an army was sent and the region devastated. Regions such as Arsi, Walayeta, and Kaffa strongly resisted Menelik's expansion and these regions suffered much more. Local rulers were removed from office and land was expropriated.

Atse Menelik introduced new things to the country. The first school, Menelik School, and the first hospital, Menelik Hospital, were opened in 1908 and 1910, respectively. The first hotel, Etege Hotel, was established in 1907. A cabinet of ministers was set up in 1907. The country became a member of the World Postal Federation during his period. Menelik minted coins and the first bank, Bank of Abyssinia, was established in 1905. An agreement was signed to construct a railway line between the French colony of French Somaliland (now Djibouti) and Ethiopia in 1894. The railway line reached Dire-Dawa in 1902 and Addis Ababa in 1917, four years after Menelik's death. A number of concession hunters came and signed agreements, but none of them materialized. Above all, Addis Ababa was established as the capital city, and in the post-Adwa period, it attracted consulates, merchants, and envoys who began to frequent the city of Addis Ababa.

Menelik encouraged the Italians against Atse Yohannes. Menelik and the Italians began their relations as friends but later became enemies. The reason for their disagreement was the Italian ambition to colonize the country. The Italians had their foothold in Assab in 1869. In the first Assab phase, the Italian Geographical Society came to Shoa in 1874 in the name of scientific research. During this period, Menelik got an agent to purchase him firearms. In 1882 Pietro Antonelli, an Italian envoy, came to Shoa. He signed the first treaty with Menelik in 1883. The terms of the agreement included consular exchange, free trade, and free movement of people, among others. The Italians got extraterritorial and protectorate rights in Shoa. With British advice, the Italians came to Massawa in February 1885 and began to expand inland. Their expansion was resisted by the governor of the maritime region, and the Italians were defeated at Dogali in January 1887.

The Italians increased their military presence in the region. They tried to isolate regional governors such as Menelik from the side of Yohannes. They signed an agreement, the Convention of Neutrality, with Menelik of Shoa in 1887. Menelik promised to remain neutral in the confrontation between Yohannes and the Italians. For this, he was promised a supply of firearms. When Yohannes died at Matamma in March 1889 fighting the Mahdists, Menelik acceded to the throne in May 1889. At the same time, the Italians were quick to sign a new treaty with Menelik.

The Treaty of Wuchale was signed in May 1889. It was designed to update the Treaty of 1883. The treaty was signed in Italian and Amharic, and there was a wording difference. Article XVII of the Italian version gave the Italians a protectorate right, while the Amharic version made the Italians an agent of the Ethiopian king. It also provided them the control of the Mereb-Melash region, which they had militarily occupied during the period of power vacuum in 1889.

Menelik realized the problem of the treaty when he wrote a letter to European rulers asking them to lift the arms embargo imposed on the country. The Italians had earlier notified the Europeans about their protectorate right over Ethiopia, and the British queen wrote to Menelik advising him not to write her directly without Italian knowledge. The news shocked Menelik and his court. The Italians refused to rewrite the agreement. In 1893, Menelik abrogated the agreement and both sides were getting ready for a showdown. The Italians also incited regional governors to their side but largely failed in this effort.

When the Italians moved southward into Tegray, Menelik called his people to arms. Every region responded positively to his call and Menelik mobilized more than 100,000 soldiers. The first engagement between the Italians and Ethiopia was at Ambalage, southern Tegray, in December 1895. The Italians were defeated and retreated to Maqalle. The Ethiopians besieged the Italian force and denied them access to water. The Italians surrendered, but to the dismay of his commanders, Menelik allowed them to go.

The Battle of Adwa was held on March 1, 1896. Before the battle, the Italians had received false intelligence that Menelik's army had traveled out of Adwa to find provisions. The army was mobilized in September 1895 and it was unable to get enough provisions as the region was highly affected by the previous period of the Great Ethiopian Famine of 1889–1892. The Italians were eager to capture Menelik when his army was away. Nevertheless, the army was intact and ready to fight back. The double-spies had also supplied a false map to the Italians that the Italian army had dispersed far and wide. The battle took less than half a day and the Italians were soundly defeated. Large numbers of Italians were captured as prisoners.

The Battle of Adwa is a symbol of independence not only to Ethiopians but also to the black race in general. When other African countries were falling under colonial yoke, Ethiopia became a bright star in Africa. Adwa was militarily successful and bolstered the independence of the Ethiopia. The idea of black consciousness and pan-Africanism had its root in the success of Adwa. A peace treaty, the Addis Ababa Treaty, was signed in Addis Ababa in October 1896 and it was a major achievement for the country. The Wuchale Treaty of 1889 was null and void. However, the boundary line between the Italian colony of Eritrea and Ethiopia remained the same. Ethiopia also did not get access to the port. These were serious limitations on the country.

Foreign consulates were opened in Addis Ababa: the Italian consulate in 1896 and the French and British soon followed. Then, the United States and Germany opened their consulates. There were also boundary agreements between Ethiopia and the neighboring colonial governments. The boundary between Ethiopia and Franco-Djibouti was signed in 1897, the boundary between Ethiopia and British Somaliland was signed in 1897, the boundary between Ethiopia and the Italian colony of Eritrea was signed in 1900, the boundary between Ethiopia and the British colony of the Sudan was signed in 1902, the boundary between Ethiopia and British East Africa (Kenya) was signed in 1907, and the boundary between Ethiopia and Italian Somaliland was signed in 1908.

Another major socioeconomic event was the Great Ethiopian Famine of 1889–1892. It was caused by the import of rinderpest-infested pack animals by the Italians. The cattle disease quickly spread to central and southern Ethiopia, and spread as far as South Africa. Approximately 90 to 100 percent of the cattle population of the country died. People had no oxen to farm, and thus, large numbers of people died of famine. People also migrated to the court and then to southern regions where the famine was less severe. In 1917, the country was struck by the influenza epidemic, which was a worldwide problem. It also took away a large number of people.

Addis Ababa was founded as the capital city of the country in 1886. It was Etege Taytu, consort of Menelik, who is credited with its foundation. She was attracted to the hot spring of Finfene rather than living in the cold Entotto Mountain. She also coined the name *Addis Ababa* (New Flower) because of the scenic beauty of the topography.

The political stability of the reign of Menelik came to an end in the beginning of the 20th century. In 1905, he had his first stroke and the likely successor Ras Mekonnen of Harar died. This brought about a problem of succession. Menelik established a cabinet of ministers in 1907 to give political continuity and designated his successor in 1909. Iyyassu was very young and a regent was assigned to him. In 1905, the neighboring colonial rulers signed the Tripartite Treaty without the knowledge of Menelik. They signed this because of the impending threat of political instability after Menelik's stroke, and also to protect their interest.

Menelik died in 1913 and Iyyassu formally assumed leadership without any coronation ceremony. He was young and was unable to properly lead his government. He was absent from the capital for months, and his absence helped his adversaries organize opposition against him. He wanted to redress past wrongs and patronized the Oromo, the Muslims, and the Somali. This was resented by the nobility and the Orthodox establishment. He also replaced the older nobility by younger functionaries and this brought him in conflict with the Shoan nobility, who had worked with his grandfather. His religious inclination and his spending more time in Harar and Jigjiga in company of Muslims were negatively interpreted as he had a Muslim background. His father was a Muslim before his conversion in 1878. He had also crowned his father Ras Mikael as king of Wallo and over Tegray, that the nobility of Shoa and Tegray were unhappy. The Tripartite Signatory powers did not also like his friendship with the Germans and Ottoman Turkey.

The nobility and the external forces wanted to get rid of Iyyassu. While he was in Jigjiga, he was removed from power in September 1916. In his place, Etege Zawditu, daughter of Menelik who was rejected from such office, succeeded him. *Ras* Tafari was assigned as regent. Then Iyyassu was defeated in the Afar region and retreated to Wallo. Ras Mikael, his father and governor of Wallo, quickly mobilized an army to Shoa but was defeated in October 1916 and taken prisoner. Iyyassu remained a fugitive until his capture in 1922. He was imprisoned in Selale and then in Addis Ababa until he was killed in 1936 under unknown circumstances during the Italian occupation.

The political settlement of 1916 brought an Etege, Zawditu Menelik, and *Ras* Tafari heir to the throne, to power. Zawditu did not have any experience in political leadership. Tafari was educated and an ambitious person. Tafari gradually undermined the little power that she had. He also removed her supporters such as *Dajjach* Aba Weqaw Birru, palace commander; and *Dajjach* Balcha, governor of the coffee-producing region of Sidamo, in 1928. Her main supporter *Fitawrari* Habta-Giyorgis, Minister of War, died earlier in 1926. Her ex-husband *Ras* Gugsa, governor of Begemder and who was made to separate from his wife in the political settlement of 1916, challenged *Ras* Tafari. He was killed in the battle of 1930 where an airplane was used for the first time to throw a bomb. A few days later, Zawditu died without knowing the outcome of the battle or of the death of her ex-husband. In November 1930, *Ras* Tafari was crowned as Haile-Selassie I.

Haile-Selassie began his reign by trying to strengthen his monarchical rule. His main emphasis was centralization of government. The first step was the enactment of the first constitution in 1931. This was to legalize his absolute power and legitimize the line of succession. It also regularized the relations between the monarchy and the nobility. The constitution was copied from the Meji Constitution of Japan. It was drafted by *Bajjrond* Takla-Hawaryat, who had been educated in Russia. The constitution allowed the establishment of a bicameral parliament. Members of the senate were elected by the emperor and an indirect system of election was used to elect members of deputies. He also appointed his own men to govern the provinces. In 1930 a Belgian mission came to train the Imperial Body Guard. Then the first military academy, Genet or Holeta Military Academy, was established in 1934 with the help of the Swedish government.

But the occupation of the country by the Italians in 1935–1936 interrupted the reforms that Haile-Selassie was undertaking. The Italians invaded the country as a revenge of their defeat at the Battle of Adwa in 1896. This time, the Italians had prepared themselves and invaded the country from three directions: two separate directions in the north from their colony of Eritrea, and from their colony of Italian Somaliland. They also used internationally prohibited poison gas, mustard gas, and airplanes. They had mobilized large number of soldiers, including colonial soldiers from Somali and Eritrea (*Askaris*). They had outnumbered the Ethiopians in terms of armaments and human resource.

Ethiopia was not prepared for such a grand battle. The centralization process had antagonized some of the regional nobility, and these disgruntled nobility joined the Italian side to get appointments. The Ethiopian army was defeated at Maychew on March 31, 1936. The army retreated in disarray and became victim of Italian war lanes. The emperor quickly arrived in the capital and a few days later left abroad with an aim of appealing to the League of Nations.

The Italians captured the capital on May 5, 1936, and declared the establishment of their colony of Italian East Africa. Before the Italians had strengthened their administration, a strong resistance struggle emerged. The resistance struggle was everywhere but was especially strong in the northern provinces. The Italian response to suppress the rebellion further alienated them. They burned down churches and killed clergy men. They killed two Ethiopian bishops, and the atrocities they committed showed the true color of fascism. Young Ethiopians also attempted to assassinate the viceroy, Graziani, by throwing a hand bomb in a ceremony in the palace. Graziani was wounded but ordered his soldiers to carry out mass killing. It was a horrendous killing as the Italian soldiers indiscriminately massacred large numbers of residents in Addis Ababa. The massacre continued for three days. They also massacred a large number of clergymen in the monastery of Dabra-Libanos, where it was believed that the perpetrators had stayed, and the monastery of Zequwala Abo.

When Italy joined World War II on the side of Germany, the British decided to support Ethiopia. The emperor flew from London to the Sudan. He organized an army there, and with British forces, a joint British–Ethiopian army was mobilized to Eritrea and Gojjam. Another British force came from

Kenya northward. The Ethiopian patriots who were fighting alone suddenly received support, and the British force from Kenya occupied the capital in April 1941. However, the emperor entered his capital on May 5, 1941, and declared the liberation of the country.

The British considered the country as an occupied enemy territory. They controlled every activity of the resorted government. The Ethiopian government did not like British dominance but had no choice as it was economically dependent on it. Ethiopia demanded that its sovereignty be recognized, and in 1942, the British did so. The British dominated Ethiopia until 1950 and were then replaced by the Americans, who helped the country until the Ethiopian revolution of 1974.

Emperor Haile-Selassie began to rebuild his administration in 1941. He revised the constitution in 1955, began to build a modern army, issued fiscal reforms, issued a five-year plan, opened schools, resumed infrastructural development, and began economic development.

The 1960s witnessed strong opposition against the government. There was a military coup in 1960 that was suppressed soon. But the coup makers killed

As the last emperor of Ethiopia, Haile Selassie brought his country into the mainstream of modern African politics. (Library of Congress)

a number of ministers. There were more radical oppositions; student, ethnic-nationalist, and revolutionary movements almost everywhere. The notable peasant oppositions were staged in Tegray in 1940 and Bale and Gojjam in the 1960s. There was also student unrest, which demanded land reform with the engaging slogan "land to the tiller." In 1974 the revolutionary fervor became strong and the government was overthrown by a military government.

The military government abolished the imperial system and declared a socialist government. It also declared the separation of church and state, and proclaimed religious equality, thus giving Muslims more rights. It imprisoned the patriarch of the Orthodox Church and later killed him. During the reign of the military government, the (Darg) two patriarchs were elected under its close control. It nationalized rural land and extra urban land and houses. This greatly affected the economy, the former nobility, and the church. It also nationalized industries.

The socialist military government established good relations with socialist countries such as Russia, East Germany, Korea, Cuba, and others but strained relations with the West. When the country was invaded by the Somali forces in 1977, it received support from Russia, Cuba, and Yemen. At the same time, it carried out a bloody political struggle against what it called local reactionary groups. The period witnessed a bloody reign of terror and a large number of young people were killed. There was a civil war in Tegray and Eritrea. This prolonged struggle and battle sapped the power of the military government, and in 1991, it was overthrown by northern insurgents.

In 1991, the Ethiopian People's Revolutionary Front (EPRDF), based in northern Ethiopia, overthrew the military government. Col. Mengistu Haile Mariam, the president of the country, fled to Zimbabwe earlier. The new government demobilized the former army. The Eritrean revolutionaries also declared the independence of the country. At first, they established good relations with Ethiopia but in the 1990s there was a terrible war between them. The EPRDF began to rebuild the country and registered good economic development.

Conflicts and Wars: Eritrea, Ogaden, and Tegray

Ethiopia had passed through periods of political and religious conflicts throughout its history. The imperial period under Emperor Haile-Selassie faced ethno-nationalist, linguistic, and religious oppositions. The major political problem was the question of Eritrea. Eritrea had been an Italian colony since 1890. In 1936 the Italians merged it in their Italian East Africa with Ethiopia and Italian Somaliland. In 1941 Eritrea was under the British military administration as an occupied enemy territory. The Ethiopian government claimed its control after liberation, based on historical, linguistic, ethnic, and social connections.

After 1941 the question of Eritrea was contested by different aspiring groups. The Ethiopian government wanted to unite it, arguing that it was an integral part of its territory. New political parties were established, which had different aspirations. The Unionist Party, based on ethnicity and religion, demanded that Eritrea be united with its motherland Ethiopia. The Muslim League wanted independence and also considered joining the Sudan. The Liberal Progressive Party campaigned for independence together with Tegray. The Pro-Italian Party, which consisted of the mixed race, wanted independence under the umbrella of the Italians.

As there was no amicable solution, the case was presented to the United Nations (UN) in 1948. The UN sent a commission of enquiry to Eritrea and later in December 1950 passed a resolution (UN Resolution 390V) that Eritrea should be united with Ethiopia by federation. The federation was gradually eroded and Eritrea was united with Ethiopia in 1962. Opposition to this political settlement had already begun in 1961 even before the process of unity.

Armed struggle was led by the Eritrean Liberation Front (ELF), which was a Muslim-dominated opposition group. It was largely supported by the Arab world, who claimed the Red Sea as an Arab Sea. Then, different splinter oppositions groups emerged. One of them was the Eritrean People's Liberation Front (EPLF or Shabiya), which emerged as a rival to ELF (Jebha) in the 1970s. The ELF and EPLF were fighting against each other for influence and dominance. These guerrilla fighters attacked the Ethiopian government. When the military government came to power in 1974, these guerrilla fighters greatly challenged it. The war in Eritrea cost large sums of money, weakened the economy, and sapped its energy, and a large number of people and soldiers died. The military government used full force, destroyed villages, and devastated areas, but was unable to suppress the rebellion. The EPLF fought the military government with the support of the EPRDF. In 1991 the military government was overthrown, and eventually, the EPLF declared the independence of Eritrea.

With the liberation of Eritrea, the Eritrean Orthodox Church declared itself independent of the Ethiopian Orthodox Church and crowned its patriarch. The new governments of Eritrea and Ethiopia worked in a close relationship. They used the Ethiopian currency. The friendship of the two governments quickly came to an end. Eritrea attacked Ethiopia in 1998 over a border dispute, which resulted in a bloody war. Despite a cease-fire, a lasting peaceful solution has not been concluded.

The problem of the Ogaden is the result of an irredentist policy of Somalia. There are Ethiopian Somalis living in the Ogaden. The Somali government not only claims the Ogaden as its own territory but also wants to take away lands in eastern Kenya and the Djibouti republic where Somali speakers live. But the boundary delimitation between the British and Ethiopia had put the region of the Ogaden under Ethiopia even if the British had administered it for a few years in the 1940s when the Italians were defeated in 1941. It was difficult to police the boundary as pastoralists were at liberty to travel here and there, and difficult to force them to permanently live on one side of the territory. This is because they had family members on both sides of the territory.

The government of Somalia invaded the Ethiopian territory of the Ogaden in the 1960s but was defeated and repulsed. There was another invasion in the 1970s. The Ethiopian army defeated and repulsed the invading force. During the early period of the revolution, the Somalis invaded and occupied large parts of the Ogaden. The Somali army was supported by the Soviet Union. When the Soviets changed sides and supported Socialist Ethiopia, the United States supplied armaments to Somalia. The Cubans and the Yemeni army also supported Ethiopia. Because of this, Ethiopia emerged victorious.

Enter Tegray. During the period of Atse Yohannes, 1872–1889, Tegray was the center of Ethiopian politics. After the Battle of Matamma and the death of Atse Yohannes in 1889, there was a shift of political center to Shewa. After this, Ethiopian ruling classes established several political marriages with Tegrean ruling classes to strengthen their relations. But following the liberation of Ethiopia from Italian fascist rule, there emerged a peasant rebellion in Tegray in 1943. It is popularly known as the Woyane rebellion. Some also call it as Woyane I. It emerged as a result of government maladministration, corruption, and taxation. The leader of the rebellion was *Blatta* Hayla-Maryam Radda. The peasant rebellion scored an initial victory over the small force stationed in some towns. But it was quickly suppressed with the support of the British airplanes, which bombed some places to crush the rebellion.

With the overthrow of the imperial regime and the coming to power of the military government in 1974, another problem emerged. This was ethno-nationalist rebellion staged by university students. Some writers consider this as the Second Woyane rebellion. It started with an aim to liberate Tegray as its name indicated, Tegray People's Liberation Front (TPLF). But it then acquired a nationalist stand to overthrow the military government. More and more youngsters joined the struggle and its guerrilla force gained strength. It also worked together with the EPLF. More importantly, former members of the Ethiopian People's Revolutionary Party (EPRP) and members of the military wing Ethiopian People's Revolutionary Army, EPRA, who called themselves Ethiopian People's Democratic Movement (EPDM) began to work together with TPLF. In due course, they established the EPRDF army and scored a decisive victory over the military government and overthrew the latter in 1991.

Politics and Government

The government of Ethiopia was based on a tradition of Solomonic dynasty. The result of their union, Menelik I, was traditionally considered to be the first ruler of Ethiopia. The Solomonic rulers were legitimate rulers who also held supreme political power and were considered as sons of god. They were head of the government and the Ethiopian Orthodox Church. The people respected their political and divine power.

In the modern period of Ethiopia, Emperor Haile-Selassie, 1931–1974, established a centralized administration. This is stated in the constitution of 1931 and the revised constitution of 1955, which regularized the succession process. The constitution of 1931 decreed that the families of Emperor Haile-Selassie were the legitimate rulers of Ethiopia. The emperor controlled every political affair in the country, had an army that protected the crown and the imperial family in addition to protecting the imperial territory, controlled land and other economic resources, appointed and demoted its officials, and claimed that the imperial king was the protector of the people. The emperor considered his citizens as his children and believed that it was his duty given by God to protect them.

The political philosophy of the military government was socialism. During its earlier rule, it claimed that its policy was based on "Ethiopian socialism." It was not exactly clear what Ethiopian socialism meant. The guiding principle of its government was Ethiopia Teqedam (Ethiopia First). It vowed to rule the country without bloodshed. However, this period turned out to be one of the bloodiest in the country's history. Every political measure was taken in the name of protecting the country from reactionary plot. It asserted that it was necessary to take such military measures to protect socialism from imperialist plot. Thus it suppressed any opposition with full force. Assassination and counter-assassination (Red Terror was unleashed against White Terror that attempted to kill revolutionary cadres) was common in the 1970s. Young boys who were believed to have been members of the opposition group were summarily killed by government forces and their bodies were strewn in the streets. This was aimed to suppress opposition and to frighten others from joining opposition forces. Such Red Terror measure was taken in urban areas, small or big, against members of EPRP. The military government also killed the leaders of Meison, who had worked with the government. EPRP and Meison were civilian political groups and rivals in their relations with the military government. These civilian political groups had hands in the Red and White Terror.

The military government also carried out a prolonged bloody battle against insurgents in Eritrea and Tegray in the name of fighting secessionist forces. To mobilize the people in its battle against such forces, the military government created a huge military force and propaganda machine in the name of protecting the unity of the state. The military government believed that internal political opposition groups were mobilized against it by imperialist forces or neighboring Arab governments to destabilize a socialist government. The economic policy of the military government was socialist.

Education

The Ethiopian Orthodox Church provided religious education. Church education had several stages, starting with identifying the Geez alphabet. Then students learned how to read. It also provided higher-level education such as church music, interpretation of the *Old* and *New Testaments*. The main aim of church education was to train deacons and priests and other clergymen to serve the church. Church scholars translated books from Coptic, Arabic, and Greek to Geez language. They were well versed in traditional church painting, book binding, the construction of buildings, and other skills. Above all, in the absence of modern education, clerics were employed in government offices.

Both Catholic and Protestant missionaries provided modern education. Missionaries also sent Ethiopians abroad and supported their education. But missionaries were not allowed to teach in Christian-dominated areas. The earliest missionary schools were opened in Eritrea by Swedish missionaries. One of their graduates, Onsimus Nasib, an ex-slave from Wallaga, translated the Bible into Oromifa. The other was Alaqa Taya, who later worked in Berlin University. The other missionary educated was *Kantiba* (mayor) Gabru. He was mayor of a Gondar town. Protestant missionaries were also active in the *Falasha* (Beta-Israel) areas of Gondar. They were encouraged to convert the people to the Orthodox Church. The most prominent educated *Falasha* was Professor Amanuel Tamarat.

Modern education began in the period of Atse Menelik. The beginning of modern education can be traced back to the opening of a school in the house of Alfred Elg, who initiated the idea of railroad construction. The first school, the Menelik II School, was opened in 1908. Coptic teachers were brought from Egypt to teach in the school because of the religious connection with the Egyptian Coptic Church. At first, there was opposition to modern schooling as the people feared missionary influence on their children.

Ethiopian children study in a classroom in the village of Katchema southeast of the capital Addis Ababa, Ethiopia, October 17, 2001. (AP Photo/Sayyid Azim)

In 1925 the Tafari Mekonnen School was opened. The medium of education was French, and the curriculum was dominated by language teaching to produce interpreters. The French also established schools in Dire-Dawa and Addis Ababa in 1910–1911.

Both Atse Menelik and Haile-Selassie sent Ethiopians to have their education abroad. The most prominent examples were Afawarq Gabra-Iyyasus, a prolific writer educated in Italy; *Bajjerond* (meaning, treasurer) Takla-Hawaryat, a Russian-educated artillery man; Nagadras Gabra-Heywat Baykadegn, an intellectual and economist educated in Germany, and Malaku Beyene, a U.S.-educated surgeon. Those educated were government functionaries who rose to prominent government ministerial posts. Some of them wrote articles on the pages of the biweekly *Berhanean Selam* newspaper about the plight of the society and advised the government to reform the administration. These intellectuals are also called the Japanizers because of their advice to take up the example of Japan.

The government of Emperor Haile-Selassie encouraged provincial governors to establish schools in their provincial towns. Thus some schools were built in the 1930s. With the occupation of the country by Italian forces, the Italians established schools. However, children attended classes only until grade four. The medium of education was also Italian and the aim of education was to produce low-level personnel to support the work of the colonial government. They also geared their work in Muslim areas as a policy of attracting formerly disadvantaged and oppressed people to their fold.

On the liberation of the country from Italian rule, the government built more schools. From 1941 onward, the government opened high schools, which were secondary schools that graduated medium-level personnel to the bureaucracy. The government also established schools for the children of the nobility who had lost their lives fighting against the Italians. The imperial government had its own language policy, with Amharic as the official language, which was also the main medium of education.

In 1950 the University College of Addis Ababa was established. Few other colleges such as engineering, agriculture, building, and health colleges were also established. These colleges later formed the Haile-Selassie I University in 1961. University education was dominated by Canadian Jesuits with an aim of preventing student radicalism. But the government was not successful in this regard. During the reign of the military government, it was renamed as the Addis Ababa University.

The military government also built a few universities. The Harmaya and Bahar Dar University, which were colleges under the Addis Ababa University, became independent universities. A new university, Jimma University, was also built. The other major work of the military government was their effort to expand adult education. They mobilized high school and university students during the summer to teach adults. This enabled adults who did not have formal education to learn how to write and read. This was conducted by an efficiently organized series of campaigns. A large number of adults who received their education under this program joined formal education and were able to continue until university level.

The EPRDF is committed to expanding education to rural areas that were neglected by previous governments. The number of primary and secondary schools has more than tripled. There is a significant increase in student enrollment. Peasant families are encouraged to send their children to school. Despite this effort, there is opposition that argues that quality of education is compromised. The government had established 31 universities and several technical colleges and enrollment has significantly increased.

Cities, Occupations, and Economy

Aksum and Lalibela were ancient political capitals during the Aksumite and Zagwe periods. The former was visited by foreign merchants from Roman, Egyptian, Persian, and Arab countries. The medieval court was mobile in nature. It was a period of expansion of an ongoing conflict between the Christian kingdom and the Muslim Sultanates that kings lived in mobile capitals as they were on war-footing and the time ready to mobilize an army where it emerged. Only Atse Zera-Yaqob (1434–1468) established the town of Dabra-Berhan, in northern Shoa, as his political seat. A member of the Portuguese envoy, Father F. Alvarez, mentioned major markets in southern Tegray, the market place of Mandley, and Asel, in Ambassal, which were visited by foreign merchants.

After the wars of the 16th century, the location of the medieval court shifted to the region north of Lake Tana. Several market centers became political centers. But none of them were permanent. Later in 1636, Atse Fasilada established Gondar as his capital. It soon had a large number of residents, including Greeks, Armenians, Indians, and Arabs. It had segregated quarters where the *Falasha*, Muslims, and foreigners lived. It had both weekly and daily markets. Gondarine kings built beautiful castles, which are now tourist attractions. The castles were built by the Beta Israel, pejoratively known as the *Falasha* and show evidence of Indian building influence. Later during the era of the princes (*Zemene Masafent*), the Yajju Oromo lords, who were kingmakers, used to live in the town of Dabra-Tabor. There were also several markets throughout the country.

The town of Makalle served as the seat of Atse Yohannes IV, 1872–1889. In the region of Shoa, several towns served as political seats of the Shoan dynasty. These towns were Ankober, Wachacha, Entoto, and later Addis Ababa. Entoto was established as a court because of its defensive location. Addis Ababa was established as a permanent capital city by Menelik in 1886. It was chosen as a suitable city by Etege Tayatu, who was attracted by its hot springs. The permanence of Addis Ababa was because of its location connected with the market centers of southern Ethiopia, the opening of legations in the post-Adwa period, and the completion of the railway line in 1917, thus attracting it to world markets.

Addis Ababa also became the seat of the former Organization of African Unity (now African Union) in 1963. It became the seat of UN Economic Commission for Africa (ECA) in 1958, and is the seat of international and nongovernmental organizations. Its population has steadily increased and is now estimated to be close to, or over, 5 million.

There are also provincial towns that have large numbers of residents. The cities of Addis Ababa, Dire-Dawa, and Asmara, now in Eritrea, were major towns of industrialization. So were Mojjo and the Aqaqi. Bahar Dar, capital of the Amhara regional state, is a major city; it attracts tourists and is a good resort city. Awassa, the seat of the Southern Peoples and Nationalist state, is another growing tourist destination. The town of Gondar is also another tourist destination. So are the ancient religious towns of Aksum and Lalibela. Other towns worth mentioning are Maqalle, Dessie, Jimma, and

Arba-Mench. Dire-Dawa and Harar are major towns in eastern Ethiopia. Dire-Dawa was founded in 1902 when the Ethio-Djibouti Railway line reached it. Harar was founded in the 14th century and was the main center of Islamic education. With the construction of the railway line, several new towns emerged along the route, and these are Mojjo, Adama, Bishoftu, Aqaqi, and others. It is also good to remember that a large number of Ethiopian live in rural villages but the number of smaller towns is increasing.

During the imperial period, the economy was mainly dependent on agricultural products. The main export commodities were coffee, hides and skin, and oil seeds. These commodities brought foreign exchange to the economy. After the 1950s, industrialization started, and in the next two decades, remarkable expansion occurred in the fields of manufacturing, import–export trade, banking, and construction.

Tenancy was a predominant form of land tenure system in southern Ethiopia before the 1974 revolution, whereas in northern Ethiopia, land was held under the lineage system. The expansion of the state in the 19th century and the need to own large coffee-producing areas facilitated the tenancy system. In most cases, peasants were driven out of their land. The mechanization of agriculture facilitated the evacuation of peasants as well. The government also provided land to patriots, the nobility, and, in rare cases, the unemployed that negatively affected tenants. Foreigners and ambassadors reported about the plight of tenants. Early Ethiopian intellectuals became champions to them too. They also argued about indigenous capitalist development and cottage industries. From the 1960s onward, university students demanded land to the tiller and land distribution.

Slaves provided surplus labor. The history of slavery is as old as the history of the country. Foreign travelers and consulates voiced their concern about slavery in Ethiopia. The *West Minister Gazette* also waged a major protest on slavery in Ethiopia. An arms embargo was also imposed on the country. Ethiopia was also prevented from joining the League of Nations because of the slavery issue. Ethiopia joined the League of Nations in 1925 only after it declared slave trade illegal in September 1923. Maji, Kaffa, Yam, and other regions in southern Ethiopia were areas greatly affected by slave raids. Slaves were also exported to Arabia and were used as domestic slaves in the country. Then a decree was issued for a gradual emancipation of slaves. A school was established to teach ex-slaves to learn some skills.

Over 90 percent of Ethiopian population are rural farmers and live in small villages. The number of industrial labor force is not that much significant. With the expansion of small-scale industries, the workforce is on the rise. Those working in the service sector are also growing. The majority of university graduates are employed by the government. The private sector, which is expanding now, also employs more workers.

In the field of banking, the first bank, Bank of Abyssinia, was established in 1905. It was subsidiary of the Bank of Egypt, owned by the British. It gave loans at high interest rates and was slow to attract customers. Etege Taytu established a society to promote trade and agriculture in 1908. The nobility bought shares and the total capital of the society was three million *Birr*. It gave loans at more reduced interest rates than the Bank Abyssinia. It was established to rival the Bank of Abyssinia, which had a monopoly status. The initial capital was three million *Birr*. Only members of the nobility bought the shares.

In 1942 the State Bank of Ethiopia was established. It provided service until 1963 and was split to form the Commercial Bank of Ethiopia and the National Bank of Ethiopia. Other banks such as the Agricultural Development Bank and the Addis Ababa Bank, a private bank, were also established. But during the reign of the military government, private banks were nationalized. Since 1991 several private banks have been established, and the market is expanding.

The Ethiopian Airlines registered a remarkable growth and it is the leading airlines in Africa, with large numbers of destinations around the world. Another remarkable achievement was in the expansion of electric power. Several dams built over the Awash, Gibe, and the Abay Rivers produce electricity. Several infrastructural developments to build dams were undertaken. One such huge project is the construction of a dam over the Abay River, the Millennium Dam, which is under construction.

The Imperial Highway Authority built roads in the country. Provincial and other important towns have road links with the capital. Since 1991, the government has given more emphasis to expand roads in the country.

With the establishment of the railway line since the beginning of the 20th century, most of the Ethiopian export was handled by the port of Djibouti. In the 1920s and 1930s, the port of Gambella handled 25 percent of the export to the Sudan. Gambella was served by the Baro River, which is navigable during the summer. The ports of Massawa and Assab, in the present-day Eritrea, also served the northern provinces. The country does not have its own port but since 1991 it has been served by the port of Djibouti.

Note

1. M. I. Bender, *Languages of Ethiopia* (London: Oxford University Press, 1976), pp. 1–19.

2

Religion and Worldview

INDIGENOUS RELIGIONS

The ancient people of Ethiopia believed in many gods, or were polytheist. According to tradition, the first god was a serpent. With the settlement of South Arabian people in northern Ethiopia between the seventh and fifth century BC, South Arabian gods were introduced into the country. These gods included Almaqah, Astar (god of heaven), and many others. Almaqah was the principal god of the South Arabians. The predominant center of their settlement and religious center was Yeha, northeast of Adwa. Here they built a temple for Almaqah. The wall of the temple was 10 meters high, and today, only one side of the temple still survives. It is believed to have been constructed between the seventh and fifth century BC. Even in later periods, the name *Almaqah* was found written in several inscriptions.

People in ancient northern Ethiopia also believed in Greek gods. Their names were also included in ancient inscriptions, including Hercules, Hermes, Zeus, Aries, and Poseidon. In addition, there was a belief in local indigenous gods such as Mahram, god of war; Baher, god of the sea; and Meder, god of the earth.

Local tradition indicates that Judaic belief was introduced into the country. This was associated with the visit of the Queen of Sheba to Jerusalem in 1000 BC. The *Beta-Israel* (*Falasha* community) were followers of the Judaic religion. There are similar customs between Judaism and Christianity. These include beliefs on circumcision, observance of the Sabbath, *Tabot* (the Ark of the Covenant), liturgical dance, avoidance of pork meat, cleanliness during the period of menstruation, sex, taking the shoes off when entering religious places, fasts, New Year, and feasts.

The origin of the *Beta-Israel* (*Falasha*) is controversial in Ethiopia's history. Ethiopian sources indicate that they were Judaic Agaws who refused to be converted to Christianity. There were several attempts to integrate the community into the medieval state but there was strong resistance against it. The chronicle of Atse Yeshaq (1413–1430) indicates that he tried to assimilate the *Falasha* community to the medieval empire. He decreed that they could inherit land if they were converted to Christianity. Those who refused to be converted were forced to evacuate their land, and thus, the name *falasi* (exile) came into use. It was from this decree that the name *falasha* was adopted.

The Ethiopian Orthodox Church had its impact on Jewish religion. A renegade monk from an orthodox monastery joined the community and copied the Old Testament to the *Falasha* community during the period of Atse Dawit (1390–1412). Some members of the royal family, who had earlier joined Orthodox monastic life, also joined the *Falasha* monasteries. Ethiopian Orthodox Church monks introduced monasticism to the Jewish community. Their youngsters also received their education in Ethiopian churches.

The *Falasha* community refused to be assimilated into the medieval state and waged a relentless struggle. The medieval rulers also tried hard to suppress their rebellion and pushed their territory further north to the Semien Mountains. The state imposed forced conversions, and the *Falasha* lands were taken away.

During the 17th and 18th centuries, the *Falasha* participated in the construction of the Gondarine castles. Atse Tewodros (1855–1868) allowed the Protestant missionaries to teach and convert the *Falasha* to the Orthodox Church. This initiated international Jewish organizations to take interest in the area and come to teach them. The local Jewish community studied Hebrew and began to adopt the language in their religious services. Some were taken abroad for study, and those who came back were instrumental in establishing closer relations with Israel. In the 1970s and 1980s, a large number of Ethiopian Jews immigrated to Israel.

There are also other forms of traditional religions that afflict people in the form of spiritual possessions. One such thing is the *Zar* cult (*bala weqabi*). *Zar* possession is known all over the country. It is inherited within a family, and both sexes can be possessed by the spirit. It can also serve as a guardian spirit, and the harmful spirit had to be appeased to get relief from problems. People who have problems come to the *Zar* cult and try to find resolutions to their problems. Such people are often advised to perform ritualistic sacrifices.

As religious leaders of their community, the *bala wuqabi* are respected and feared.

The indigenous religion of the Oromo people is called *Waaqeffanna*. Waqa is the sky god, creator of life, who knows all and lives in heaven. Nothing happens without his knowledge. His name should also be referred to with respect. People address Waqa as *Rabbi*. He is the guardian of truth and justice. He protects all but withdraws his support from evildoers. Thus, misfortune comes when he withdraws his support. Believers pray to him for peace, health, rain, and good harvest.

It is believed that there are also different spirits that benefit or harm human beings. The *qallu* (male) or *qallitti* (female) are officiating priests or priestesses and are protectors of the law. The *ayana* is a divine agent that represents man in his relation to *Waqa*. The spirit of a dead person is called *ekera*. A sacrifice is held for the dead person so that the ghost of the dead does not affect his or her relatives. *Sanbata* is a guardian spirit for cattle, and people make sacrifices for more cattle wealth. The *ayole* spirit helps women conceive and bear children. The *atete* (ceremony) is held by women who want to become pregnant. The name *Maram* (as St. Mary of the Christians) is invoked during delivery.

The religion of the Oromo highly emphasizes good moral values such as respecting elders and restraining from doing evil things that harm the society. There are also some cultural connections in which some Christian concepts such as *Sanbat* (Sunday), St. Mary, *Satan* (devil), and spirits were adopted by the Oromo from Christians, as well as other concepts from Muslims.

ORTHODOX CHRISTIANITY AND ITS IMPACT

According to the New Testament, Christianity was introduced to Ethiopia during the period of the Apostles. An Ethiopian eunuch of Queen Candace, who was in charge of her treasure, was traveling back from Jerusalem after Pentecost and was eventually baptized. The eunuch became the first man to be baptized after the Apostles, and Ethiopia was the first country to be Christianized after Jerusalem (Acts 8: 26–29). However, the historical sources that have been discovered so far in northern Ethiopia reveal that paganism was the predominant belief in pre-Christian period.

The introduction of Christianity to Aksum was the result of Ethiopia's commercial relationship with the Greco-Roman world. Christian merchants and envoys visited Aksum, and their local people obtained information about Christianity. The official introduction of Christianity was in the first half of the fourth century AD during the reign of Atse Ezana.

The story is that there was a philosopher of Tyre who had traveled with his students to India. On his way back, his ship anchored in the coast of the Red

Sea. But it was attacked by pirates and all the crew were put to death. His two students, Frumentius and Aedesius, survived the incident and were taken to the court of Aksum. They stayed in Aksum for a number of years and were finally set free. Frumentius traveled to Alexandria to report the presence of Christians in Aksum, and asked for the appointment of a bishop to Aksum.

Athanasius, the patriarch of Alexandria, wanted to send an Egyptian to become the bishop of Aksum. But none of the Egyptian bishops were interested in traveling. Thus, in AD 328, he ordained and appointed Frumentius as the first bishop of Aksum. This is evident from his two letters sent to the king of Aksum.

Frumentius was happily received in Aksum and is known as *Abba-Selama* (father of peace) and *Kesate-Berhan* (revealer of light). He is canonized as a saint by the Ethiopian Orthodox Church, the Greek Orthodox Church, and the Roman Catholic Church. A church is dedicated to him in Tamben, southern Tegray.

The official conversion of Atse Ezana to Christianity occurred following the arrival of Frumentius in Aksum. According to tradition, two brothers, Abreha (Ezana) and Asebeha (Sayzana), who are said to have been co-regents, accepted Christianity. They were canonized as saints and a church is dedicated to them near Weqro, in Tegray.

Ezana lived both as a pagan and a Christian ruler of Aksum. In his pagan inscriptions, he called himself the son of Mahram, pagan god of Aksum. After his conversion to Christianity, he called himself the son of Jesus Christ. The later coins of Ezana also bore the symbol of the cross. The letter of a Byzantium Emperor to Ezana indicated the introduction of Christianity to Aksum. The letter was written in AD 356 and its content was on religious issues. The emperor invited Ezana to accept the doctrine of Arianism as an official religion rather than the doctrine of Nicaea, which believed in the Trinity of God.

The later inscriptions of Ezana started with the invocation of "In the faith of God and of the Father, and the Son and the Holy Ghost who have saved my kingdom. I believe in Your Son Jesus Christ." The earlier name—"the son of Mahram"—was replaced by the new saying "by the power of the Lord of heaven." Ezana also mentions "Lord of Heavens," "Lord of Earth," and "Lord of All." Ezana built the church of Aksum Seyon, the first church in Ethiopia.

Toward the second half of the fifth century AD, a group of Christian missionaries arrived in Aksum. The pioneers were called the *Sadqan* (the Righteous Men). They came and settled in Matara, now in Eritrea. However, due to unknown reasons they were persecuted by the local people. The second group who later came to the country were called the Nine Saints. They came from the eastern Mediterranean because they were persecuted there. They were supported by Aksumite rulers. Their arrival in Aksum is regarded as the second Evangelization. They built churches and monasteries in the surrounding regions of Aksum. One of them built the monastery of Dabra-Damo. The Nine Saints converted and baptized the non-Christians to Christianity, translated most parts of the Bible into Geez, and introduced monastic life.

The other major development in the church in the sixth century AD was the emergence of St. Yared. He was the father of Ethiopian church music, introducing religious singing to Ethiopia. The development of church music was the greatest achievement in the sixth century. He is also considered to be the founder of traditional education. *Qene* (pottery) is his creation. *Qene* had a double meaning, gold and wax. The gold is the hidden, or inner, meaning, while the wax is the literal or overt meaning, which is easily understandable. He also composed the Degwa, a collection of hymns. The music of Yared had three modes or musical notations. Yared is highly praised for all his achievements and is canonized as a saint.

The church gradually expanded to the south of Aksum. During the period of the Zagwe dynasty, the church expanded to the Lake Tana region, and

Bet Giyorgis (St. George's), one of a number of rock-hewn churches built under Lalibela, a Christian king of Ethiopia during the 12th and 13th centuries. (iStockPhoto.com)

the Zagwe rulers built several rock-hewn churches. The establishment of the rock-hewn churches of Lalibela was intended to emulate the significance of Jerusalem. In the Ethiopian church tradition, the church of Aksum and Lalibela are considered the second Jerusalem.

The earliest church established in Amhara land dates back to the ninth century. With the southward shift of the political center and the settlement of Christian communities in Amhara region, the first church was established in the region of Lake Hayq in 1248. The founder of the monastery, Abba Iyyassus Moa, had closer relations with the founder of the new dynasty. By about the 13th century, the church had expanded as far as northern Shoa. The monastic school of Debra Hayq became the first traditional school to be established, which was very important in the expansion of the church in Amhara land and Shoa. The graduates of this school traveled back to their regions and founded churches and monasteries in Amhara land, Shoa, and Lake Tana.

The other monastery that played a major role in the expansion of the church was that of Dabra-Libanos. It was established by *Abuna* Takla-Haymanot in 1284 in the region inhabited by the pagan community of Damot, which was located in northwestern Shoa and south of the Abay River. It was established in the direction of the expansion of the Muslims. Beyond the Abay River was the pagan region of Gojjam. The graduates of this monastery founded churches in Damot, Gojjam, across the Abay River, the *Falasha* (Beta-Israel) regions of Lake Tana, Semen, and Wegera.

The head of the Ethiopian Orthodox Church was an Egyptian national. He was appointed for life by the patriarch of the Egyptian Coptic Church. The Egyptian Coptic bishop was a rather isolated figure because he neither spoke the local language nor understood the customs of the country. Only very few Coptic bishops spoke the local language and wrote books. The bishops were helped by interpreters, Copts who knew the local language or Ethiopians who knew Arabic. He was assisted by the Abbot of the monastery of Dabra-Libanos, who had the title of the *echage*. The *echage* was the administrator of the church.

The Egyptian Church did not allow the Ethiopian clergy to appoint their own bishops. This was a major restriction imposed by the Coptic Church. The expansion of the church and the literary developments in the church was the work of Ethiopian clergymen. Reforms in the church were also initiated by the Ethiopian clergy.

The major reform attempt in the 14th century was to observe the Sabbath as a holiday. The movement was led by Abba Ewostatewos. The Coptic Church declared the Sabbath as a Jewish holiday, and it became a point of conflict in the church. The monastery of Dabra-Libanos supported the position of the Coptic Church. The movement was initiated by a monastic leader in Tegray, and churches in northern Ethiopia supported the Sabbath. The movement began in the 14th century and continued to be a point of conflict in the church. Unable to get royal support to his religious question, the leader of the movement, Abba Ewostatewos, went into self-imposed exile to the Holy Land and thence he died in Cyprus in the second half of the 15th century.

The disciples of Abba Ewostatewos came back and established the monastery of Dabra-Bizan, in Eritrea in 1390, and began to teach their religious doctrine. Gradually they gained supporters in northern Ethiopia. Later during the period of Atse Dawit (1380–1412) they were given freedom of movement and were allowed to teach their doctrine as they had secured some support from court officials and clergymen who lived in the royal court. The problem was solved during the period of Atse Zera-Yaqob (1434–1468), who had his church education in Tegray. In a religious council, the Council of Dabra-Mitmaq, Shoa, held in 1450, he presided in the council and declared that the Sabbath should be an equal holiday to that of Sunday. The monastery of Dabra-Libanos was given the right to collect taxes from Shewa for accepting the decision. It should be noted that the question of the Ewostatewos movement was also to achieve religious independence from the Coptic Church of Alexandria.

Another religious controversy that emerged during the period of Zera-Yaqob was the movement of Estifanos. Abba Estifanos was a known church scholar in Tegray who urged his followers to live by their labor, advising them to produce their own food and asking the clergy not to accept gifts from officials. This earned him opposition from the clergy. But the clergy accused him of not respecting the cult of Maryam (St. Mary), of not bowing when the king's name was mentioned, and of other issues. He was summoned to the court where he and his followers were beaten and ordered to account for their stand. They were termed *Sera Maryam* (enemy of Mary) and those who welcomed these people were persecuted. His followers were also persecuted. Unlike the followers of Ewostatewos, the followers of Estifanos continued to receive holy orders from the bishop and remained under the umbrella of the church. The followers of Ewostatewos were denounced by the bishop, and they did not have enough priests and deacons to serve in their churches.

Atse Zera-Yaqob was a religious nationalist and did not attempt to import bishops from Egypt after the death of the Coptic bishops. He encouraged the clergy to travel to areas where churches were not established to teach the people. He wrote religious books and struggled to root out pagan beliefs. The religious nationalism of the period of Zera-Yaqob continued, and during the period of his son and successor, Ba'eda-Maryam (1468–1478), a religious council was held in 1477 to appoint an Ethiopian bishop. In this council, a majority of the participants, numbering 400, decided to appoint an Ethiopian bishop. However, the king decided to import a Coptic bishop, and the decision of the council did not materialize.

There were periods when there were two or three bishops in the country. Sometimes clerics arrived in the country with claims that they were appointed by the Coptic Church. But their true identities were soon discovered, and they were quickly banned from the country and, in some cases, put to death.

In the modern period of the country, Atse Yohannes IV (1871–1889) brought four bishops. He kept one of them to himself, and sent the others to Gojjam, Shewa, and Wallo. They were sent to these regions administered by *Negus* Takla-Haymanot, *Negus* Menelik, and *Ras* Araya-Selassie, son of Yohannes IV, respectively.

In the early 20th century, a widespread movement to appoint an Ethiopian bishop emerged during the period of Atse Menelik (1889–1913). The call for the appointment of an Ethiopian bishop was spearheaded by the early intellectuals of the period. These intellectuals published their ideas on the pages of *Berhanena Selam*, a weekly Amharic newspaper established in 1925. They accused the Coptic Church for not appointing an Ethiopian bishop. The religious nationalism of the period grew in strength from time to time and people from all parts of the country sent articles to be published on the pages of *Berhanena Selam* newspaper. They also accused the Coptic bishop in Ethiopia for accepting simony (giving money for ordination) and for making the Ethiopian Church dependent on the Coptic Church.

The Ethiopian government asked the Coptic patriarch to appoint an Ethiopian bishop. The government also tried to control the movement so that it could take the credit itself. Through a long process of negotiation, the Coptic patriarch agreed to appoint Ethiopian bishops. Thus, four clerics traveled to Cairo and were appointed as bishops in June 1928, and another in Addis Ababa in January 1929. This was a landmark event in the history of the Ethiopian Church, and five dioceses were created because of it. The Ethiopian Church achieved its autocephalous status, but Ethiopian bishops were still not allowed to appoint their own patriarch.

The negotiation with the Coptic Church was interrupted because of the occupation of the country by the Italian fascist forces from 1936 to 1941. The Italians attacked the church and killed two of the Ethiopian bishops. One of the bishops was taken as prisoner to Italy and then was brought back to serve the colonial government. Large numbers of churches were burned down during the war, clergymen were killed, and church property looted or destroyed. The Italians declared the independence of the church, isolated it from the Coptic church, appointed several bishops, and opened several dioceses. With the independence of the country from Italian colonial rule, the Italian-appointed bishops, who were earlier excommunicated by the Coptic Church, were imprisoned and lost their bishopric position.

The negotiation with the Coptic Church resumed soon but it took a number of years to reach a compromise. Finally, the first patriarch was appointed in Cairo in 1955. In 1971 the second Ethiopian patriarch was appointed and crowned in the country by the Ethiopian clergy. The Coptic Church was not invited to preside in the coronation ceremony. Gradually, the Coptic Church lost its dominance over the Ethiopian Orthodox Church, but the relationship still continues on an equal basis.

Since 1959 six Ethiopian patriarchs have been appointed; they were Abunas Basliyous, Tewoflos, Takla-Haymanot, Marqoriyos, Pawlos, and Matyas. A large number of archbishops have also appointed. The numbers of dioceses have increased and several other dioceses have also been opened in the United States, Canada, Europe, Africa, and the Middle East to serve a large number of Ethiopia Diaspora.

With the outbreak of the 1974 revolution, the church–state relation took a different course. The revolution did away with the monarchical order and the old church–state relations came to an end. The church was no longer the official religion of the country. The military rulers declared religious equality. They nationalized church lands and extra urban land and extra houses. The church thus lost its economic income. The military rulers imprisoned patriarch Tewoflos and later killed him. Gradually, the government improved its stance and worked with the church. Two patriarchs were appointed during the period of the military regime. After the downfall of the military regime, the second patriarch appointed by the military government was forced out of office by the current government (by Ethiopian People's Revolutionary Democratic Front). Remarkably, a large number of churches were built during the military regime as local urban dwellers and peasant associations provided land to churches. The current government that came to power in 1991 appointed a patriarch, who had spent some years in prison during the period of the military government and who lived in exile in the United States. He died in August 2012, and his successor was elected and appointed in March 2013.

The Ethiopian Orthodox Church had a huge impact on the social, cultural, and political aspects of the country. The church was established as the official religion of the country when Atse Ezana was converted in the fourth century AD. It received imperial protection and the state allocated land and other economic resources to the church. As the religion of the state, the church was not persecuted. Kings who acceded to the throne received their legitimacy when they were anointed by the bishop. The legitimacy of the kings was due to their claim that they were the descendants of Solomon of Israel and the Queen of Sheba. Throughout the history of the country, church and state worked together until 1974.

The church contributed its share as a center of learning. Young children had access to religious education. The curriculum of the church had several stages, including a higher level of education. Before the introduction of modern education, the clergymen staffed government offices. Clergymen were chroniclers, religious advisors, and scribes in the court. They supported the expansion of the state, and through religious propaganda, they mobilized people for battles and they themselves participated in theaters of war.

Clergymen translated religious books from Arabic, Coptic, and Greek into the Geez language. Monastic leaders had their own hagiography, which had some references to succession, power struggle in the court, expansion of the state, trade and trade routes, and other historical events. They were also experts in book binding.

Clergymen built churches and monasteries, and the building technology of some of the ancient churches is remarkable. The rock-hewn churches of Lalibela are recognized as world wonders by the United Nations Educational, Scientific, and Cultural Organization (UNESCO). There are also large numbers of such churches that stand as a living proof of the impressive and long-lasting building technology of ancient Ethiopia. Traditional religious paintings adorn the interior of churches. The style, colors, design, and their aspects of Ethiopian church painting had their own unique features. According to the 2007 census, the percentage of religious groups

Painting of Mary and Jesus at an Ethiopian Orthodox monastery in Laka Tana, Ethiopia. (iStockPhoto.com)

is as follows: Orthodox Christians 43.5 percent, Protestants 18.6 percent, Catholics 0.7 percent, Muslims 33.9 percent, and traditional believers 2.6 percent.

THE ISLAMIC IMPACT

Ethiopia is one of the earliest countries to establish early contact with the Islamic world. In fact, its relationship with Arabia predates the sixth century. When the early Islamic converts were persecuted in Arabia, the prophet Mohammed sent his followers to the kingdom of Aksum. The refugees came in two different waves. They were received warmly and allowed to live there freely. The rulers of Arabia sent envoys to Aksum to take back the Muslim refugees. But the king of Aksum refused to hand them over, and they stayed in Aksum until the prophet Mohammed gained political control of Mecca. Thus, Arabia and Aksum had good relations. It is reported that Mohammad had advised his followers not to attack Ethiopia for their support to Muslim refugees. But a few years after the death of Mohammad, their relationship turned sour.

Then there was commercial rivalry between Arabia and Aksum to dominate the Red Sea trade. The ports of Adulis, on the side of Aksum of the Red Sea, and Jeddah on the Arabian side became rivals. The commercial rivalry turned into armed conflicts, which resulted in the destruction of the Aksumite port of Adulis in AD 875. Aksum lost its commercial hegemony over the Red Sea and its economy declined. The Muslims also controlled the Dahlak Islands in the Red Sea in the 10th century AD. By the 10th century, the Dahlak Muslim Sultanate was established. However, Islam never penetrated deep into the highland regions of northern Ethiopia.

The main gateway of Islam to Ethiopia was the port of Zeyla in the Indian Ocean coast. Islam came to Ethiopia through trade. Muslim merchants from Arabia settled along the trade routes and intermarried with the local population. They were also able to convert the local population. Zayla had a rich and profitable hinterland, and several items of commodities were exported to Arabia. Muslim Arabs also settled along the coasts of the Indian Ocean and established several other states in Somalia.

The Sultanate of Shoa was the first Muslim Sultanate established in AD 896 in eastern highland Shoa, by the Makhzumite dynasty that traced its descent from Arabia. The founder of the dynasty was Mahzumi Khalid b. Al-Wald. Its rulers had an Arabic chronicle, which is translated only into Italian. The sultanate had a political rivalry with the sultanate of Yifat. The rulers of Yifat later controlled the sultanate of Shoa in 1285.

The Muslim sultanate of Yifat, the second sultanate, was established in northern Shoa. It was ruled by the Walasma dynasty and its founder was

Street scene with mosque, Harar, Ethiopia. (Guiziou Franck/Hemis/Corbis)

Umar Walasma, who also claimed descent from Arabia. In the beginning of the 14th century, Yifat put up a strong resistance against the Christian kingdom, as it did not want to lose its monopoly of the trade routes. The rulers of Yifat, supported by other Muslim states, rebelled one after the other and refused to pay tribute to the Christian court. But the Christian kings quickly suppressed their rebellion, and Yifat became a tributary state under the Christian kingdom. Later in the 15th century, some of the rulers of Yifat broke away from Yifat and moved away from beyond the Awash River, settling in the arid regions of Adal. Here they established the sultanate of Adal, also called Harar. The new rulers of Adal adopted a militant attitude and were committed to be independent. They also did not want to be a tributary state under the Christian kingdom. Later on, the rulers of Adal from the Walasma dynasty were dominated by army commanders, including Mahfuz and Ahmed Gragn. The latter defeated the Christian kingdom and dominated the country from 1525 until he was killed in 1543.

Hadya was another Muslim sultanate that was established in southern Shoa. The rulers of Hadya supported the Walasma rulers of Yifat and were partners in the slave trade. But it was made a tributary state of the Christian kingdom. Hadya was also a center of the slave trade. Atse Zera-Yaqob (1434–1468) was married to a Hadya queen, Elleni, who became a prominent member of the court and served as a member of regency. She also wrote the first letter to Portugal to establish relations in 1512. Other medieval rulers were also married to Hadya women.

Bali was a Muslim state that was established in the river basins of Ganale and Wabi-Shebelle. Bali was a supporter of the Yifat but it was integrated into the Christian state. The medieval rulers had also stationed an army in Bali to protect the frontier regions from Adal. The ruler of Bali was defeated in 1527 by the ruler of Adal, which opened the way for the success of Adal.

The Muslim sultanates of Sharaka, Dawaro, Dera, Fetegar, and Arababni were all defeated, and were either integrated or made into tributary states under the medieval court. The medieval rulers had also stationed an army in Dawaro and Fetegar to protect the frontier regions from Adal. Nevertheless, all of them became supporters of Adal in the wars of the 16th century.

The Muslim sultanate of Adal was established east of the Awash River. It was also called the sultanate of Harar. The rulers of Adal were members of the Walasma dynasty who had broken away from Yifat. They were militant, and mobilized the pastoral community against the medieval court. The relative location of Adal in the arid regions of eastern Ethiopia helped them carry out raids and loot regions under the Christian kingdom. They also carried a *Jihadi* spirit and raided the neighboring regions. Such raids affected the peace of the region and the conduct of trade. The medieval rulers were also forced to mobilize an army, which also affected the settled life of the people. Atse Dawit (1380–1412) followed one of the Adali rulers into Zayla and killed him in 1402–1403. This brought a relative period of peace but the problem continued. The military commanders of Adal dominated the ruling classes of Adal, and in early 16th century, they were able to defeat the Christian kingdom.

Since the introduction of Islam into the country, Muslim clerics have played a major role in expanding Islam. Muslim educational centers were established, and young people received their education. The medium of education was, and still is, Arabic. Books were produced locally. Harar, Wallo, Jimma, and other areas became main educational centers.

The Ulama traveled to different places to gain their education. The Muslims felt that they were politically dominated and marginalized in state affairs. Thus, there was a period of rebellions against the state in the medieval period and also in modern periods. The Muslims sought support from Egypt in medieval period, and in the modern period, they received it from other Arab countries.

Muslims did not participate in modern education in large numbers. They also wanted Arabic to be the medium of instruction. They resented that Amharic was the main language of education. They also felt that the government had not built enough schools in their areas. Only in rare cases did the state allocate land for building mosques. It was during the military regime, 1974–1991, that Muslim holidays became publicly recognized. In April 1974, during the early period of the military regime, a large number of Muslims staged a huge demonstration to achieve religious freedom, and since 1991, they have been enjoying religious freedom.

In the modern period, Ethiopia has witnessed the emergence of Muslim opposition against the centralizing policy of the imperial regime. Young Muslim students, who received their education in Egypt or other Arab countries, mobilized rebellions against the government. Some of them traveled to neighboring Muslim countries and opened armed struggles or rebelled in their regions. Some of these oppositions were not strong enough to overthrow the government. But mass discontent erupted in the revolution of 1974 in which Muslims took active part in these political events. According to the 2007 census, Ethiopian Muslims comprised 33.9 percent of the population.

Apart from these Muslim states, there were also several other Omotic states—Damot, Kaffa, Enarya, Bizamo, Walayeta, and Yem—that were established along the Omo Valley. Most of them were traditional believers or pagan states. The prominent state in early 13th century was the kingdom of Damot, which was established on the bend of the Abay River but had tributary states in the southern regions such as Walayata and Kaffa. Damot was brought under the medieval court in the early 14th century. These Omotic states were rich in commodities and were raided both by the Muslim and by Christian rulers for slaves and to control the trade routes. Later, the medieval court established its power over these states as mentioned earlier.

RELIGION AND POLITICS

Religion and politics were interconnected. The medieval Christian state or the Muslim sultanates used religion for their legitimacy. The medieval state economically supported and protected the church. The Ethiopian Orthodox Church was the state religion and its followers were not persecuted. The state allocated land to the church. The church also gave legitimacy to the Christian state. It also propagated to its followers that the people should be loyal to the Ethiopian "Solomonic" rulers. The kings considered themselves as head of the church. When religious councils were held, they were presided over by kings. They controlled the appointment of bishops and it was their duty to import bishops to Ethiopia, They also appointed known clerics to important churches and monasteries.

The church took part in state politics. Clerics were members of the regency and acted as father confessors to kings. They provided religious advice to the king and the royal family. They were called to give their views on important state issues. The head of the church played a major role in denouncing the coup leaders of 1960 and rallying the loyalist forces of the army to suppress the coup leaders.

The imperial rulers did not economically benefit Muslim religious places. They had only supported the construction of some mosques, particularly in Eritrea. Muslim holidays were not officially observed. Only Muslim leaders were allowed to visit the palace to pay their respects to the king on important Muslim holidays. Muslims thus held resentment on several Muslim religious issues and were against the policy of the state that did not respect their rights. Since 1974 the rights of Muslims have been respected. Religious freedom is also guaranteed by the constitution.

3

Literature and Media

ORAL LITERATURE

Ethiopia has a rich tradition of oral literature in terms of fables, stories, poems, and riddles. Parents and older people tell stories and fables to children, who in turn enjoy telling stories to their friends. As most of the Ethiopian ethnicities and cultural groups do not have their own script, there was a great deal of orality, as traditions are passed by word of mouth from generation to generation.

Other kinds of oral literature are recited through traditional methods of communication such as proverbs, folklore, poetry, and legendary stories. These stories teach moral values, as well as the history of the society and the people's past. These stories appear as myths, legends, and symbolic accounts of political structures, praise songs, epic poetry, folktales, riddles, proverbs, and magical spells. These are just a few examples that display Ethiopian oral culture, which is passed down from one generation to the next. As Ethiopia is home to many ethnicities, they have similar traditions of oral literature. Sometimes the stories are similar in content or overlap in their content.

Ethiopians tend to have a very good sense of humor and are witty when they converse with other people during their leisure time or on a period of duty. Most witty statements have a double meaning of "wax and gold." The wax is the unconcealed or overt meaning that can be understood easily. The gold has the inner, covert, or hidden meaning. The covert meaning is not clear and may contain stealthy or blatant meaning. Thus, people need to think to get the real meaning of the gold rather than simply smile with people who immediately get what it means.

A very famous legend of witticism was *Alaqa* Gabra-Hana of Gondar. Almost all kinds of wits are attributed to him and his name is often mentioned. His riddles are widely spoken when people have leisure time. He served as *liqa kahenat* (head of priests) of Gondar. He was also interpreter of the *Fetha-Nagast* (*Law of Kings*) and a judge in the court of Atse Tewodros (1855–1868). He also served as *alaqa* (head) of the Chalaqot Selassie church in Tegray. He was the teacher of *Aquwaquam* (chant). During the period of Atse Menelik (1889–1913), he came to Shoa and taught *Aquwaquam* at Entotto Raguel church. He was on good terms with Menelik, and he was often invited to the palace. He left Shoa in 1905 because he had displeased Empress Taytu with his biting wits. His legacy to the church is the new style of church dance that he developed. His teaching was later developed by his son, and it is called *Ya Tekle Aquwaquam*. *Alaqa* Gabra-Hana is very well remembered for his quick wit.

Mahtama-Selassie Walda-Masqal, Minister of Pen during the period of Emperor Haile-Selassie, collected and published an Amharic fable, *Enqilif Lemine* (*Why Would I Sleep*). It is a children's book but useful for adults too.

LITERATURE IN GEEZ

Most of the literature written in Geez are religious books produced by the clerics of the Ethiopian Orthodox Church. The Geez language was employed in writing as far back as the third century AD. It was gradually vocalized with the use of signs in lieu of vowels.

The Bible was translated into the Geez language in the fifth century AD. Atse Kaleb's inscription erected in South Arabia in the sixth century AD has a quote from the Bible (Psalm 23:8). This indicates the existence of a Geez version of the Old Testament. The Geez inscriptions of Atse Ezana are more readable and are easily understandable.

The Ethiopian Orthodox Church clerics translated religious books from Greek, Coptic, and Arabic books. Such work began during the period of the Zagwe dynasty. Translation work continued vigorously during the medieval period when the church and state greatly expanded to the south of Shewa, the Lake Tana region, and Gojjam. Ethiopia contributed the lost book of Enoch to the world.

Books were written on parchments. Clerics also prepared the ink from different leaves, grains, and other natural sources. Their work was sponsored by the court. Usually, the court had a scriptorium where clerics were assigned to prepare chronicles of kings and books to be distributed to major churches

A priest holds an ancient manuscript at the monastery of Kebran Gabriel, on an island on Lake Tana, Ethiopia. (Andrew McConnell/Robert Harding World Imagery/ Corbis)

and monasteries. One such monarch who distributed religious books to churches and monasteries was Zera-Yaqob (1434–1468). Other monarchs continued the tradition and distributed religious books.

We do not know when the chronicles began to be written. Most of the medieval Ethiopian monarchs of the 14th and 16th centuries had their own chronicles. Several of the Gondarine rulers of the 17th and 18th centuries had chronicles. There is a chronicle for the period of the *Zemene-Masafent* (era of the princes) that was collected by someone named Eshete Haylu, who was of royal descent. His collection has been translated into English by Crawford. All of these chronicles have been written in the language of Geez.

The only exception is the chronicle of Atse Tewodros (1855–1868), which was written in the Amharic language. The chronicler, who wrote this in good Amharic prose, was *Alaqa* Zanab. Zanab was a cleric of the church who later converted to Protestantism. He had also written the first Amharic stories (riddle). Two others had also written the chronicle of Tewodros a few years after his death. One of them was Walda-Maryam, and the other was unknown. All of these chronicles were edited and published: Zanab's by Enno Littman in 1902, Walda-Maryam's by Mondon Vidailhet in 1904, and the unknown chronicler by Guji Fusella in 1959.

Atse Yohannes IV had a Geez chronicle. Atse Menelik II had an Amharic chronicle. The chronicler was a renowned cleric named *Alaqa* Gabra-Selassie. Gabra-Selassie became the first Minister of Pen in 1907. He has excellent skills in writing and prose. Emperor Haile-Selassie published his own autobiography in Amharic, in two volumes. Both were translated into English by Ullendorff and Harold Marcus.

When reading medieval chronicles, we should note that these chronicles have some problems. Some are incomplete even for the reign of a monarch. Some of them mention only about a certain aspect of the work of the king. Some are also brief and left out important historical events. Sometimes the chronicler's emphasis was only on religion, and he interpreted everything through a religious prism, leaving out discussion on important political and administrative reforms. As the chroniclers were dependent on the court, they could not write contrary to the interest of the king. The works of the king were also explained in light of a known saint, and were often more glorified. Some medieval chronicles were written after the death of the king and from memory. Most of these chronicles have been translated into Italian, French, Portuguese, and German.

These chronicles are very important in reconstructing the history of medieval Ethiopia. They contain information about the expansion of the state, conquered people, tribute payment, trade and trade routes, the Muslim–Christian conflict, the army, regional government, the movement of the court, the expansion of the church, external relations, and other key issues throughout history.

Geez hagiographies (or *gadel*) are the largest number of sources that chronicle the life history of Ethiopian saints, Ethiopian church history, the study of Ethiopian literature, and the history of the country. These served as biographies of saints, depicting their ascetic lives and religious work. It was largely to enhance the sanctity and prestige of the monastery where the saint lived and worked.

Hagiographies were mostly written after the death of a saint and were repeatedly copied and rewritten thereafter. Sometimes they were written from memory. The date of their composition is not clear but can be known in comparison to other historical dates. Zagwe kings also had hagiographies. The earliest hagiographies deal with saints and martyrs of the early Christian church. The other group includes the medieval Ethiopian saints who lived between the 13th and 16th centuries.

The writing of a hagiography had its own format. The first chapter deals with the life history of the saint. The second part contains the pact, an agreement that God had given the saint in a special place. The saint was given the power to intercede or mediate on behalf of sinners who prayed to God, or had given alms to the needy in his name. People who made donations to the monastery or those who visited the monastery were given promise in their later life. The last chapter contains the miracles performed by the saint during his lifetime or those achieved posthumously. The miracles were intended to build the prestige of the monastery and to attract admirers to the monastery.

Hagiographies are the practice of not only Christian people but also of Muslims. There are some hagiographies of local Muslim saints in Jimma, Bale, Wallo, and other areas. The hagiographies are written by local scribes in Arabic. The chronicle of the Muslim Sultanate of Shoa of the 13th century was discovered by Cerulli and translated into Italian in 1941. Chihab ad-Din Ben Abdel-Qader (also known as Arab Faqih), a Yemeni chronicler, wrote the history of the wars of Ahmed Ibn Ibrahim al-Gazi (Ahmed Gragn).

Another aspect of Geez literature in medieval Ethiopia is the *gult* (land) charter. Granting of land to churches began during the Aksumite period, and was much practiced in the medieval period. *Gult* was given to churches and monasteries. Land was also given to officials of the state as a reward to their services. The writing of land charters had its own format. It started with a religious formula or invocation. The name of the granter—that is, the name of the king and his throne name or the name of another granter—the place where the grant was made, sometimes the date when the grant was made, the grantee, and the list of estates were documented.

The reason why the grant was made is explained. This reason for the grant was mostly pious in an attempt to get into heaven, but was also for the commemoration of the granter, provision of incense, or the death of a person.

The type of the grant was also indicated: temporary or hereditary. Lands granted to religious institutions were on a hereditary basis but there were cases where the grant was renewed.

Lastly, the grant had the list of contemporary officials who witnessed and validated the grant. The tradition of including this list of officials began during the period of Atse Zera-Yaqob. Eyewitnesses who had witnessed the delimitation of the boundary were indicated. The grant also had the immunity clause. The sanction cursed people who would try to take away the land. This was to protect the land grant. Sometimes officials were not allowed to enter the estate.

THE LEGEND OF THE PRESTER JOHN

The celebrated legend of the Prester John was associated with Ethiopia, even though the country did not have a priest king named John. It was simply related to Ethiopia because Europeans did not have an accurate geographical knowledge of the world.

Europeans developed knowledge of Ethiopia after the revival of the Mediterranean trade in the 10th century AD. Their interest to get direct access to the Far East and to bring valuable products such as silk and spices from there increased their curiosity about Ethiopia.

The main quest of the Crusaders to liberate Jerusalem from the Muslim Arabs also persuaded them to find a strong Christian ally against their enemies. The major motive, however, was to safeguard their trade and to get fiefs outside Europe. The wars of the Crusades considerably increased the knowledge of Europeans about Eastern Mediterranean and the civilizations that the latter had achieved.

The origin of the story of the Prester John is unknown. Sometime in the 12th century, the story of the Prester John was introduced in Europe. It seems that the story was fabricated by a zealous and passionate Crusader who wanted to see the defeat of the Muslim Arabs by the Crusaders. The emergence of the story increased the eagerness of the Crusaders to continue the war.

The story depicted the Prester John as a wise and mighty ruler of a Christian nation. He was believed to have been a powerful ruler who had a strong army.

Details from a portolan chart of the Indian Ocean show Prester John seated on a throne, by Diego Homem, about 1558. (The British Library/Robana via Getty Images)

The story related his interest to enter the war in support of the Crusaders. It also stated that his kingdom was located in the East.

In c. 1165, a forged letter about the Prester John reached Europe. The letter was sent to the pope of Rome. It was said that the letter indicated his desire to join the Crusade war on the side of the Christian world. The letter increased the inquisitiveness of Europeans to know the exact location of or the whereabouts of his kingdom. They were also eager to know more about the priest king and his rich empire. They tried to identify where he was, but were unable to know the exact location of his kingdom. Some travelers to the East also came up with their fictitious stories of the priest king.

Among the European travelers of the 13th century, Marco Polo, who visited China, reported a probable story. He tried to identify the king with one of the chiefs of the nomadic tribes of Central Asia. He further related that the said king was defeated by the nomadic tribe chiefs of Genghis Khan of Tarar. The Europeans refused to accept the story but continued to find out his whereabouts.

The locus of his kingdom was believed to have been somewhere in India. According to the then geographical knowledge, India had three parts, including the north-east African region. Much later on, they came to identify his location. They believed that he was the king of Ethiopia. In the early 14th century, a monk indicated that Ethiopian kings could be identified as Prester John of the Indies. Spanish geographers also stressed that he was the king of Ethiopia or Nubia. Finally, they believed that his country was Ethiopia. Ethiopia was well known to the Arab travelers and merchants, and it was the Arabs who related the exact location of Ethiopia.

By the 14th century, European travelers learned that the East was not ruled by a Christian king, Prester John. Ethiopian Christian kings had waged a relentless struggle against the Muslim sultanates since the 13th century. This information persuaded Europeans to establish relations and, if possible, some kind of alliance with Ethiopia.

Ethiopian kings also wanted to establish relations with Christian European rulers. They wanted to have direct contact to benefit from Europe's technological development. They wanted to import firearms, artisans, and military officers to train their army. Thus, there was a mutual interest on both sides.

The first known European letter to Ethiopia arrived in 1400. It was written by King Henry IV of England. Henry IV had widely traveled in the Eastern Mediterranean in the 1390s. He had met Ethiopian pilgrims in the Holy Land and others who knew Ethiopia. Atse Dawit's (1398–1412) victory against the ruler of the sultanate of Adal, Sa'adadin, in Zayla in 1402–1403 might have been widely circulated in the region so that the British king might have also received the same information. Henry IV's letter was addressed to the king of Abyssinia, Prester John. He asked the Ethiopian king to cooperate on the issues of the Eastern Mediterranean.

In 1402 Atse Dawit sent the first embassy to Europe. Dawit indicated his interest to establish relations. The mission was led by a Florentine merchant, Antonio Bartoli. The mission also included some Ethiopians. Atse Yeshaq (1413–1430) and Zera-Yaqob wrote letters for the same reason. Yeshaq also sent an Ethiopian embassy to Europe in 1427. The embassy was led by a Persian merchant, Tabrizi, who had lived in the country for a long time. His embassy was sent to the kingdom of Aragon, northern Sicily. On his way back, Tabrizi was intercepted and killed in Egypt for dealing with two religions. But some of the craftsmen sent to Ethiopia succeeded in returning to Ethiopia. Zera-Yaqob's letter to Europe was sent in 1450. The mission was led by a Sicilian, Petro Rumbulo. This mission arrived back safely. Between 1451 and 1453, two missions were sent to Ethiopia by the king of Aragon. Some craftsmen also arrived. Gradually, Europeans gained more knowledge about Ethiopia. The maps prepared in the second half of the 15th century by European cartographers included Ethiopia. By the 16th century, a direct contact was established with the kingdom of Portugal.

By the 16th century, Portugal was the leading power in the world. The Portuguese desire was to reach the Far East in search of spices and silk. The other major power was Spain. In 1498 a Portuguese navigator, Vasco da Gama, reached India, and Portugal also wanted to explore the Red Sea region. When the Portuguese were established in India and East Africa, they wanted to establish relations with Ethiopia. Since the Portuguese were confronted by Egypt, which had monopolized the Red Sea trade, Portugal wanted to strengthen its relations with Ethiopia. It also became easier for Ethiopia to establish relations with the Portuguese in India. In addition, the Portuguese wanted to establish commercial contact with Ethiopian kings.

The commander of the Portuguese force in the Indian Ocean, Afonso de Albuquerque, wanted to monopolize the trade. Portugal was very much interested in receiving military support from Ethiopia, which it believed was ruled by Prester John. The Portuguese thus began to come to Ethiopia. The first man to arrive was Pedro da Covilha, arriving in the country in 1494. When he arrived, there was a power struggle in Ethiopia and he never went back to relate his findings. He was married to an Ethiopian, received land grants, and remained in the country. When the Portuguese mission arrived in the country in 1520, they met him there.

In 1508 Atse Lebna-Dengel (1508–1541) came to power. His regent was Etege Elleni, former wife of Zera-Yaqob from Hadya. She wanted to establish relations with the Portuguese in India and wrote a letter to the Portuguese king in 1512. Her mission to Europe was led by Matthew the Armenian. She indicated that Ethiopia and Portugal could block Muslim power, Ethiopia by land and Portugal by sea. Thus, there was a mutual interest to establish relations.

Then the Portuguese began a series of campaigns in the Red Sea region. They attacked Jeddah and Aden. In 1516–1517, the Ottoman Turks invaded Egypt and posed a new threat against the Portuguese. In response to Elleni's letter, Portugal sent envoys together with Matthew to Ethiopia. Nevertheless, Matthew died on his way back to Ethiopia at the monastery of Dabra-Bizan, now in Eritrea. The Portuguese mission arrived in 1520. Elleni died a few months before their arrival. Atse Lebna Dengel was not interested in them and did not believe that Portugal, located far away, could be taken as a serious support to his kingdom. This was because of his fresh victory against Mahfuz, the sultan of the Muslim sultanate of Adal.

One member of the mission was Father F. Alvarez. The mission stayed in the country between 1520 and 1526. Alvarez and his friends lived in the court and had toured the country with the king, whose court was mobile in nature. Alvarez visited important religious centers, market towns, and regions. He wrote a book (two volumes) and titled his book as the *Prester John of the Indies,* though he very well knew that the Ethiopian monarch he met was neither a priest nor named John. He did this for publicity, hoping people would read his book and believe it was based on the famous legend of the Prester John.

When the Portuguese mission left the country in 1526, no major agreement was signed. A year later, the Sultanate of Adal waged its raid against the Christian kingdom. Adal defeated the Christian kingdom in 1529, and Atse Lebna-Dengel requested for Portuguese support in 1540. Four hundred Portuguese soldiers came in 1541 and helped defeat the sultan of Adal. Later, the Jesuit missionaries arrived in 1557. Their interest was to convert the people to Catholicism. This brought about a civil war that lasted from 1622 to 1632, resulting in the expulsion of the Jesuit missionaries.

MODERN LITERARY WORKS

Modern literature began in the beginning of the 20th century. The first modern literary work/novel was written by Afawarq Gabra-Iyyasus. He was one of the early intellectuals. He was educated in Italy. Back in Ethiopia, he worked as a customs official in Dire-Dawa and Addis Ababa.

During the Battle of Adwa against Italy in 1896, he defected from Ethiopia and supported the Italian cause. When he decided to return to his country, he wrote an Amharic book titled *Atse Menelik Enna Ityopiya (Atse Menelik and Ethiopia)* in 1908–1909. The book was first published in Rome. It was written as a kind of apology for his defection. He extolled the achievements of Menelik, but painted the period of Yohannes IV in a dark light. For his biased writing, he was sharply criticized by another early intellectual, Gabra-Heywat Baykadagn. Gabra-Heywat indicated that Afawarq need not have to demonize Atse Yohannes to just think highly of Atse Menelik.

Afawarq was also Ethiopia's ambassador to Italy before the battle of 1935–1936. But he again defected and served in the Italian colonial administration in Addis Ababa. He diligently worked in the Italian press in Addis Ababa. He thus earned the name *Afa Qesar* (Mouth of Caesar). After liberation, he was exiled.

Afawarq's Amharic novel was titled *Tobiya* (Ethiopia). This Amharic book was the first novel in the country and was published in 1900. The main theme of the book is a battle between a Christian kingdom and a non-Christian region, and the devastation of the territory by the latter. The main character, *Tobiya*, and her family are uprooted and forced to flee. But they are captured and ultimately saved from being sold as slaves because the king falls in love with *Tobiya*. She saves not only her family but also her country. The book is reminiscent of the medieval period when the country overcame several destructive wars. The book was translated into English by the late professor Taddesse Tamarat (d. May 2013) and appeared in the *Ethiopia Observer,* published by the Institute of Ethiopian Studies of Addis Ababa University.

Gabra-Heywat Baykadagn was educated as a surgeon in Germany. He came to Ethiopia toward the end of Menelik's period. He was not given an opportunity to examine and administer medicine to Menelik. Later he was a supporter of the young *Ras* Teferi, who later became Emperor Haile-Selassie. Gabra-Heywat served as the chief of merchants and customs official in Addis Ababa and Dire-Dawa. His main achievement was his book on economics. He discussed Ethiopian backwardness and advised on its progress. He was against the policy of having several customs posts where taxes were collected. He was also against the monopoly status of the British Bank established in 1905. He advised the government to expand cottage industries and education. He had also written another book advising *Lej* Iyyassu, successor of Menelik, how to develop the country. He died at an early age.

Alaqa Tayye Gabre-Maryam was a traditional historian, linguist, and Geez language teacher in the University of Berlin. Earlier he taught Amharic and Geez and wrote a grammar book and a dictionary while working in Eritrea in a Protestant school. He wrote a history of Ethiopian nationalities and their language classification.

Blatten-Geta Heruy Walda-Selassie was a noted cleric. He was also a famous writer. He wrote a history of ancient Ethiopia and books that dealt with morality and traditional values. He was minister of foreign affairs before the

Italian invasion of 1936. He died in London in exile. His children were also killed while resisting the Italian invasion.

Alaqa Asme-Giyorgis Gabre-Mesih (popularly known as Asme) served as a clerk in the court of Atse Menelik. His famous work is on the history of the Kingdom of Shoa and the Oromo people. He left us their genealogy and the process of their movement and settlement.

Takla-Sadiq Makuriya worked as head of the National Archives and Library of Ethiopia, and later as a minister. He was best known as a traditional historian. He wrote the history of the country from ancient times to the modern period. In particular, he wrote the history of Ethiopian modern rulers: Tewodros II (1855–1865), Yohannes IV (1871–1889), and Menelik II (1889–1913). Unlike the ancient chroniclers, he provided sources and cited both local and foreign sources. He was recently awarded an honorary doctorate degree by the Addis Ababa University.

Ras Bitwaddad Mekonnen Endalkachew was an aristocrat. He was minister of the interior, chairman of the council of ministers, and prime minister. He also served as representative of his country when the United Nations Charter was signed in San Francisco in 1945. He is well known for his novel *Almotkum Beya Alwashem* (*I Shall Not Lie That I Am Not Dead*). One of his chapters is about an Ethiopian patriot who campaigned to defend his country against fascist Italy in 1936. After Ethiopia's defeat in 1936, he returned to his village to find out that his wife had married a fascist. He witnessed the happy lives that the new couples were leading. Heartbroken, he killed them and went to join the resistance movement.

There were also lexicographers noted for their major works. They were Tesemma Habte-Mikael, who compiled an Amharic-Geez dictionary, and Desta Takle-Wold, who complied an Amharic dictionary. Desta actually completed the work of his teacher Kidane-Wold Kefle. Germa-Seyon Mabrahtu also compiled a Tegregna dictionary.

Two people stand out as prominent writers of children's books, which were used as school textbooks. These were Kebede Mikael and Bemenet Gabre-Amlak. Kebede Mikael was a prolific writer who published several books, including the children's book *Taretena Mesale* (folk tales and examples). Most of his books are plays, poetry, and social and historical works. His children's' books were used as school textbooks. In his writings, he also introduced the history of European philosophers, explorers and travelers, and Western thinkers. He also translated Shakespeare's work such as *Romeo and Juliet*. Like Takla-Sadiq Makuriya, he also recently received an honorary doctorate degree from Addis Ababa University.

Bemenet Gabre-Amlak's famous book is *Lijjinat Temeleso Aymtam* (*Childhood Never Returns*). His book was reprinted several times by the Ministry of Education and used as school textbook. Yared Gabre-Mikael also wrote children's books.

The earlier intellectuals were worried about the backwardness of the country and wanted Ethiopian rulers to expand education. They advised that Ethiopian rulers take up the example of Japan to speed up the technological development of the country. These writers were termed Japanizers by Professor Bahru Zewde. Some of these were *Blaten-Geta* Heruy Walda-Selassie, minister of foreign affairs before 1935, and Kebede Mikael. In his Amharic book, *Japan Endemen Seletanach* (*How Japan Modernized*), Heruy strongly advised that Ethiopia follow the example of Japan. He argued:

> The only country that had succeeded in safeguarding her independence and in charting her own path of educational progress is Japan. If we examine her history and follow her example, we can achieve a lot in a short period of time.[1]

Blatta Deressa Amante also published several articles on the pages of *Berhanena Selam* Amharic newspaper about the accomplishments of Japan. Some other writers indicated the role of educated intellectuals in the development of the country.

Blatta Walda-Giyorgis Walda-Yohanne served in the Ministry of Information as editor of the Amharic daily newspaper *Addis Zemen*. He also worked as editor of Amharic newspapers during the Italian invasion of 1936–1941. He also worked hard to develop Ethiopian journalism. He wrote several books. His main Amharic book is *Agazi,* about the attempt of an educated young man to develop his country.

Haddis Alemayehu was a famous novelist. He was a patriot during the Italian invasion of the country in 1936–1941. He was imprisoned in Italy by the colonial rulers. He was Ethiopia's ambassador to Jerusalem, the United Nations, the United Kingdom, the Netherlands, and vice minister of foreign affairs and minister of education. His famous novel is *Feqer Eska Maqaber* (*Love unto Death*). The book served as a school text and was published several times. He introduced a new way of writing in Amharic by avoiding repetitive alphabets. His book reflects his experience of the traditional/rural and urban culture. The main theme of the novel is that an orphan and student of traditional school was employed in the house of a rural nobility to teach one of the daughters who lived there. He fell in love with the girl. The girl was not married at her young age because her families were choosing her a suitable mate from members of the nobility. Afraid that his illicit love affair would be uncovered, he ran away, leaving his beloved in distress. She also ran away to find her lover. She could not make the journey in the lowland regions of the

Valley of the Nile (Blue Nile) River to reach the town of Addis Ababa. When she made it to the other side of the valley, in Shoa, she found her lover sick and bedridden with typhus. He did not recognize her and died soon. She was heartbroken and soon followed him in death.

Haddis had also written a book on traditional folk tales. His other novels included *Wanjalagnaw Dagna* (*A Criminal Judge*) and *Yelme Zat* (*Plenty of Dreams*). All of his books are about traditional life and corruption. He also wrote his memories as a biography in Amharic. He was recently awarded an honorary doctorate degree by the Addis Ababa University.

Germachew Takla-Hawaryat was the minister of information and agriculture in the post-1941 period. His Amharic novel is *Araya* (*Good Example*). It is about a French-educated Ethiopian and his attempt to introduce some elements of modernization. It also explains the problem of returnees to implant seeds of modernization. He was imprisoned for several years by the military government in 1974.

Germachew's father, *Dajjazmach* Takla-Hawaryat Takla-Mariam, was educated in Russia. He was trained as an officer. He drafted the first constitution in 1931. It was a copy of the Meiji Constitution. He also wrote a book on farming and modern agriculture, which was intended to be a textbook. He believed that modern agriculture was the basis of the country's development. He wrote his biography, which was recently published by his son several years after his death.

Dagnachew Worqu's Amharic novel *Adferes* illustrates the traditional and modern side of the country. A young man loves a traditional rural girl and at the same time he also falls in love with a prostitute, who thinks of herself as modern. He likes to live with the prostitute and makes her his mistress. But he also admires and wants to live with the traditionalist girl. The traditionalist represents rural Ethiopia, while the modern represents the new urban centers where the Italian colonialists had left their mark. The young, educated man finds it hard to combine the old and the new ideas. Dagnachew had also published a collection of poems and plays.

Birhanu Zerihun was a regular contributor and later editor of the Amharic newspaper *Addis Zemen*. He published several novels such as *Del Kamot Bahuwala* (*Victory after Death*) and *Ya Emba Debedabewoch* (*Letters of Tears*). The latter is about the life of prostitutes in Addis Ababa who joined the profession from rural areas. He also published *Amanuel Darso Melse* (*In and Out of Amanuel (Hospital) for the Lunatic*) and wrote *Ya Tewodros Enba* (*Tewodros's Tears*). This is the story of Atse Tewodros (r. 1855–1865) as a hero of the young generation. It was written as a response to some writers who depicted Tewodros as cruel and vindictive. Later he wrote *Ya Tangut Mister* (*The Secret of Tangut*). It is a historical novel about Tewodros. He also wrote several short stories, as well as a trilogy of books on the famine of Wallo in the 1970s. He felt that the government did not try to alleviate the plight of the famine-affected people of Wallo.

Ba'alu Girma was one of the most admired novelists of all time in Ethiopia. He was the editor of the Amharic daily *Addis Zemen* and other newspapers. His editorial was not popular among university student revolutionaries due to his support for the government. The students considered him a supporter of the imperial regime. During the military regime, he served as head of the Ethiopian News Agency, vice minister of information, and was responsible for the propaganda office in the ministry. His novel *Ya Helina Dawal* (*The Bell of Conscience*) was published before the Ethiopian revolution of 1974. The book is about a young educated man who wanted to introduce modernization. His other book *Haddis* (*New*) is the continuation of his novel indicted earlier.

The other novel *Darasew* (*The Author*) is about a struggle against corruption, intrigue, and injustice. The book depicts the life of a French-educated man, Sebehat Gabre-Egziabher, who had a hard time adjusting himself with the waves of the revolution and the flight of his family abroad, who were members of the nobility. His other novel, *Qay Abeba* (*Red Flower*), is a revolutionary book that mentions the work of revolutionary intellectuals in developing a backward country.

His other book, *Oromay* (*The End*), was written during the Red Star Campaign in Eritrea in the 1980s. It is about the failure of the military government in solving the political question of the Eritrean people for independence. It illustrates how the military governors and commanders of the army in Eritrea, and, in general, in the country, were corrupt and had drawn the country to a bloody civil war. Within a short period of time that the book was published, it was withdrawn from the market. Those who managed to buy the book were even afraid to carry the book in public. No reason was given for its withdrawal from market. It was clear that anybody could identify his characters in the book. Although there is an indication that he was on good terms with Mengestu Haile-Mariam, head of the military government, he had created strong enemies in the establishment. A few months later, he disappeared and died in unknown circumstances. His book was published only after the downfall of the military regime. Eritrea, now independent since 1991, was part of Ethiopia and had waged a relentless struggle for self-independence.

Another noted writer was Abe Gubegna, whose writings often criticized the imperial regime. His book *Alewoldem* (*I Refuse to Be Born*) is a critique of the government for its policy of discrimination and social injustice. He was exiled for some years because of this. Abe Gubegna was a visionary and was against oppression, corruption, and exploitation. He asked people to struggle for justice, development, and better lives. He had also written a book, *Gobland Acehberbarew Tota* (*Gobland the Deceptive Ape*), about those who think that they are educated and work for the good of the society, but who actually do nothing for the welfare of the society. He was killed during the period of the military government for not respecting the curfew imposed by the government. But people believe that he was killed by the government for his writings.

Mamo Wudenenh started to work in the U.S. Information Center in Addis Ababa. He was a regular contributor to several Amharic newspapers. He was the editor of a newspaper, *Policena Ermjaw* (*Police and Its Progress*), and made it a popular paper among people who like to read stories of crime and the progress of the force. He also worked as press officer of the Eritrean representative of Emperor Haile-Selassie in the 1960s and 1970s.

Wudenenh's first novel is *Ya Gabar Lej* (*The Son of a Tenant Farmer*). It deals with the feudal system. He wrote a short history of Eritrea where he advised how to resolve the Eritrean political issue. He also wrote social issues about social associations such as *Equbtagnchu* (members of local saving association), *Mahbertagnochu* (a religious association in the name of saints), and *Edertagnochu* (association to bury people and console the bereaved).

Wudenenh's major work was the translation of books into Amharic, mostly spy stories. He wrote a historical novel on the life of Atse Yohannes IV (1972–1989) and his army general, *Ras* Alula Abab Nega. He had also written his autobiography in three volumes. He continued writing novels to the last days of his life. He died in February 2012.

Andarge Mesfin picked up the issue of blood feud that was prevalent during the imperial regime. Blood feud arose because of disputes over land, property, and other social issues.

The late Sebehat Gabre-Egzia'bher is remembered for his romantic short stories and books. He was educated in France, and thus, he is heavily influenced by French romance and love stories. His admirers are mostly the young.

Since the 1980s, several writers have focused mainly on short stories.

POETRY AND POPULAR LITERATURE

Several Ethiopian authors published poetry books. The prominent poet was the late Segaye Gabre-Medhen. One of his books is *Esat Woy Abeba* (*Fire or Flower*), which was published in 1973–1974.

Mengestu Lema was a playwright and poet. He published *Ya Getem Gubae* (*Poetic Session*). He also wrote traditional stories, *Ya Abotch Chewata* (*Tales of Our fathers*). One of the lovely pieces in this book is about a naïve lover who was embarrassed when he was instantly slapped by girl when he tried to kiss her. Mangestu interviewed his father about his life history and experiences, and turned the interview into an Amharic book. His father, *Alaqa* Lemma Haylu, was a renowned cleric and teacher of the New Testament.

Other noted poets are the late Debebe Seifu and Seifu Matafariya. Recently, several young poets, both women and men, have emerged and have published books.

NEWSPAPERS AND MAGAZINES

The establishment of newspapers was a late development that began during the period of Atse Menelik (1889–1913). The first small press was established by missionaries in the town of Keren, in the present-day Eritrea, in 1879. It printed religious books for their evangelization program. In 1885 the Swedish Evangelical Mission established a press in Munkullo, now in Eritrea, to print religious books. The press was later transferred to Massawa, a port in Eritrea. The Italians also established a secular press at Massawa in 1885 when they transferred their base to Massawa from Assab. The first Tegregna publication, a religious one, was published in Eritrea by the Swedish Evangelical Mission between 1912 and 1915.

The beginning of an Amharic newspaper was in Addis Ababa by *Blatta* Gabra-Egzia'bher Gila-Maryam, an Eritrean, who came to live in Addis Ababa, in 1897. He was an irredentist who advised Atse Menelik to drive out Italian colonists from Eritrea. The newspaper had 15 copies, and it was written by hand, as there was no printing press then.

The first newspaper, *A'emro,* was founded in 1902. It had a small edition and was distributed to the nobility. It was a weekly newspaper. Its publication was stopped in 1916 because the editor was pro-German. Later in 1924, it resumed its publication, and its editor was A. E. Kavadia. Between 1916 and 1918, the Allies, under the Italian legation, printed *Ya-Tor Ware* (*War News*) about World War I to inform the public about World War I.

Ras Tafari, regent of Etege Zawditu, established the Berhanena Selam Printing Press, which published a newspaper with the same title, *Berhanena Selam,* in 1925. It was a biweekly Amharic newspaper. It also had a French language section. The Ethiopian intellectuals contributed articles and had a wide circulation in Addis Ababa, the provincial towns, and where Ethiopian students were learning abroad. The intellectuals were trying to inform and educate the people in their aim of modernizing the country. Some of the themes that attracted its readers were expansion of education, the call for the Ethiopianization of the episcopacy of the church, modernization of the government bureaucracy, and the introduction of government reforms.

When the Italians invaded the country in 1935–1936, *Berhanena Selam* carried reports of the war. It got reports from the battlefield. The then-editor of the paper was also killed by the Italians in the summary killings following the Graziani Incident of 1936. The incident was a response of the attempted killing of the viceroy.

The Italian colonial government established Amharic newspapers as their colonial propaganda machine. The newspapers were *Ya Roma Berhan* (*The Light of Rome*), *Ya Qesar Mengest Melketagna* (*Messenger of the Government of Caesar*), and *Zena Beta-Krestiyan* (*News of the Church*) in Amharic. The main editor was Afawarq-Gabra-Iyyasus, who was educated in Rome. Afawarq was named as *Afa-Qesar* (Mouth of Caesar). He got this name because of his devotion to the Italian colonial policy. As he was educated in Rome, he thought that the Italians would try to bring civilization to the country. He had supported Italian colonial ambition all along, even when they were defeated at the Battle of Adwa in 1896. After 1941, he was imprisoned and exiled by the restored government of Emperor Haile-Selassie. The *Zena Beta-Krestiyan* was devoted to church news.

In the war of liberation, a newspaper called *Bandirachen* (*Our Banner*) was printed by the liberation forces. The paper was dropped as a leaflet by airplanes over the Italian-occupied regions to inform the advance of the British and Ethiopian forces. It was then renamed *Sendeqalamachen* (*Our Flag*) after the liberation of the country. *Sendeqalamachen* was printed in Amharic and Arabic languages.

After liberation, Emperor Haile-Selassie founded the *Addis Zemen* (*New Era*) Amharic newspaper in 1941. It was a weekly and later a daily newspaper. Its name signifies the beginning of a new era after the liberation of the country from Italian colonial rule. *The Ethiopian Herald,* an English newspaper, was established in 1943. *Addis Zemen* and *Ethiopian Herald* were published daily except on Mondays. These government-owned newspapers and their circulation were limited to the capital and other provincial towns.

In 1952 a French and Amharic language weekly newspaper, *L'Ethiopie D'aujourd 'Hui,* appeared in the capital. It later became a weekly Amharic paper known as *Ya-Zareyetu Ithiopiya* (*Today's Ethiopia*). *Al-Alam,* an Arabic weekly newspaper, was published by the Ministry of Information in 1942. The military government also began the publication of a newspaper *Oromifa* in the Oromo language.

During the period of the military regime and the current government, there were party newspapers whose circulation was among party members and, to some extent, the public. *Sarto Adar* (*Working Class*) was published by the military government, while the *Abiyotawi Democracy* (*Revolutionary Democracy*) is published by the current regime. Under the current government, several privately owned newspapers were published. They were opposed to the government and their editors faced some jail terms. All these have since stopped publication.

There were few Amharic journals that came out both during the period of the imperial and the military regime. *Menen* (after the late empress Menen, consort of Emperor Haile-Selassie) began to come out in 1962. It began as a bilingual journal but in 1973 it began to be published in Amharic. It was a monthly journal. Its publication came to an end during the military regime. There was also an English quarterly magazine, *Ethiopia Mirror.* In 1965 with the establishment of the Organization of African Unity (now Africa Union), a French daily newspaper, *Addis Soir,* was founded. The military government had an Amharic journal called *Yakatit* (*February*—denoting the outbreak of the Ethiopian Revolution in February 1974), which carried revolutionary ideas and articles. There was also the publication of party-affiliated monthly Amharic journals opposed to the military government. The most famous one was *Goh* (*Dawn*). But they were short-lived.

Under the EFDR, with freedom of the press less domineering, several monthly Amharic journals began to be published. *Tobiya* (*Ethiopia*), *Itop* (*Ethiopia*), *Mogad Reporter* are cases in point. In addition, most privately owned newspapers such as *Reporter* and *Admas* are out of publication after a fallout with the government after the election of 2005–2006.

RADIO AND TELEVISION

Radio and television broadcasts began during the imperial regime. The first telegraph line was introduced to Ethiopia during the period of Atse Menelik II in 1894. It connected some major towns during the period. At present, the country has an efficient telephone line system and has expanded its mobile connection. The Ethiopian Telecommunication Cooperation (ETC) has made good progress in this regard.

Emperor Haile-Selassie introduced radio-telegraphic station in the capital in 1935. The site of the transmission was at Qaliti and the receiving station installed at Nefas Selk. This radio station broadcast programs about the impending Italian invasion to listeners in the capital as of September 7, 1935. It was operating under the Ministry of Posts, Telephone, and Telegraphs. Before the Italians occupied the capital on May 5, 1936, the patriots had already destroyed the station. The Italians built their radio station near the old Ethiopian Radio Station, near St. Giyorgis (George) Church. They installed loudspeakers in different neighborhoods to transmit their propaganda. They also destroyed the station when they were defeated in 1941.

The restored government of Haile-Selassie rebuilt another radio station with the help of the British in 1941. Radio Ethiopia was put under the directive of the Ministry of Information. Radio broadcasting before 1950 was live transmission. Musical bands were invited to the station to transmit

Emperor Haile Selassie broadcasts, via short wave to the United States, a plea for a peaceful resolution of the Italo-Ethiopian dispute in Addis Ababa, September 13, 1935. (AP Photo)

their song live to the people. In 1950 recording for broadcasting began. In addition to local broadcasts in Amharic, Radio Ethiopia broadcast programs to listeners in French and English to West and Northwest Africa, in Arabic to North Africa and the Middle East, and in Swahili to East and central Africa. In 1970, a radio program was broadcast for 18 hours daily in nine languages from Asmara, Addis Ababa, and Harar. The languages were Amharic, English, Somali, Arabic, French, Afar, Tigergna, and Tegre. The Ministry of Education had its own educational radio. During the military regime, there were several educational radio stations in the provinces.

In 1959 the government allowed the World Federation of Lutheran Churches to build a short-wave radio station. The station, established in Addis Ababa, began its transmission in 1963 as Radio Voice of the Gospel. It was allowed to broadcast its programs 70 percent evangelical (religious) and 30 percent informational. The station had power to transmit to areas in parts of Africa, the Middle East, and parts of Asia. Its transmission to the nation was only in Amharic language.

The Ethiopian Radio now broadcasts for 18 hours daily, and it also has an FM radio station. The Ethiopian Radio and Television, as it is now called, recently began broadcasts through satellite system using rented satellites and the Internet to the United States, Europe, Africa, the Middle East, and other areas.

Under the government of Prime Minister Meles Zenawi, some privately owned FM radio stations have been established. They serve the metropolis of Addis Ababa and the nearby towns. They had a 16-hour broadcast and one government-owned FM station affiliated to the Ethiopian Radio serve for 24 hours. Some FM radio stations have also been established in provincial towns that are owned by regional governments or by the ruling party. The ruling party owns the *Radio Fana* (Radio Torch), which have also built other stations in the provincial towns.

Attempts to establish a television station began in the 1950s when Emperor Haile-Selassie celebrated his 34th anniversary of coronation. On November 2, 1964, the Ethiopian television began its first regular transmission. It began its broadcast from the Addis Ababa municipal office building. Then, it had 29 workers—British and Ethiopians. Until 1984, it transmitted its program in black and white, and then later in color. It broadcast its programs in Amharic and English six days a week between 5:00 P.M. and 10:30 P.M. In 1965 it signed an agreement with the Ministry of Education to broadcast educational programs to schools.

Until 1964, the Ethiopian Television was serving the capital city. But in 1964 with the building of microwave stations in major towns in northern Ethiopia, the Ethiopian Television began to broadcast to major towns. It was then only in black and white programming. During the military regime, color transmission started. The Ethiopian Television's broadcast covers most of the country. Major expansions were undertaken by the current government, and the Ethiopian Television broadcasts with rented satellite stations or using the Internet, to Europe, the United States, the Middle East, and other countries. Its daily services have grown from a few hours in the evening during the imperial era to 24 hours service a day at the moment.

NOTE

1. Quoted in Bahru Zewde, "The Concept of Japanization in the Intellectual History of Modern Ethiopia," Proceedings of the Fifth Seminar of the Department of History, 1990, p. 2.

4

Architecture and Art

INTRODUCTION

Studying Ethiopian art and architecture is very difficult, if not impossible, due to a number of reasons. Ethiopia is a country with a population of about 80 million, of diverse ethnic and cultural groups that are best explained in linguistic terms such as Cushitic (Oromo, Afar, Somali, etc.), Semitic (Amhara, Tigre, Gurage, etc.), Omotic (Welaytta, Dorze, Gamo, etc.), and Nilo-Saharan (Agnawak, Nuer, Berta, etc.). Despite this diversity, the available literature on Ethiopian art and architecture is focused only on the Semitic speakers, who roughly reside in the central and northern parts of the country. Even this is incomplete because most of the works of art and sculpture revolve around palaces, churches, and religious art, especially those of the Ethiopian Orthodox faith—a faith that Ethiopians have practiced for more than 1,500 years. Although Ethiopian Christian art has prospered since the introduction of Christianity in the fourth century AD, it has also suffered tremendously as a result of the Wars of Ahmad Gragn (AD 1522–1543). Thus, the study of Ethiopian art remains incomplete.

Meanwhile, other forms of art such as basket making and pottery were not usually considered, within the context of "Ethiopian Studies," to be artistic expressions until very recently. Similarly, though Ethiopia was one of the first countries to accept Islam, and despite its decisive help in saving Islam from destruction in its early age, and in spite of the prophet Mohammed's favorable regard to Ethiopia, and Ethiopians' cultural and geographic proximity and ties to the birthplace of Islam, there is very limited or no study regarding Ethiopian Islamic art and architecture.

ARCHITECTURE

Ancient Period

The Aksumite State's (500 BC–AD 1000) strategic location on the Red Sea littoral, its position as a center and thoroughfare for caravan trade that crisscrossed the African continent in general and the Horn of Africa in particular, and the existence of an agrarian community that produced surplus helped in the development of a class of artisans and masons with exceptional skills.

Archaeological excavations in Aksum, the surrounding area, and its port city, Adulis, revealed that its artisans were minting bronze, silver, and gold coins, making jewelry and pottery, while its masons built palaces, temples, and churches. With the exception of coins and obelisks, much of the Aksumite building and architecture has been lost, save some of the building layouts uncovered by archaeologist in southwestern part of Aksum at Enda Mikael (28 square feet), Enda Semon (110 square feet), and Ta'akha Maryam (390 × 260 feet). Archaeologists were able to determine these settlement sites were of the Aksumite elite, which indicate the existence of spatial differentiation based on class and occupation. Yeha, Matara, and the port city of Adulis were other urban centers of the Aksumite period where ruins of monuments and extensive settlement sites were found.

Aksumite coins, which were made of bronze, silver, and gold, revealed the skilled workmanship of Aksumite artisans. Coin minting in Aksum was believed to have begun as early as the third century AD. These coins depicted images, probably actual portraits, of kings wearing a crown, a bonnet, or a cape that was pulled down to the nape of the neck. Until the reign of *Niguse Negest* (King of Kings)[1] Ezana (r. AD 330–356), the first Christian king of Ethiopia, Aksumite coins also contained depictions of the disk and crescent, representations of the sun and the moon, which were symbols of pre-Christian beliefs. Since Ezana's time, however, the cross and phrases such as "by the grace of the Lord" or "thanks to God" were engraved on Aksumite coins. The inscriptions on the coins were written in Greek and, later on, Geez (an ancient Ethiopian language).[2]

Although wooden materials have not survived, the iron nails and bronze fittings unearthed in and around Aksum have retained traces of woods. This, coupled with the studies of the layouts of Aksumite buildings, convinced archaeologists that Aksumites must have had wooden objects such as chests and other artifacts. Aksumites were also noted for a high standard of artistry in their ivory carvings. Ivory panels (each measuring 19 × 6 inches) found in Aksum in the third-century Tomb of the Brick Arches revealed an intricate design of vines, human-headed animals, and a tiny female statue with long, straight hair.

Similarly, archaeologists have uncovered various sizes and makes of pottery in and around the city of Aksum. These fragments indicate that Aksumites made their pottery without the use of potter's wheels and that glazing was unknown among Aksumite potters. Despite this, Aksumites produced a wide range of flasks, bowls, and beakers with decorations primarily based on surface relief, motifs on the surface of the soft clay. Jars surmounted with human heads and rims with elaborate figures of birds or other representations were common features of Aksumite pottery.

Archaeologists and historians of the classical period noted that Aksumite masons were masters in the art of stone cutting, which is further confirmed by the many obelisks (stele) of colossal proportions found in and around the city of Aksum. Some of the obelisks are taller than the Egyptian steles.

The specific date on which the obelisks were hoisted is unknown. Yet, because of the non-Christian symbols found on them, the steles might have been erected between second century BC and the introduction of Christianity in Ethiopia, around AD 350. Some of the obelisks weigh between 400 and 500 tons, while their heights vary between 60 feet and more than 100 feet above the ground. The engineering skills of the Aksumites must have been extraordinary, for they were able to put up such mammoth structures in those days.

Though the Aksumite obelisks mimic buildings as high as 13 floors, the exact purpose of these giant edifices is not known. However, there are indications that they might have been used as burial monument or statues dedicated to gods. While some of the steles are plain, others are dressed on all four sides. The architecture on the obelisks represents a huge story building that prevailed in Aksum at the time of their erection, probably around the third century AD. At the base of each dressed obelisk, one also finds representations of a doorway with bolts and ring handles in relief. On top of the false door, imitations of rows of smaller and larger windows separated by protruding beams (monkey heads) are also found. Both sides of the apex of the giant obelisk have been affixed with metal ornaments representing the disk and the crescent, symbols of pagan gods.

Archaeologists were unable to ascertain the existence of 13-story building as depicted on Aksumite obelisks. However, the architectural design found at the Debra Damo monastery, which was built around the sixth century, exhibited projecting square beams and rows of windows similar to the designs found on Aksumite obelisks. The interior of the church contains

Aksumite obelisk, Ethiopia. (Siempre Verde/Dreamstime.com)

well-preserved architectural features: "The roof is supported by square-sectioned monolithic pillars connected by flat lintels. Above them is a good example of the so-called Aksumite frieze: a band of false window apertures constructed entirely of wood. The horizontal wooden ceiling is divided into square coffers, each containing a relief geometric or zoomorphic carvings; the species depicted include lions, camels and antelope."[3]

The tradition of stone cutting, shaping, and dressing continued after the decline of the Aksumite Empire sometime around the 10th century. The Zagwe dynasty (11th to 13th centuries) that succeeded Aksum established its capital at Roha, some hundreds of kilometers south of the ancient city. The new capital, where 12 individual churches were carved out of granite rock, exhibits the refinement of the art of stone cutting in ancient Ethiopia. These churches are collectively referred to as the Rock-Hewn Churches of Lalibela, named after one of the kings of the Zagwe dynasty, King Lalibela, who was known for his piety, and in fact, the construction of these churches was attributed to his desire to re-create Jerusalem in Ethiopia. Consequently, some of the rock-hewn churches have names similar to those found in the Holy Land (e.g., Golgotha). There is also a river, Jordan, which passes through these churches and cuts them into roughly two groups.[4]

Besides the continued tradition of stone cutting, the churches of Lalibela reflect the architectural designs of Aksum. The Medhane Alem (the Savior of the World) church, which is the largest of all churches measuring (109 feet by 76 and 36 feet high), stands supported by rows of rectangular columns and is believed to replicate the features of the original cathedral of Aksum Tsion (Zion). Both the exterior and the interior of Medhane Alem are supported and divided by massive columns, respectively. However, these columns are devoid of decoration.

The smallest among the rock-hewn churches of Lalibela is the St. Mary. However, it is also one of the most well-decorated churches. An elaborate entrance leads into a three-aisled interior with delicately curved and decorated columns, arches, and ceilings. The nave reflects one of the characteristic features of Aksumite architecture, "Aksumite frieze" of false windows.

The exteriors of the church of St. Emmanuel and St. George, with features like protruding false wooden beams and doorways represented in stone, clearly reflect the Aksumite architecture that was depicted on obelisks. St. George has another unique architectural element. Its structure is a cruciform. Similarly, the church of Golgotha is noted for its series of life-size relief carvings in its chapel.

Though the relationship between the Aksum and Zagwe dynasties on one hand and the people of the Walita-Soddo (south-central Ethiopia) on the other was not clearly established, archaeologists have come across some 40 obelisks. The height of these stone statues ranges from one to two meters. Archaeological excavation revealed that these stones were used as markings of burial grounds. Engraved on the statues are swords, disks, and other markings. Though ethno-historians and anthropologists concur that these stone statues are of the pre-Christian era, their exact date is unknown. The local people, however, associate these statues with Ahmad Ibn Ibrahim al-Ghazi (1506–1543). This, too, is doubted because of the age of the stones. The Cushitic-speaking people who reside in southwestern Ethiopia, the Konso, are noted for carving wooden statues. These wooden statues were carved and planted commemorating successful men and women.

Medieval Period

The ascension of Yekuno-Amlak to the imperial throne around AD 1270 marked the end of the Zagwe rule and the beginning of the medieval period in Ethiopia. Although ruins of buildings that suggested the continuity of the architectural styles of Aksum and Zagwe were found in northern Shoa (central Ethiopia), there are no palaces and churches that survived the wars of Ahmad Gragn (1522–1541). What is more significant is that until the establishment of Gondar (northwestern part of Ethiopia) as the capital at the beginning of the 17th century, the medieval kings of Ethiopia ruled their country without having a permanent seat or capital. The period thus witnessed what is now known in Ethiopian history as the "roving capital," which also implies the absence of the development of a meaningful urban center. The king of kings and queens lived in tents that could be pitched and dismantled at short notice. In this regard, and because of its unique architectural style, the city of Gondar is an exception. It was the first permanent seat of the empire and urban center after the absence of such tradition for centuries. The style of construction is markedly different from that of Aksum and Lalibela. Stone and mortar were used to build palaces, churches, and bridges. The architectural style of the Gondarian period (1620s–1880s) though primarily of indigenous origin and credited to the Beta Israel, pejoratively known as Falasha, exhibited foreign input from Armenians, Greeks, Indians, and the Portuguese.[5]

Of the many castles and churches built at that time, the most imposing palaces and churches that survived time and many of the wars are that of King of Kings Fasiladas (r. 1632–1667), Fasil Castle, King of Kings Iyasu I (r. 1682–1706), and Dabra Birhan Sillassie church. Iyasu I, who was the grandson of Fasil, has meticulously decorated the interior of his church, including the ceiling with paintings of saints and angels that are still visible today.

King of kings and queens who reigned in that city followed the example set by Fasil. Consequently, 14 palaces, castles, and 44 churches were built in and around Gondar. The unique element of the Gondarian architecture as exhibited on the palaces and churches was two- or three-story buildings with rectangular and doomed angle towers, turrets, and embattlements. Wooden balconies, windows edged with red volcanic tuff, and an outside staircase were other features.

However, some of the churches and palaces that the Gondarian kings and queens built were destroyed by the Mahdist invasion of 1887. During the Italian occupation (1936–1941), too, the Italians destroyed some of the churches and used them as military camps. The British, on their part, bombed some of the castles such as the palace of Iyasu I. Despite these setbacks, the city has some of the old churches such as Debre Birhan Sillassie, Fit Abbo, St. Gabriel, Mikael, and Mariam. Except for Debre Birhan Sillassie, the aforementioned churches have been renovated, though at the cost of losing their historic value.[6]

Modern Ethiopia

The monarchial tradition of building churches and palaces has continued in modern Ethiopia as well. After transferring the capital from Gondar to Addis Ababa in 1889, King of Kings Menelik II and Queen Taitu continued building churches and palaces. Some of the churches they built included Selassie Balewold, Baata Mariam, St. George, and Intoto Mariam. These churches exhibit the Ethiopian traditional as well as Western architecture, while the city reflected the traditional pattern of settlement. The site where the imperial palace was built was on a commanding place, a hilltop. The palace, oftentimes referred to as the *Gibe*, served as the central locus around which the residences of prince and princess, notables, and generals were constructed. Next to the palace was always a church where the king and empress conducted their daily prayers. There was also an open ground that served as a public space. The latter could be used as a place of litigation, a mini-market, or a public square. Each notable, in return, served as a mini locus where his or her entourages and servants set up their residences. This is how towns were "planned" in pre-19th-century Ethiopia; and each town, including the capital, reflected the aforementioned pattern of settlement. Each locality is named after the notable, prince, or general. Even today, in Addis Ababa and other towns we hear the names of localities that reflect the earlier trends. In Addis Ababa, local names such Ras Meknonen local *(safar)*, Dejach Habite Giyorgis *sefer*, and Dejach Balacha *sefer* are still prevalent.[7]

Intoto Mariam Church was built by Emperor Menelik II in 1882 on Mount Entoto in Addis Ababa, Ethiopia. (Derejeb/Dreamstime.com)

The Italians developed a master plan for Addis Ababa and other major Ethiopian towns such as Gondar, Jimma, Desse, Harar, and Dre Dawa. Each of them served as seats of provincial administrators. In the process of their planning, the Italians zoned the city into white (European) and black (Ethiopian) residential areas. Then, they subdivided the city into administrative, residential, commercial, and industrial areas. Italian-designated names such as *mercato* (market), *piazza* (downtown), *caza* (inches), and *caza populare* (residential places) tried to replace names of some of the older neighborhoods. To some degree, indeed, the Italians succeeded in leaving their colonial imprints despite their short-lived stay in Ethiopia. Names like *piazza* and some of the city plans they outlined in the 1930s remained the basis for urban planners in 20th-century and contemporary Ethiopia.[8]

It was only after the Italian occupation (1936–1941) that Ethiopian cities began witnessing "modern" urban planning. Even then, urban planners found it hard to remake major cities like Addis Ababa. Thus, Addis Ababa continued to be, according to one of the city planners, an urban center where "shops, factories, and houses compete with one another for street access, daylight and fresh air."[9]

In terms of architecture, too, the Italian legacy is very visible. Most urban centers in Ethiopia retained the colonial buildings: two- to three-story rectangular buildings with arched windows, doors, and high ceiling. After the departure of the Italians, Ethiopians who did not have their own trained architects and urban planners but who had been working under the Italians continued mimicking the Italian style. Residential houses, which used to be round with thatched roofing, ceased to exist in the urban centers, though they are still very visible in rural areas. Villas, with rectangular shape and French windows, were the favored architectural design for residential houses. Today, Ethiopia, especially Addis Ababa, as one *Washington Post* reporter observed, "is a jumble of architecture, the legacy of the shifting alliances in the country, which was occupied by Italy from 1936 to 1941. Monuments displaying the communist red star with hammer-and-sickle inset, gifts from Moscow during the nearly 20-year rule of Marxist dictator Mengistu Haile Mariam, mix with gleaming glass-and-steel banks and high-rises emblematic of Western capitalism."[10]

ART

Painting and Graphic Arts

Half a dozen researchers have tried to categorize Ethiopian art but failed to concur either on the periodizations or on the themes that define the periodization. However, all have agreed that the monastic school of painting is the basis for Ethiopian art and that the Wars of Ahmad Gragn (1529–1543) was a landmark in categorizing Ethiopian art. They also have come to an understanding on the existence of what they termed as "Gondarian" art or "Gondar" style (17th to 19th centuries), which they further divided into early and second Gondar art, where painters were observed to include court and domestic scenes as well as social life.[11] Stanislaw Chojnacki, an expert on the study of Ethiopian art, believes that between the late 16th and early 17th centuries "a dramatic change occurred in Ethiopian church architecture with the round form generally replacing the rectangular, and this in turn dramatically altered the arrangement of wall paintings in churches. . . . This change certainly had as much relevance to the evolution of wall paintings as the destruction of churches by the invading Adal warriors [Ahmad Gragn's soldiers]."[12]

Hence, until the post-Adwa period (the period after 1896), Ethiopian art and sculpture remained more spiritually oriented, exclusively dedicated to religious themes such as paintings that depicted angels, God, St. Mary, and the Trinity; all these paintings were found, again exclusively, inside churches on walls, icons, and in religious manuscripts. Occasionally, however, one also finds the images of the benefactors of the church, or the legend of the Queen of Sheba and King Solomon, and battle scenes from the wars of Ahmad Ibn Ibrahim Al-Ghazi, Maqidala (a war fought between Britannia and Ethiopian in 1868) and Adwa (a battle fought between Ethiopia and Italy in 1896). It is very hard to find paintings that illustrate the day-to-day lives of ordinary people. Consequently, Ethiopian art and sculpture remain primarily in the domains of the Ethiopian Orthodox Church and hence in the hands of its clergy. Finally, though the country was almost evenly divided into Christian and Muslim, the art and sculpture of the country largely remained Christian, which further compounded the problem of studying Ethiopian art and sculpture.

In the aforementioned Christian-Semitic art of Ethiopia, in addition to being an expression of religious devotion and aesthetic feelings, some common themes can be discerned. Almost all painters were clergymen such as priests, deacons, monks, and *debteras* who learned to paint by studying the works of painters who existed before them. They were self-taught. Except probably for the images of the Trinity and Jesus Christ, the hairstyle of almost all individuals is in the Afro style, while St. Mary's head is always covered. What is more, all the images of the wicked, the enemy, and the plebian, including the devil, were portrayed in profile, while the faces of the righteous, the angels, and saints were portrayed in full. Size is another important mark of distinction. The size of the images of king of kings, empresses, and queens were always larger than that of nobles and commoners. In the absence of king of kings and empresses, the size of the kings or other notables is larger, and thus, the traditional artist illustrates the sociopolitical and military position of the individual in his paintings. Having a handkerchief on hand, wearing large tropical hats, and being surrounded by large number of retunes are symbols of higher status that the traditional painter employed to depict individual's position in paintings. Another trait of Gondarian art/painting was that the painter did not put his name on his work. If he did, it was considered (by the church fathers, his colleagues, and the populace at large) as snobbery. This practice of not placing one's name on paintings continued even after the development of folk/popular art; however, the reason is different. In traditional Ethiopian art, the church prohibited the portrayal of secular themes. In addition, it was considered improper to put one's name on paintings. Thus, when folk art emerged at the turn of the 20th century, many painters found it hard to place their name on their paintings, at least initially. As a result, many of the painters of Ethiopian traditional and folk art are unknown.[13]

The transition from traditional to modern art happened in the late 19th century with the rise of King Menelik of Shoa to the imperial throne (r. 1889–1913) and the transfer of the imperial capital from Gondar to the newly established city, Addis Ababa. There, the royal court began commissioning artists to paint newly built churches in the city and its environs. The painters were mainly from Gojam (a province found in western Ethiopia and adjoining Gondar) but trained in the late Gondarian style.

The influx of devotional pictures from Europe also influenced the painters. The presence of European dignitaries who came to pay homage to the victorious Ethiopian King and foreign travelers and residents in the country served as a conduit for newer ideas and styles of painting. As Walter Raunig sums up, "In the 1920s the stimulus of European models—above all of prints and photography—as well as European artists active in the land, and their schools, as well as the education of Ethiopian artists in Europe, led a number of Ethiopian painters to deviate from their country's artistic tradition and develop their own, so called modern, style."[14]

The foreign diplomats, businessmen, and adventurers who came to Ethiopia also wanted some memento that showed they were in Ethiopia and began commissioning painters. Their interest, however, was not confined solely to religious paintings. They wanted paintings that depicted secular themes. The response of Ethiopian traditional painters resulted in the transformation of Ethiopian traditional art into popular painting. Initially, battle scenes and wars were the favorite themes. This was followed by paintings of the story of the Queen of Sheba and King Solomon, and finally paintings that portrayed day-to-day lives of kings, notables, and their people and hunting scenes. Thus, while the pre-20th-century Ethiopian art was primarily religious and chiefly commissioned and acquired either by the Ethiopian Orthodox Church or by the royal court, the commercialization of art and its increasing separation from the sole domains of the church and the royal court became its 20th-century feature. As the demand for Ethiopian art increased, so too did the number of artists and secular themes such as royal banquets, hunting, and faming life.

After a momentary lull due to the Italian occupation in 1935–1941, postwar Ethiopia experienced a surge in folk art. Most of the paintings during the immediate aftermath of the war were patriotic. They depicted leaders of the patriotic resistance with their long Afro hair and aggressive stances, and their counterparts, the Italians, despite their impressive attire, were always portrayed as losers. King of Kings Tewodros and "mother Ethiopia," with a background of the Ethiopian tricolors, were other themes of postwar folk art that now are interchangeably referred as "Tejbet," or "airport art."

The training of Ethiopians in Western-style painting and the influx of cheap Western paintings into Ethiopia challenged the postwar traditional Ethiopian artists. This, coupled with the growth of tourism industry, an additional challenge to Ethiopian traditional art, also provided stimulus and demand for folk paintings. The classic materials used were cotton or linen and skin (goat or sheep). Sometimes, artists used paper, calabashes, ostrich eggs, and other materials. Folk artists, however, used paper and cotton cloth. The use of imported paint also became another feature of folk art. Above all, folk art was primarily intended for sale to foreigners who had little understanding of the art and the language written on the paintings. This "airport art" was poor in quality and often "devoid of the country's spiritual and emotional background."[15] Yet, folk art, though relatively poor in quality, is diverse in its themes. Unlike earlier paintings, it often contains depictions of landscape, ethnographic details, and information on customs, clothing, and traditions of the time. Its customers, too, are different. Tourists and urban dwellers are the primary buyers of folk art.

The arrival of the first Western-educated art students from Europe in the early decades of the 20th century had also introduced Western concepts and styles of painting and thus ushered in what is now known as Ethiopian modernist art. The first Western-educated painters were educated in France, including Abebe Wolde Giyorgis, Agegnehu Engida, and Zerihun Dominik. Nevertheless, their impact on Ethiopian art was very limited. They were either realistic painters or sculptors. They were employees of the state, and their art was commissioned by the state, primarily by the king. The king gave these paintings to foreign dignitaries or simply kept them in the palace, or gave them to the various governmental offices and Ethiopian notables. Much of their work was confined to making portraits of important personalities in Ethiopia, the usual reproduction of biblical themes that often adorned church walls, the legends of the Queen of Sheba and King Solomon, and the Battle of Adwa. Thus, the emergence of a truly modernist art in Ethiopia had to wait until the post-Italian period and the opening of the Addis Ababa School of Fine Arts in 1957.[16]

In the aftermath of the Italian occupation, the Ethiopian state had to re-build the state apparatus, including educational institution, from scratch. Unlike other colonies in Africa where the colonial state structure remained operational after the departure of the colonizer, in Ethiopia this did not hap-pen. The British, who helped Ethiopia defeat the Italians, forcefully deported the Italians out of Ethiopia. During their five years' occupation of Ethiopia (1936–1941), the Italians totally decimated both the traditional- and Western-educated Ethiopians. The latter were considered a threat to Italian colonial aspirations. Therefore, King Haile Selassie feverishly began establishing in-stitutions such as the Ministry of Education and Fine Arts. He, meanwhile, employed the few survivors of Italian occupation to run the Fine Arts Depart-ment of the Ministry of Education. These were the French-educated artists mentioned earlier. The king also sent Ethiopians abroad for various training, including arts. Among those who studied modern art in the post-Italian period, who tremendously impacted Ethiopian art, and who truly introduced modern concepts of art and sculpture were Afawarq Takle, Ale Felege Selam, Gebre Kirstos Desta, and Skunder Boghosian.[17]

Afawarq Takle was born in Ankober (north central Ethiopia) in 1932. The king sent Afawarq in 1947 to the Central School of Arts and Crafts in London. Upon completion of his studies, he was admitted to the famous British School of Art, the Faculty of Fine Arts at Slade, and the University of London, also known as "the Slade," to study art. He was the first African to enroll at this prestigious institution. He returned to Ethiopia in 1954 soon after, and at age 22, Afawarq exhibited his work in Addis Ababa. Afawarq, who is one of the most renowned artists of 20th-century Ethio-pia and who is also known as "establishment artist," received one of the most coveted prizes in Ethiopia, the Haile Selassie I Award for Fine Arts in 1964. The trustees recognized Afawarq, among other things, "for his con-tribution in being among the first to introduce contemporary techniques to Ethiopian subject matter and content."[18] Maitre Artist World Laureate Afawarq Takle lived in Addis Ababa in his self-designed 22-room house, art gallery, and a studio, "Villa Alpha." Afawarq Takle died on April 10, 2012. Some of his early works include the stained glass triptych that depicts African enslavement and liberation that covers the walls of the Africa Hall, statues of Ras Mekonnen, *the Last Judgment, Fish and Shell, War and Peace, Mother Ethiopia, Telecommunications*, and murals and mosaics covering two inner walls of St. George's Cathedral. He also painted portraits of heads of states such as K Nkrumah, and designed various commemorative postage stamps.[19]

Gebre Kristos, who became to be associated with Ethiopian abstract expressionist art, was born in Harar (eastern Ethiopia) in 1932. He received his training at the Cologne Academy of Fine Arts, Kölner Werkschulen, in Germany where he was introduced to abstract art. Like his contemporaries, Gebre Kristos won the coveted Haile Selassie I Prize in 1965. Apart from his paintings that were exhibited at home as well as abroad, Gebre Kristos' contribution to Ethiopian modernist art was phenomenal in mentoring and influencing a new generation of modernist Ethiopian artists. He taught in the only fine arts school, the Addis Ababa School of Fine Arts, since his return from Europe in 1962 until his exile to the United States in 1980. His success, however, was not an easy one. During the prerevolution years, his art was often criticized for neglecting, and even abandoning, Ethiopian traditional art in favor of the Western world. During the turbulent days of the *Derg* (1974–1991), Gebre Kristos was compelled to adhere to principles of socialist art, Socialist Realism, and forced to produce posters for the revolution, which ultimately led to his exile to the United States. As a professor and one of the forebears of abstract expressionist art in Ethiopia, Gebre Kristos was one of the best known modernist artists among the art community of Ethiopia. Some of his paintings include *Age, My Neighborhood, Gugs, Golgotha, Daisies, Tam Tam,* and *Interior.* An art critic and historian of Ethiopian art, Professor Stanislaw Chojnacki, commented on some of the earlier works of Gebre Kristos such as the *Interior* and *Daisies,* which he described as "an appealing blend of transparent softness and the charm of evocation of nature . . . [while] Daisies [is] a virile and powerful painting, Gebre Kristos succeeded in expressing at the same time the fragility of the flower and the irresistible power of attraction of nature."[20] Gebre Kristos died in exile, as a refugee, in the United States in 1981, at the young age of 49.

Ale Felege Selam was born around 1924 in Fitche, central Ethiopia. In 1949, unlike the aforementioned colleagues of his, Ale was sent to the United States, the Chicago Art Institute, one of the premier institutes of art in America. After completing his studies, Ale returned to Ethiopia in 1954. Though Ale was engaged in designing postage stamps, portrait and flyer paintings, illustration of books and texts, and paintings that adorned cathedrals in central and eastern Ethiopia, his notable contribution to Ethiopian modernist art lays in institution building. Ale was instrumental in the establishment of the only fine arts school in Ethiopia, the Addis Ababa School of Fine Arts, in 1958. Ale also served as the director of the school since its establishment until he was forced to resign in 1974. During these years, Ale recruited the youngest and brightest Ethiopian art teachers, including men like Gebre Kristos and Skunder Boghossian. Despite such contributions, Ale was accused of living a petit bourgeoisie lifestyle in the early days of the revolution. According to Esseye G Medhin, "Ale only contributed to his sinking reputation when he interfered regarding the works of graduating students' subject matters. . . . Ale was unhappy to see contemporary and radical subject matter displayed on students' diploma works. Staff members were unhappy with his involvement." This portrayed Ale as a person who was oblivious to his surrounding and out of touch with the tide of change. Accordingly, some students dared to portray "Ale sleeping on the roof of the school . . . provide[ed] the final blow."[21] He was forced to resign from his post in 1974. Despite such setbacks, Ale continued pursuing his profession. As recently as 2006 at the age of 82, he was engaged in adorning one of the Ethiopian Orthodox churches in Maryland.[22]

Less known in Ethiopia and yet very influential at home and abroad as an Ethiopian artist with an African Diasporic vision was Alexander "Skunder" Boghossian. He was born in July 1937 in Addis Ababa. Skunder studied art

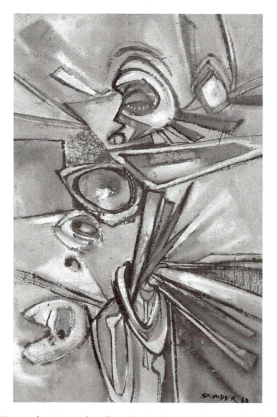

Painting titled *Eye in the Mirror*, by Skunder Boghossian (b. 1937). (Private Collection/ The Bridgeman Art Library)

informally at the Teferi Mekonenn School and at the University College of Addis Ababa (later renamed Haile Selassie I University). His informal art teacher was the librarian of the college, Stanislaw Chojnacki, who was also a historian of Ethiopian art. Skunder was one of the Ethiopians sent by the king to study art in England sometime in 1955. He studied art at St. Martin's School, Central School, and the Slade School of Fine Art for a couple of years. Then in 1957, Skunder left London for Paris, France, where he studied at the École nationale superieure des Beaux-Arts and stayed for almost a decade. In those years, he was a student as well as a professor at the Académie de la Grande Chaumière. While there, he met the founder of Surrealism, Andre Breton, and worked with him for some time. It was also in Paris that he studied the works of prominent African and Latin American painters such as Cuban Wilfredo Lam and Chilean surrealist, Roberto Matta, and a German-Swiss artist, Paul Klee. Skunder explains his encounter in Paris in the following manner:

> I discovered two things: First African Art and then Paul Klee. For a year I made daily visits to the African section of the *Musee de l'Homme* studying The masks, the totems, and fetish dolls. . . . I was discovering African Art, apart from my Ethiopian tradition. . . . After this came Klee. In his work I found everything—magic, poetry, humor, mysticism. . . . In his masks I saw a soul in close communication with the roots of Africa. . . . [While] passing I just happened to be in a small gallery. . . . So impressed by the dramatic play of forces and the supernatural quality in that work, I really could not move. . . . That was Lam. when I finally went inside I was startled again by Matta. In his paintings, there was cosmic coordination in space and time and his metallic rhythms vibrated in such a way that the canvases seemed to move. The effect of all this was confusion about my work but eventually that confusion became suggestion.[23]

In addition to the aforementioned encounters, Skunder's African Diasporic art was influenced by two interconnected events of the 1960s in Africa and across the Atlantic. The year 1960 was referred to as the Year of Africa. Many African countries gained independence from colonialism in the 1960s. Some Africans in Africa and beyond were celebrating Africanness through art and philosophy such as Negritude. Meanwhile, the civil rights movement was making inroads in the United States.[24]

It was also in Paris that he met his wife, an African American woman from Tuskegee, Alabama, whom he married in 1966. In the same year, he returned to Ethiopia with his wife and a baby girl. While in Addis Ababa, like some of his Ethiopian contemporaries, he joined the Addis Ababa School of Fine Arts as instructor, exhibited his work, and won the coveted Haile Selassie I Prize. However, after only three years of stay in Ethiopia (1966–1969), he left for Atlanta University, Georgia, where he was invited as a resident instructor in sculpting, painting, and African design at the Atlanta Center for Black Art. From Atlanta, he moved to Howard University, Washington, D.C., in 1971 where he taught art until his death in 2003. Thus, Skunder was part and the product of his time. As Elsabet W. Giorgis, who was a friend of Skunder, summed, "Skunder was intimately involved in the struggle for independence and liberation movements in Paris, where he lived for a decade, and the Civil Rights Movement in the United States, which he was part of."[25] Thus, it was a combination of all these that shaped Skunder's art, which more often than not depicts African spirituality, symbols, and myth that meanwhile reflect tension, resistance, and the cultural unity of Africa.[26]

Some of his works are *The End of the Beginning, Time Cycle III, Jacobs Ladder, Fragment, Fertility*, and the *Grass Sprit*. His work was the first modern African art that was bought by the New York's Museum of Modern Art. In spite of such achievements, Skunder's work remained associated with "native" art, while he was identified as "honored guest of the art world than a bona fide star." As a result, Elsabet says, Skunder "was the victim of the failure of congruence between the art of the 'Other' and an accepted European formalized system of art."[27]

Compared to the artists mentioned earlier, Julie Meheretu, another Ethiopian modernist artist, is less burdened by tradition. Unlike her Ethiopian modernist artists' predecessors and contemporaries who reside in the United States, Julie never passed out from the Addis Ababa School of Fine Arts nor has she been mentored by one of the graduates of that school. Though Julie was born in Ethiopia in 1970, she left for the United States with her Ethiopian father and an American mother at an early age. Raised in Michigan, she studied at the Universite Cheikh Anta Diop (UCAD) in Dakar, Senegal, in 1990–1991 and then at Kalamazoo College where she received her BFA. Julie also studied at the Rhode Island School of Design in Providence, where she earned her MFA in 1997.

Julie's art is also unique in that it "has forged a new tradition of landscape painting—one with a language of forms that includes architectural plans, topographical and airport maps, weather charts, street girds, animated explosions and popular culture imagery—everything from tattoos to graffiti, science fiction elements to Kung Fu kicks."[28] While this summarizes the gist of her art, it also reflects her time and life experience. Elizabeth Harney remarks, "Meheretu's history and practice illustrate the fluid, shifting and highly personal means through which individuals negotiate definitions of diaspora. While she clearly feels an affinity and connection to things Ethiopian, her works move beyond any narrow definition and speak to global concerns."[29]

These days, American cities such as Washington, D.C, Los Angeles, and others have a sizable Ethiopian immigrant/refugee population that left its country seeking better life, education, or asylum due to political oppression in Ethiopia. With these Ethiopians, as demonstrated earlier, we find the best and brightest artists, who benefited from the rich and diverse Ethiopian culture, from the Ethiopian ecclesiastical paintings, and from their immigrant/refugee experience in America and beyond. One apparent result is the infusion of newer concepts of art into Ethiopian modernist art and its transformation that transcends boundaries.

Today, Ethiopian/African artists are receiving due recognition in the art community in America. Their arts are being exhibited in major art museums, sought after by private as well as institutional art collectors. There are more Ethiopian artists and art exhibitions in the United States than in Ethiopia. Though it cannot be matched with what is going on in America, there are signs of revitalization in Ethiopia among artists and Ethiopian art lovers. There are even private art galleries in cities like Addis Ababa. But, here too, the revitalization is spearheaded primarily by Ethiopian returnees from the Diaspora. Thus, while Ethiopian modern art is engaged with the Diaspora and globalization, the Ethiopian Diaspora is equally occupied with Ethiopia in Ethiopia.

NOTES

1. Although Western as well as Ethiopian scholars often refer to Ethiopian kings as emperors and the country as empire, Ethiopian rulers were never emperors and the country an empire. The title that Ethiopian monarchs used, either in their letters or during their coronation ceremonies, had been always *niguse negest,* which exactly means king of kings. Unlike the European term, *emperor,* the *king of kings* reflects Ethiopia's power structure and manner of rule. The king of kings is a monarch who rules over other kings and that he cannot appoint his own person as a king over a territory/province that has hereditary rulers. These hereditary rulers could be kings, *rases, dejazmachs,* and so on. If the king of kings is dissatisfied with the performance or loyalty of the provincial king, he can replace the king with another king from among the local magnate but not from outside. Such practice entails the limited power of the king of kings vis-à-vis the provincial kings and that the king of kings was never an absolute monarch, as was the case in Europe until the Industrial and the bourgeoisie revolutions. Therefore, the Ethiopian state structure was a sort of federation (for lack of better terms) where the regional/provisional rulers were relatively free to do whatever they wish in their domain as long as they pledged their allegiance to the king of kings. Equally important is that the provincial king could also become king of kings if he or she was related to the monarchy through blood, a bloodline that hails from King Solomon and the Queen of Sheba.

2. Sergew Hable Selassie, *Ancient and Medieval Ethiopian History to 1270* (Addis Ababa, Ethiopia: United Printers, 1972), pp. 82–85, 201; David W. Phillipson, *Ancient Ethiopia, Aksum: Its Antecedents and Successors* (London: British Museum Press, 1998), pp. 71–95.

3. Phillipson, *Ancient Ethiopia*, p. 131.

4. Phillipson, *Ancient Ethiopia*. See also Yuri M. Kobishchanov, *Axum* (University Park: Pennsylvania State University Press, 1979); Jean Doresse, *Ethiopia: Ancient Cities and Temples* (London: G. P. Putnam's Sons, 1959).

5. See Richard Pankhurst, *History of Ethiopian Towns from the Middle Ages to the Early Nineteenth Century* (Wiesbaden: Steiner, 1982); Manuel Joao Ramos and Isabel Boavida, eds., *The Indigenous and the Foreign in Christian Ethiopian Art* (Burlington, VT: Ashgate Pub. Co., 2004).

6. See Solomon A. Getahun, *A History of the City of Gondar* (Newark, NJ: Africa World Press, 2006).

7. See Richard Pankhurst, *History of Ethiopian Towns: From the Mid-Nineteenth Century to 1935* (Stuttgart, Germany: Franz Steiner Verlag Wiesbaden GMBH, 1985).

8. For the various Italian urban planning, see Ferdinando Quaranta, *Ethiopia, An Empire in the Making* (London: P.S. King, 1939), pp. 94–110; "Sir Patrick Abercrombie's Town Plan," *Ethiopia Observer* I, no. 2 (March 1957): 35–44.

9. "Sir Patrick Abercrombie's Town Plan," p. 35; See also Francis J. C. Amos, "A Development Plan for Addis Ababa," *Ethiopia Observer* VI, no. 1 (1962): 5–14.

10. Emily Wax, "Ambitious Plans for Ethiopia's Capital: Mayor Envisions Addis Ababa as Hub for E. Africa," *Washington Post*, June 11, 2004, p. A14.

11. Stanislaw Chojanacki, "Attempts at the Periodization of Ethiopian Painting: A Summary from 1960 to Present," in *Proceedings of the Six International Conference of Ethiopian Art*, ed. Birhanu Teferra and Richard Pankhurst (Addis Ababa, Ethiopia: Institute of Ethiopian Studies, 2003), 3–27.

12. Chojanacki, "Attempts at the Periodization," p. 7.

13. Richard Pankhurst, "The Battle of Adwa (1896) as Depicted by Traditional Ethiopian Artists," in *Proceedings of the First International Conference on the History of Ethiopian Art* (London: The Pindar Press, 1989), 78–103; Girma Fisseha, "The Ethiopian Avant-grade in the Thirties and "Tejbet" Painting," in *Proceedings of the History of Ethiopian Art*, ed. Birhanu Teferra and Richard Pankhurs (Addis Ababa, Ethiopia: Institute of Ethiopian Studies, 2003), 221, 227.

14. "Ethiopian Folk Art Painting," in *Proceedings of the First International Conference on the History of Ethiopian Art*, ed. Birhanu Teferra and Richard Pankhurs (London: The Pindar Press, 1989), 70; Girma Fisseha, "The Ethiopian Avant-grade in the Thirties and "Tejbet" Painting," in *Proceedings of the History of Ethiopian Art*, ed. Birhanu Teferra and Richard Pankhurs (Addis Ababa, Ethiopia: Institute of Ethiopian Studies, 2003), 221; Chojanacki, "Attempts at the Periodization," pp. 23–25.

15. Raunig, "Ethiopian Folk Art," p. 70; Girma Fisseha, "The Hunt in Ethiopian Folk Art," in *Proceedings of the First International Conference on the History of Ethiopian Art*, ed. Birhanu Teferra and Richard Pankhurs (London: The Pindar Press, 1989), pp. 104–14; Girma Fisseha, "The Ethiopian Avant-grade in the Thirties and "Tejbet" Painting," in *Proceedings of the History of Ethiopian Art*, ed. Birhanu Teferra and Richard Pankhurs (Addis Ababa, Ethiopia: Institute of Ethiopian Studies, 2003), p. 225.

16. Shiferaw Bekele, "A Modernizing State and the Emergence of Modern Art in Ethiopia (1930s–1970s) with Special Reference to Gebre Kristos Desta (1932–1981) and Skunder Boghossian (1937–2003)," *Journal of Ethiopian Studies* XXXVII, no. 2 (December 2004): 11–45.

17. Sheferaw, "A Modernizing State"; See also Sydney W. Head, "A Conversation with Gebre Kristos Desta," *African Arts* 2, no. 4 (Summer 1969): 20–25.

18. Quoted in Shiferaw, *A Modernizing State*, p. 26. See also Tseday Alehegn, "Maitre Afeworq Tekele's Odyssey," *Tadias: Ethiopian-American Lifestyle Magazine* II, no. II (June–July, 2004). http://www.tadias.com/v1n7/coverstory.html.

19. Unknown, "Afework Tekele," *Ethiopia Observer* VI, no. 3 (1962): 189–240; RKPP, "The Art of Afeworq Tekele," *Ethiopia Observer* IX, no. 3 (1965): 162–208.

20. Stanislaw Chojnacki, "Gebre Kristos Desta: Four Years Later," *Ethiopia Observer* XI, no. 3 (1967): 176–78; See also Sheferaw, "A Modernizing State"; See also S. Chojnacki, "Gebre Kristos Desta: Impressions of His Recent Exhibition," *Ethiopia Observer* XIV, no. 1 (1971): 10–24; Gebre Kristos, "Desta: Some Press Comments from Germany," *Ethiopia Observer* XIV, no. 1 (1970): 25; Solomon Deressa, "Gebre Kristos Desta: Somber Colors and Incantatory Words," *Ethiopia Observer* XI, no. 3 (1967): 162–75; The 4th Annual Blen Art Show, "Honoring the Painter-Poite Gebre Kristos Desta," http://www.blenartshow.com/fourth/honorary.htm (accessed February 5, 2008). All citations have some of the artist's work.

21. Esseye G Medhin, "Ale Felege Selam: The Modernization of Art," Debre Hayq Ethiopian Art Gallery (May 29, 2007), http://www.ethiopianart.org/articles/articles.php?id=80 (accessed January 5, 2008); See also Esseye G. Medhin, "Ale Felege Selam," *Lissan: Magazine for Ethiopian Art and Life Style* (January 19, 2008), http://lissanonline.com/blog/?p=98.

22. Esseye G. Medhin, "Ale Felege Selam: The Modernization of Art," Debre Hayq Ethiopian Art Gallery (May 29, 2007), http://www.ethiopianart.org/articles/articles.php?id=80 (accessed January 5, 2008). See also Seferaw, "A Modernizing State."

23. Quoted in Sheferaw, "A Modernizing State," pp. 31–32. See also Solomon Deressa, "Skunder: In Retrospect Precociously," *Ethiopia Observer* X, no. 3 (1966): 174–84.

24. National Museum of African Arts, "Ethiopian Passages: Dialog in the Diaspora," http://africa.si.edu/exhibits/passages/boghossian.html# (accessed February 5, 2008.)

"This image depicts the burning of Axum and Lalibela, two historically significant sites in Ethiopia. Here, the artist-seer prefigures the Ethiopian revolution of 1974 and illustrates the overturning of church and imperial hegemony in modern Ethiopia. The white bird in the center, poised as a phoenix, is witness to and survivor of the destruction, while the spirit figure on the right represents the past hoping to escape the violent present. Skunder has deconstructed spatial order to convey a sense of collision and shock, a metaphor for revolution and change."

25. Elsabet W/Giorgis, "Modernist Spirits: The Images of Skunder Boghossian," *Journal of Ethiopian Studies* XXXVII, no. 2 (December 2004): 140, 139–61; see also

Elsabet W/Giorgis, "Skunder Boghossian: Artist of the Universal and the Specific," http://www.the3rdman.com/ethiopianart/articles/boghossian.html (accessed February 5, 2008).

26. National Museum of African Arts, "Ethiopian Passages: Dialog in the Diaspora," http://africa.si.edu/exhibits/passages/boghossian.html# (accessed February 5, 2008).

"During a trip to Uganda, Skunder collected bark that was used locally for burial. He worked the bark into a somber, totemic composition, one that derives its strength as much from the beauty of the material's natural hues and textures as from the mysterious forms with which he endows it. One senses a profound narrative about the grandness of Mother Nature complete with volcanoes, lava flows and mountain formations. . . . The artist's ongoing fascination with the cosmological is here given an abstract, lyrical form."

27. Elsabet, "Modernist Sprits," p. 140.

28. Elizabeth Harney, "The Poetics of Diaspora," in *Ethiopian Passages: Contemporary Art from the Diaspora* (London: Philip Wilson Publishers, 2003), p. 27.

29. Ibid., p. 29.

5

Cuisine and Traditional Dress

INTRODUCTION

Ethiopia has a diverse topography and climate. Its lowest point is 100 meters below sea level, while the highest point is almost 5,000 meters above sea level. The country has abundant water resources. So much so it is referred as "the water tower of East Africa." Ethiopia is also endowed with fertile soil. This, coupled with other favorable circumstances, helped the country become one of the cradles of the world where the domestication of a variety of plants and animals occurred in prehistoric times. It has been practicing ox-plow agriculture for thousands of years that continues with very little change to this day. Chat (*Catha edulis*), coffee (*Coffea arabica*), nug (*Guizotia abyssinica*), enset (*Ensete ventricosum,* also known as false banana), teff (*Eragostis abyssinica*), finger millet (*Eleusine coracana*), and red chili pepper (*Capsicum frutescens, C. abyssinicum*) are some of the plants indigenous to Ethiopia. On the other hand, lentils, chickpeas, barley, sorghum, and wheat were additions from the outside world and yet whose cultivation in Ethiopia dates back to the antiquities. Sometime around the 16th century, Portuguese emissaries introduced maize (which Ethiopians call bahir mashila, "maize that came from across the sea"), tomatoes, potatoes, and oranges into Ethiopia.[1]

Ethiopians divide the wide-ranging topography of their country into three climatic zones: *qolla* (lowlands/hotter climate) rising between 1,400 and 2,000 meters above sea level; *woyna-dega* (temperate) between 2,000 and

2,600 meters above sea level; and *dega* (highlands/cold climate) varying from 2,600 to 3,600 meters above sea level.

The diverse nature of the climate very much affects the demographic pattern of the population, way of life, and economic endeavor. Most Ethiopian reside in the *woyna-dega,* away from the bitter cold of the highland and the steaming heat and the ruthless sun of the lowlands. People who reside in the lowlands are mostly pastoralists, while those in the *woyna-dega* are primarily farmers.

These circumstances along with the Ethiopian Orthodox Church's dietary restrictions and the presence of other religious traditions such as Judaism and Islam in Ethiopia make the culinary history of the country much more complex. This, together with the seeping of Western culinary tradition into Ethiopia since the turn of the 20th century, gave Ethiopian cuisine an added element.

ETHIOPIAN VEGETARIAN DISHES AND THE ROLE OF RELIGION

Religious diversity such as Judaism, Christianity, and Islam affects the dietary habits and attitudes of Ethiopians, probably more than anything else. Ethiopia is one of the few Christian countries in the world where the Old Testament's rules of "clean" and "unclean" food is strictly adhered to. It is also in Ethiopia that one finds "Muslim" and "Christian" meat. Here we witness the social symbolism of food in identifying and defining a certain group of people vis-à-vis others, or creating a common bond from within and without.[2] When an Ethiopian remarks *"inena anta islamina amra nan"* (you and I are Muslim and Amhara), he or she is implying that "we are no more in agreement or, we are different."

The Ethiopian Orthodox Church, which was a privileged national religious institution until the 1974 socialist revolution, has molded the country's norms and people's behavior. The church believes in the Old and New Testament, and thus, all meat sources are classified as "clean" and "unclean." Accordingly, pork/ham, for instance, is unclean. Moreover, even those that are categorized as "clean" can only be considered and consumed as "clean" if and only if the animal is killed by an ordained priest or a deacon. Ethiopian Muslims also follow similar dietary rules. Both bless the animal to be slaughtered with their monotheistic words common to both religions such as *Basima Ab,* which means "in the Name of the Father" in the clerical language, Geez, while Muslims say *Besimilah* in Arabic, which also means "in the Name of the Father." Yet, while there is no difference in their dietary habits and cuisines, and although they sometimes eat together, Christians and Muslims never share food together if it has meat in it. The British Imperial envoy,

Henry Salt, who visited Ethiopia in 1809 and 1810, expressed his difficulty understanding this custom, "We this evening experienced some difficulty in supplying our followers with provisions. Part of them being Christians, and part Musselmauns [sic], it became necessary, (as neither would eat of the meat slain by the other) to kill two cows each day, [one for Muslims and one for Christians]."[3] Another European traveler who ventured into Ethiopia in the 1920s reiterated that in Ethiopia "Christians will not touch meat unless it is killed by one of themselves, nor will Moslems eat any which has been killed by a Christian."[4] This norm is very much alive today. Keeping with this tradition, if there is a feast, or a holy day in which Muslims and Christians are invited, the host has to provide, depending on his or her resources, a goat, sheep, or ox/cow, or chicken to Muslims and Christians alike.[5] So much so, in urban centers in Ethiopia, where meat is now sold, it is very common to find *Yekiristiyan siga bet* (Christian butchery house) and *Yesilam siga bet* (Muslim butchery house). It is also common to come across a *Yesilam migib bet* (literally, Muslim's food house, i.e., restaurant). Thus, both groups avoid each other's restaurants. If a Christian is observed entering in a Muslim restaurant, or eating with a Muslim, he or she is considered a Muslim. Salt, whose countryman was witnessed eating with a Muslim, reported his agonizing experience:

> We had not long taken up our quarters, before an attendant was sent by the lady, with the present of a sheep and a quantity of bread [*enjara*]. On my requesting him, according to the custom of the country, to get permission for one of his master's people to kill the sheep, he replied, that 'none of them would kill for *Christians* [emphasis original] who eat with Musselmanus [sic],' . . . a practice of which he at the same time asserted, Mr. Stuart had been guilty. I was extremely alarmed at this account, knowing how fatal an act of this kind would have proved to our interests.[6]

In such circumstances, the father confessor, *yensiha abat,* would inquire if the alleged person has eaten Muslim meat. If the person confessed to committing such sin, he or she undergoes one or all of the following measures of absolution. These include a symbolic baptism (*meshafe-qedr*), performing a certain number of prostrations (*sigdat*) at church, and fasting (*tsome*) for a number of days, as prescribed by the priest.

While Muslims and Christians share or borrow household goods and utensils as long as these are washed, Christians and Jews do not. The latter, who refer to their Christian neighbor as *Goim,* strictly keep utensils designated for use by non-Jews outside their house. If there is a social occasion such as birth, death, or wedding that brings the two religious groups together, each must come with his or her own drinking cup and eating plate. If they do not, then the host provides one. In the latter circumstance, the utensils are always kept outside. Or, both break the drinking utensil that they used.[7] Like the rest of Africa, Ethiopians use the gourd (also referred to as calabash) for various purposes, one of them being using it as a drinking cup.[8] These types of drinking utensils made of gourds are known as *shikina* or *wamira*. Ethiopians also use clay or horn-made cups for drinking and other purposes. The calabash and clay cups are, therefore, cheaper and easier to break. Of course, the European penetration of the country also introduced cups made of glass, tin, and plastics that are increasingly pushing out the traditional household items.

Unlike their Muslim and Arab neighbors, Ethiopian Muslims do not eat camel meat. There are exceptions, however. These are Muslims of northwestern and northeastern Ethiopian lowlands (the present-day Eritrea) and southeastern lowlands, dwellers of the Ogaden desert. These groups of people, the Beni Amir, the Rashida (both reside in the present-day Eritrea), and Ethiopian Somalis, respectively, have closer contact with non-Ethiopian Muslims of the surrounding countries who are highly influenced by Arab culture and whose lifestyle is nomadic. These Arabicized nomadic Muslims, unlike the Ethiopian Muslim highlanders, depend on the camel for survival. In addition to eating camel meat, they drink camel milk and blood. The latter often happens not as a way of life but as a survival strategy. In the absence of choice, these people pierce the camel's vain and drink the blood.

For the followers of the Ethiopian Orthodox Christian faith, fasting is a very different matter compared to other Christian sects, as Henry Salt notes, "[It] is customary during the season of Lent, which . . . Abyssinians observe with strict and scrupulous attention."[9] During the Lenten season, *arba tsom*, the church and the community expect all people above the age of 13 to fast until 3:00 P.M. During these times, they do not drink water and avoid dairy and poultry products as well as meat. The foods they eat consist of vegetables (boiled beets, boiled kale, collard greens, pumpkin sauce, potato stew, spinach sauce, etc.) and legumes (broad beans, chickpeas, lentil sauce, etc.).[10] The Orthodox Church also advocates and enforces sexual abstinence during the fasting season. Fasting during Lent becomes even more intense during the Passion Week. Beginning from Good Friday and lasting until the dawn of Easter Sunday, nothing is eaten or drunk. Children, the sick, and the very old are exempt. Accompanying this fasting is *sigdat* (prostration), which is done all day on Good Friday and Saturday.

The stringent dietary rules of the Ethiopian Orthodox Church and the many fasting days—followers of the Ethiopian Orthodox faith are expected to fast 208 days, including Lent, Wednesdays, and Fridays of every week and other fasting seasons[11]—resulted in the development of a complex set of vegetarian dishes, *atakilt wot*. These vegetarian dishes, which are also known as *yatsom wot* (fasting dishes), have a various blend of seasoning. One of the well-known fasting dishes is *ye-shnibra assa* (chickpea-flour fish). This dish is made of chopped red onions (*qay shinkurt*), red-hot spiced pepper (*barbare*), cooking oil (*zayit*), various spices (*qimama-qimam*), and a thick chickpea flour paste shaped like fish, and is fried in oil. *Goman wot* (it can be kale, collard greens, or spinach) which is boiled, finely chopped collard greens combined with cooked/fried onion and garlic, topped with green jalapeño pepper is another side dish that goes with the *shimbra assa* dish. *Shiro wot,* which is a powdered bean, chickpea, or peas, is combined with boiled water, oil, fried red onions, and red-hot and spiced chili pepper. Or *kik wot,* which consists of split peas, chickpeas, or beans, is mixed and cooked in fried onions; oil and red pepper is another main fasting dish in Ethiopia. If the aforementioned dishes are cooked without the red-hot and spiced chili pepper, but with additional ingredients such as garlic, diced ginger, and green pepper, they are known as *alicha shiro* and *alicha kik wot.* These can be used as side or main dishes. There are also other fasting-season dishes such as *dinich wot* (potato stew). The potato is peeled and chopped into four or eight parts depending upon its size. This is boiled with chopped and fried red onions and oil for some time. Then some garlic, diced ginger, turmeric, and fresh chilies (chopped green pepper) are added. Like the *kik* and *shiro* sauce, the *dinich wot* could be made with or without *barbare,* the red-hot and spiced chili pepper.[12]

In urban areas like Addis Ababa, exposure to Western dietary habits and socialist revolutionary ideas has eroded the grip of religion on Ethiopian dietary habits. The introduction of a new type of dish, *shifinfin* (which literally means covered up), in the 1970s is one example in which Ethiopian Christians tried to evade public embarrassment by eating meat during a fasting season or day. *Shifinfin,* as its name implies, is primarily a meat/chicken dish but covered with one of the many fasting dishes. It is served in such a manner to evade public scrutiny and the wrath of the church.

As in Christianity, fasting is an integral part of Islam. It is one of the pillars of Islam, and thus, Ethiopian Muslims rigorously adhere to this practice. In addition to the fasting that Ethiopian Muslims do to cleanse their body and mind from evil temptations, there is the Ramadan where they fast all day. They do not even swallow their saliva during the Ramadan. However, before 6:00 A.M. and after 6:00 P.M., Muslims dine. Unlike their Christian counterparts, Ethiopian Muslims consume meat, dairy, and poultry products during Ramadan. Some unique foods that Ethiopian Muslims prepare during Ramadan include, but are not limited to, *sambussa* (a triangle-shaped crust fried wheat dough stuffed with spiced lentils, meat, or spinach), a variety of soups, *fool* (boiled beans, finely chopped green peppers, and red onions mixed with spiced butter/oil), and *baklava*. The *baklava* and to some degree the *sambussa* are used as desserts. *Chat* (*Catha edulis*), which is a mild stimulant that is chewed, is part of the after-fasting feast among Ethiopian Muslims. While Muslim highlanders use *chat* for special occasions such as *doa* (prayer) and during the fasting season, for Muslims of the lowlands such as Ethiopian-Somalis and their Muslim Oromo neighbors of eastern and southeastern Ethiopia, *chat* is consumed casually.[13] However, since the 1980s, the role of *chat* as a Muslim cultural mark has begun to blur. Ethiopians, especially the youth, begin consuming *chat* regardless of religion and region. This is because of the following circumstances and developments. The Ethiopian revolution was one of the most traumatic periods in Ethiopian history. To overcome this traumatic experience, the younger generation turned to *chat* and drinking. Due to the breakup of cultural norms that the socialist regime regarded as feudal and thus deemed irrelevant, parents lost control over their children. This development further exacerbated the already worsening situation. Meanwhile, the revolution's attempt to respect all religions and cultural practices also contributed to the introduction of chewing *chat* to areas and cultures hitherto unknown. The higher commercial value of *chat* and its relatively draught resistance nature and less labor intensive character made the plant attractive to farmers who previously shunned it for cultural and religious reasons. These days, however, farmers of Gojjam, Gondar, Tigray, and Wello that roughly account for the other half of the country produce *chat* for local and international consumption. The ever-increasing Ethiopian Diaspora community is the latest market that stimulates the production and export of *chat*. This is in addition to the already existing markets such as Somalia, Djibouti, and the Muslim Arab world, especially the modern Middle East. Currently, foreign currency earning from the export of *chat* is more than $250 million annually and it is continually rising.

Coffee Ceremony, *Injara* and *Doro Wot*: The Culinary Markers of Ethiopian Identity

Coffee, one of Ethiopian's contributions to the world, got its name from one of the southern provinces of the country, Keffa. There, and in much of the southern, southeastern, and southwestern parts of Ethiopia, coffee grows in the wild. The people who cultivated coffee and probably the first to use it as a beverage were the Oromos. It is also among the Oromos that one finds the consumption of coffee in many ways and forms than any other ethnic group in Ethiopia. As mentioned earlier, the Oromo use coffee as *qolo* (*bunaqalla*), which is a form of snack. The green coffee beans are roasted and then soaked in a spiced butter. The soaking of the roasted coffee beans in spiced butter adds flavor and is rich in food value. It is also partly intended to preserve the aroma and partly to guarantee the longevity of the roasted coffee. The Oromos also use coffee leaves as a substitute for coffee. The coffee leaves are roasted, powdered, and then boiled. Such a brew of coffee is called *qutti*, and it is usually made in the absence of coffee beans either due to scarcity or because the coffee beans are not yet ripe. *Qutti*, however, smells and tastes as good as coffee. The most commonly known coffee preparation, however, is roasting the green coffee beans until they turn dark brown, pounding the roasted coffee in a wooden mortar, *mugacha*, with a wooden pestle, *zanazana*, and finally brewing the coffee powder in a small clay pot, called *jabanna*.

Until the late 19th century, the consumption of coffee was limited to the southern half of the country, among the Muslims and the Oromos. In the northern half of the country, where the Ethiopian Orthodox Church has a stronghold, the clergy prohibited its consumption. The clergy believed that coffee was among the few plants (tobacco, *chat*, and marijuana) that did not dry while all other plants did when Jesus was crucified and died on the Cross. Thus, said the clergy, coffee is a cursed plant. However, when the public witnessed Menelik II, king of kings of Ethiopia, drink coffee, and when the then patriarch of the Ethiopia Orthodox Church, a certain *Abba* Matewos (Mathew), rebuffed the aforementioned assertion as baseless, people of northern Ethiopia (the Amharas and Tigrians) began drinking coffee.[14] So much so today Ethiopia is one of the two major coffee-producing countries in the world, the other being Brazil, where more than 50 percent of the coffee produced is consumed locally. Coffee has become a national beverage with an elaborate ceremony that has become the symbol of Ethiopia and Ethiopians.

Throughout much of Ethiopia, though the size and type of coffee pots vary and the ingredient(s) with which they flavor their coffee is (are) different, the ritual is almost uniform from place to place and from one ethnic group to another. If a guest comes, the first thing the host does is to invite the visitor to have coffee. The guest might be reluctant indicating lack of time, or he or she just had coffee a little while earlier. It is, however, customary for an Ethiopian to entreat and insist that the caller have coffee, saying that it will not take that much time or giving other such excuses. The guest then accepts the request of his or her host and enters the house. The lady of the house then brings her coffee pot, *jabana*, coffee table (*rekebot*), a four-legged round wooden plate (being replaced these days with a mass-produced plastic, tin, or a small wooden box with a drawer for coffee cups), coffee cups, *finjal* more commonly known as *sine*, (about a dozen), and green coffee beans on a metal pan.

While the coffee is getting ready, the husband instructs his wife to bring something to eat. The wife then brings *injara* with *wot*. The latter, depending on the day (Wednesdays and Fridays are fasting days) or the season (fasting or nonfasting), could be a vegetarian or beef dish, or a combination of both. The

Coffee ceremony, Addis Abba, Ethiopia. (Karen Kasmauski/Corbis)

food brought also depends on the resource of the host. With the food, *tella* (a homemade beer) or *taji* (honey mead) is served. Usually, it is more common for rural households to have *tella* at home. If it is in urban areas, a servant or one of the children or neighbors' children are sent to buy from one of the many beer vendors in the locality.

In the midst of this, fresh green grass is cut and spread on the floor. Then, the lady of the house/servant/daughter roasts the green coffee beans on an iron pan. The roasted coffee is brought to the guest so that he or she can have a whiff of the aroma. The roasted coffee is ground and the powder along with water is put into the pot and boiled. When ready, the pot is taken off the hearth or stove and is placed on small round pot-seat made of straw, *mawatot,* so as to allow the coffee to settle. Then, the lady of the house burns incense on a small funnel-shaped clay, *itan-machesha* (incense burner) or just places the incense on the hearth.

Like all activities in Africa, coffee-drinking is a social event. Accordingly, the host summons his or her neighbors for coffee. It is very rude and unbecoming of someone not to invite his or her neighbors for coffee if coffee is made in his or her home. It is because of the socializing nature of coffee that every household in Ethiopia has more than a dozen coffee cups.

Coffee time is also an occasion where the host introduces his or her guest to neighbors and relatives. Coffee time is also a moment where the business of the day, gossip, or information is exchanged, or even match making and other deals are done. It may be because of this association of coffee with "business" that the Ethiopian coffee ceremony has three stages. The first round of coffee is called *abol.* After everyone returns his or her cup to the person who is making (brewing) the coffee, more water is added to the pot and placed on the hearth for a second round, *tonna.* Each stage is accompanied with incense burning. The final, or the third, round of coffee is named *baraka,* blessing/blessed. Any person/guest who comes at this stage is considered blessed and viewed as a good omen. While it is inappropriate to drink the first round of coffee and leave, it is also equally improper to drink or serve lukewarm coffee—hence the centuries-old adage "the pleasure of coffee is its burning." Throughout the ceremony, coffee has to be drunk hot. After the final serving, neighbors and guests alike express their gratitude by saying "*yabaraka yasesay bet yarigaw,*" which literally means "May He make the house blessed and prosperous."[15]

Whether a person has a guest or not, coffee is made three times a day (in the morning, at midday, and in the evening) almost in every household, be it in rural or urban areas. It is also customary to offer something to eat during coffee time, *yabuna quris* (coffee breakfast). The "coffee breakfast" depends on the resources of the household. It could be *injara,* boiled beans/wheat (*nifro*), roasted beans/barley/wheat, or a combination of all (*qollo*), or a full meal such as breakfast, lunch, or dinner. Thus, in traditional Ethiopia and even today, inviting someone for coffee entails more than just drinking coffee. These days, however, with the commercialization of labor and the increasing awareness of time and cost of living, people (both in rural and in urban centers, more so in the latter), though they drink coffee three times a day, it is shared among neighbors. For instance, if the morning coffee is served in X's house, the mid-day and evening coffees are held in Y and Z's households, respectively. The ever-increasing market penetration of Ethiopia, the commercialization of coffee, and the growing demand for coffee in the international market might have made the three-times-a-day coffee consumption at home an expensive proposition and thus might have resulted in the rotation of having coffee ceremonies among neighbors.

HOLIDAY, SPECIAL OCCASIONS, AND *DORO WOT*

If the guest is a relative, or a dear friend who came from afar, the man/lady of the house will ask the person to spend the night, or stay for a few days. Naturally, the guest desires to continue journey but his or her host literally begs him or her to stay; and oftentimes, the guest accedes to the host's request. It is customary to accept someone's hospitality; otherwise, it is considered mean and brutish. The willingness of the guest to pass the night, or stay for some time, makes the day particular. As a result, a special preparation would soon commence. Depending on the resources of the host, a chicken or sheep, or both, will be slaughtered. It is worth mentioning that in rural households both chickens and goats/sheep are raised in the backyard. Thus, it is not difficult to kill a chicken for one's guest(s). Similarly, people raise chickens in urban centers, for the rural–urban dichotomy is still blurry in much of Ethiopia. Otherwise, chickens are cheap and available in the local open-air daily market. In Ethiopia, it is customary to kill a chicken for a guest/relative, hence, the traditional saying *saw lawadaju chachut yardal* ("even if he or she has nothing, a person would kill at least a chicken for his favorite kin"). It is the association of friendship and hospitality, and the *doro wot* that makes the latter as one of the major culinary markers of Ethiopian identity. As Igor Cusack, in his article "African Cuisine," aptly sums, "The development of a national cuisine will involve the summoning of a variety of dishes into the ambit of the discourse of the nation, and the very mention then of some national dish will quietly flag the nation. Thus, for example, the serving of Doro Wat . . . , one of the national dishes of Ethiopia, will gently remind the Ethiopian diner of the nation."[16]

The preparation of chicken stew, *doro wot,* is laborious and requires skill. That is why chicken stew is a dish for special occasions such as the ones mentioned earlier, or for one of the many holidays like the Ethiopian New Year (*Inqutatash*), commemorating the finding of the True Cross (*Masqael*), Christmas (*Ganna*), Epiphany (*Timqat*), and Easter (*Tinsae*).

Once the chicken is killed, it is immersed in boiling water so as to make it easier to pluck its feathers. Then, the chicken is lightly placed over the flame of a burning fire so that the remaining feathers, which are invisible to the naked eye and difficult to pluck, can be removed. Removing the skin and cutting the chicken into 12 parts known as *bilits* then follows. After that, the chicken is placed in a big wooden bowel, *gabate,* and thoroughly washed for hours. The washing continues until the chicken meat looks ashen white. The washed chicken is then soaked in salted water with lime juice until the stew is ready. A good chicken stew does not smell like chicken. If it does, then the cook is a lousy one and she will become a mockery of the neighborhood. Because of this, the preparation of a chicken stew is one of the moments in which the lady of the house exhibits her skills as a refined cook.

Aside from the washing and cleaning of the chicken, the most important ingredient that makes chicken stew best is the spiced red-hot pepper, *dilh/chew.* The lady of the house prepares the *berbare,* a mixture of dried red-hot peppers (*Capsicum frutescens* and *C. abyssinicum*), garlic, fresh ginger roots, chopped red onions, scared basil, cloves, cinnamon, cardamom, bishop weed, salt, and water. Depending on the size of the chicken, a good amount of chopped red onions is added in a clay pot, *dist,* and roasted until it turns brown; a small amount of water is added now and then. This is then followed by the addition of the spiced red-hot pepper and mixing it with the onion and cooking it with some cooking oil, preferably with spiced butter. When the mix is thick and cooked well, the chicken is added until the latter soaks the stew. Salt is added into the stew and stirred, on and off so that the stew would not burn, until the chicken is fully cooked. Sometimes before taking out the chicken stew, a dozen hard-boiled eggs are added and left to soak the stew for a while. Then, lunch/dinner is ready.[17]

Despite the variety of food crops grown in Ethiopia and the availability of numerous locally produced foods, *teff* (*Eragrostis teff*), from which *injera* is made, remains the staple cereal, and *injara* (a soft, spongy, and sour bread) is the indispensable bread of the country. Thus, a chicken stew is unthinkable without a *teff-injara* (bread made of *teff*). *Teff,* a highly nutritious cereal grain, is unique to Ethiopia. Until the migration of Ethiopians to the United States and other parts of the world, it was only grown in the Ethiopian highlands. However, recently some farmers in Canada and the United States (Idaho) began growing *teff* in a limited quantity.[18] The cereal is ground into a fine powder. The *teff* flour is then mixed with water and yeast. The mix is kept in a tightly closed container for two to three days to allow fermentation. On the third day, after the water is discarded, the thick dough is mixed with hot water. After a while, the dough, which has thinned, is ready to be backed. It is baked on a round clay pan, *mitad* (a term used in central Ethiopia), also known as *mugogo* (a name used in the northern half of the country).

The *injara* is served on a common plate, *massob,* a basket-table, which can hold as many as 20 *injaras*. The *massob* and all other household goods such as *agaligil* and *muday* are woven by coiling fiber plants. The most common grasses are *sindado* (*Pennisetum schimperi*), used to form the coils, *akirmma* (*Chloris*), and *gramita* (*Cyperus fischerianus*) that are split and used for wrapping the coils. A metal punch (*wasife*) is used to make a hole in the coil. While the metal punch is made by the ironsmith, usually a Beta Israel, dying the *akirma* is the profession of Muslim women. However, all basket making is done by the women of the house. Basket weaving is, thus, another skill that measures the quality of a lady. A skillful woman adorns her basket with various colors and patterns. To keep the longevity of the edge and to waterproof it, the edges and the top part of the basket table is bound with fine leather that has been treated with *qulquwal* (aloe) juice. These finely made basket tables are not used daily. They are brought out on holidays, or to honor a guest.[19]

On the basket table, many layers of *injara* are placed, and in the middle of the *injara,* the chicken stew is placed. The guests, invited neighbors, and family members sit around the basket table. The eldest among the diners blesses the food. If the man of the house happens to be the oldest, as a gesture of honoring the guest, he invites the guest to bless the food. However, if there is a priest, an *imam,* or a *qadi* among them, then it is his prerogative to do the blessing.

During dining, Ethiopians do not use knives and forks. Ethiopians, like the rest of Africa, use their fingers to eat. Hermann Norden who visited Ethiopia at the beginning of the 20th century and who was appalled by the absence of spoons, knives, and forks remarked, " [I]t was etiquette to tear off a piece of bread, fill it with meat, dip it into the sauce, and as adroitly as possible carry the dripping mass to our mouths. Forks, spoons, or plates there were none."[20]

It is also customary for the host to now and then feed the guest, give *gurisha.* For Ethiopians, feeding the guest with one's own hands signifies affection and closeness. C. F. Rey, who was in Ethiopia in the 1920s and 1930s, described his experience:

Injara served with various side dishes. (Ton Koene/Visuals Unlimited/Corbis)

I happened on one occasion to call on an Abyssinian chieftain . . . who was a particular friend of mine, just as he was sitting down to a late lunch . . . surrounded by his principal vassal chiefs. I had to sit down on the divan next to him; as he was of course eating *à l'Abyssine* his cook kept on rolling up succulent morsels of terrifically hot curry or stewed meat or raw flesh in bread [*injara*] with his fingers, and pressing them on my jaded palate. Any of his chiefs whom he desired to honor was similarly distinguished.[21]

During these times, the guest might protest saying that he or she is full. But, the man/woman of the house will insist that it is customary for the guest to accept the *gurisha*. The mid-19th-century traveler and British representative in Ethiopia Walter Plowden also noted that giving *gurisha* to a servant signifies appreciation by the master: " [E]ach servant likes to feel that his master thinks of him occasionally, and to receive a mouthful from his [master's] hand makes him happier than much wage."[22] In addition to *gurisha,* the man or lady of the house expresses affection, respect, and closeness to the guest by inviting the latter to sit next to him or her. If a visitor is motioned to sit on the right, it reflects the highest honor, the next highest being on the left. Offering one's own drinking cup to the guest is another expression of honor and favor bestowed upon the visitor.[23]

HOLIDAYS: CUISINE (*QURIT* AND *KITFO*)

The Ethiopian New Year (*Inqutatash*), commemorating the finding of the True Cross (*Masqael*), Christmas (*Ganna*), Epiphany (*Timqat*), and Easter (*Tinsae*), and *Mawiled* (the birth of the prophet Mohammad) and *Id-al-fatir* (the end of the fasting of the Ramadan) are national holidays. The latter two became so after the 1974 revolution. During these holidays, *doro wot* is prepared, but depending upon one's means, a lamb/goat or even an ox/cow is slaughtered. These days, because a cow/ox is expensive, villagers and neighbors pool their financial resources together and buy a bull. Or, someone with a means buys the bull and shares it among those who are interested and willing to pay for their share. Such arrangements are called *qircha*. The number of people who participate in the *qircha* depends on their financial strength. Hence, the bull is apportioned into 10, 15, or 20 equal parts. While this is customary in the present-day Ethiopia, where virtually everything is commercialized and thus up for grabs by anyone who can afford to pay, the pre-20th-century Ethiopian scenario of meat sharing was very different. For one thing, no one sold or bought meat. For another, the various parts of the ox/cow or goat/sheep that were killed had claimants based on military and civilian rank or professional occupation. Henry Salt expressed his admiration for Ethiopians concerning their skill and knowledge with which they shared meat. He further indicated that such refined skill was the result of the necessity that each person should have his meat according to his entitlement: "I may here mention, that the Abyssinian are, in general, very expert in the dissection of a cow, a circumstance owing to the necessity of a very exact division of the several parts among the numerous claimants, who are entitled to a certain portion of every animal that is killed."[24] Plowden, who visited Ethiopia almost half a century later, and who partook in some of the military campaigns in Ethiopia, concurs: "[In] slaying an ox, for example, each portion of meat, which, in their fashion of separation, must be a hundred or so, has its particular claimant, such as the wood-cutter, the grass-cutter, the shield-bearer, the singer or minstrel, the butcher, the maidservants, the *gambo* carriers, the *tej*-maker, and numerous others, all which are scrupulously exacted."[25]

Thus, in such holidays, in addition to the *doro wot*, raw meat (*brindo*, these days it is called *qurt*) is a common dish. The origin of *brindo* eating is not clearly known. Some attribute the development of raw meat eating to the endless military campaigns that Ethiopian monarchs conducted to secure their domain from internal usurpers or external aggressors such as Ottoman Turks, Mahdists, Egyptians, and Europeans. During such campaigns, soldiers were strictly ordered not to light fire so as not to betray their position to the enemy. Hunger after a long march, as Henry Salt indicated, can be another reason.[26] Be that as it may, one thing is very clear: Ethiopians love raw meat. European travelers who visited the country between the 18th and the early decades of the 20th century unequivocally attested that during holidays and special occasions, raw meat was part of a meal. Some travelers such as C. F. Rey went to the extent of saying, "Among other customs which are peculiar and interesting, pride of place must surely be given to their fondness for raw meat or *broundo*. This form of diet is preferred to any other by the masses of the population, and indeed by practically all sections thereof, beef being liked better than mutton."[27]

In the present-day Ethiopia, though raw meat dish is still associated with holy days and special occasions, people can have it anytime. In fact, urban centers like Addis Ababa are abundant with butchery houses that sell raw meat to anyone who can afford it at any time of the day. The difference, compared to the previous times such as the pre-1990s, is that instead of raw beef, people, especially those who can afford it, prefer to have goat raw meat. This is so because of the belief that goat meat is healthier than beef. Raw meat eaters consider that beef is rich in cholesterol, which in turn leads to cholesterol-related diseases than goat meat. The preference for goat meat is partly to avoid the consequences of the "modernization": fattening of cattle using artificial hormones instead of the normal, traditional, and open-range feeding and fattening of cattle. Another development witnessed in the present times is that the price of raw meat has skyrocketed. In the early 1990s, kilos of raw meat used to fetch 5.00 birr (about $1.00). But today it costs about 200 birr and thus has become unaffordable to many.

There is another raw meat cuisine, *kitfo,* a minced beef mixed with spiced butter. Among the Gurage, people of central Ethiopia, whom the rest of Ethiopians view as the best chefs of *kitfo* and probably its origin, the dish is accompanied with Ethiopian cheese (homemade traditional cheese) and cooked collard greens. Among the Gurage and other peoples of south-central Ethiopia, *kitfo* is eaten with *qocho,* a highly nutritional bread processed from *inset (Ensete edulis,* false banana) rather than the usual *injara.*[28]

Among the Gurage, most of them are strict followers of the Ethiopian Orthodox faith; the *Masqael* holiday and *kitfo* have special place. As Osseo-Asare indicated, "There is a deep African spirituality, whether it is expressed in worship of God or gods, or on respect for the elders or ancestors, or in understanding of the spiritual forces in the world. There is often a profound connection to one's homeland."[29] Accordingly, during the *Masqael* holiday, all Gurages who are away from home will return to their village. The return-ees, usually migrant laborers, are expected not only to buy new clothes for themselves and their kin, but also to buy or provide the money for a bull to be slaughtered on that day.

In order to understand the celebration of the *Masqael* holiday, a brief historical background is imperative. The European Christian tradition has it that Queen Helena, upon finding the True Cross, ordered her entourages to light a bonfire to signal its discovery. The bonfire lit in Palestine, the legend indicates, was seen as far as Constantinople. Ethiopians, on their part, replicate the story differently. They ascribed the *Masqael* tradition to King of Kings Dawit (David) I (1382–1411), who died fighting Muslim incursions into Ethiopia, while some attribute the festival to King of Kings Zara Yaqob (1434–1468).

Commemorating the Finding of the True Cross, a bonfire (*damara*) is lit in each and every Christian household throughout Ethiopia. In addition, a much bigger bonfire is lit at a central location of each and every village, town, and city in Ethiopia. So much so the public square in Addis Ababa, Ethiopia's capital, is known as *Masiqal Adabababy* (Meskel Square). There, the Ethiopian head of state accompanied by the patriarch of the Ethiopian Orthodox Church lights the *Masiqal Damara.* The patriarch blesses the *damara* before it is lit. The direction to which the central pole on which a cross is affixed on its top-end and on which logs of wood and the golden-yellow

Masqael daisies (*Aday Ababa, Coreopsis negriana*) are piled is important. The populace believes that it is a good omen for the provinces (states), villages, and towns toward which the pole falls. These provinces or regions will have a bumper crop and thus a prosperous year. It should be remembered that the *Masqael* festival is celebrated on Maskram 16 (September 24), after the end of rainy season and the beginning of harvesting time.

The lighting ceremony is accompanied with the Orthodox Church's chant, followed by traditional folk music and dance. In bigger and multiethnic cities like Addis Ababa, one catches a glimpse of the music and dance of the many ethnic groups of the country such as the Oromo, the Amhara, the Tigrians, the Gurage, and the Dorze.

People who are returning from the festivity mark their forehead with a cross with ashes of the *damara*. Almost everyone who attended the event tries to have access to the ash or charcoal to mark his or her forehead with the cross.

While it is the head of state or governors and administrators of respective areas who light the bonfire, in villages and households it is the head of the household or the village elder who does it. After the bonfire is lit, the head of the family or the elder of the village kills the bull in the morning, and with that, the festivity commences and will last for weeks.

HOLIDAYS AND ETHIOPIAN TRADITIONAL DRESS

During holidays and special occasions such as weddings, christening, or attending church, Ethiopians attire themselves with the best dress they have. The exact date when Ethiopians began weaving and wearing clothes is not known. However, life-size stone statues found around Aksum at Hawulti Melazo depict a well-dressed lady. Her dress covers her hands all the way to her wrist and her body all the way to her ankles. The earliest Aksumite coins also depict busts of well-dressed kings with a bandanna or a bonnet tied at the nape of their neck. Ethiopian church paintings also exhibit colorfully dressed individuals, saints, and angels. The earliest of these paintings, however, do not go beyond the 15th century, for all were destroyed during the wars of Ahmad Gragn. In addition to church paintings, we have travelers' accounts that inform us that Ethiopians wear *shamma*, a cloth that is made of locally grown cotton.[30]

The cotton is spun by women and woven by men with the handloom. Prior to the Italian occupation of Ethiopia, the finest cotton cloth was produced in Gondar, followed by Adwa. In those days, there was very little distinction between the rich and the poor in terms of the style of dress. It consisted of a pair of trousers that were either above, or a little below, the knee. The latter is known as *bat-tahulat*. The upper body of a man was covered with a loosely fitting *shama,* a Roman toga–like cotton cloth. Hence, according to Walter Plowden, it was King of Kings Tewodros II (r. 1855–1868) who "began to reform . . . the dress of Abyssinia, all about his person wearing loose-flowing trousers, and upper and under vests, instead of the half-naked costume introduced by the Gallas [now called Oromo]."[31] Since then, it seems, men have been obliged to wear a shirt that reaches the thighs, which is slashed on both sides below the waist, with tight-fitting sleeves, which is known as *ija-tabab.* Women wear a very loose dress with sleeves to the wrist and descending to the ankle. They use a strip of the same material to tie around their waist. The difference between the rich and poor in Ethiopia in the manner of dress stems from the embroidery and ornament that adorns the hems of the dress, the edges of the sleeves, and collars. The embroidery is usually done with the finest and lightest material, usually silk, or with various vivid colors woven in an artistic design into the edge. On top of this, both men and women of eminence wear the finest cloak (*kaba*) made of silk and embroidered and ornamented with silver-gilt.[32]

For women and, to some degree, men, such attire is incomplete without styling hair. Both men and women plait their hair in various forms, the common being cornrow. For women, the end of the plait, which could be more than four inches or so long, is tied at the nape of the neck or let loose, becoming a kind of a frame for the face. Sometimes, the women's plait is parted in the middle. For men, besides beautifying, plaiting hair has more meaning. The number of cornrows varies from man to man. Men who were noted for killing enemies and hunting wild animals had their hair fully plaited in 10 rows. Earrings made of ivory, which implies the person has killed a lion, or an earring, and a ring(s) made of silver are common. Women, on their part, in addition to the earrings, have bracelets, necklaces, and anklets. They also apply butter mixed with oils of cloves, sandalwood, and other perfumes on their plaited or baby-afro hair. Their hands and feet are dyed with a root known as *insosila,* which gives the dark rose tinge that henna produces. With this, one's beautification is complete and everyone is ready, for a holiday or a special occasion.[33]

However, the color of one's *shamma* and hairstyle conveys the circumstances a person is in. Rey indicates that a *shamma* "worn in pink or blue or even yellow . . . is a sign of mourning."[34] Norden, on his part, states that "if a dirty garment is seen it is a sign of mourning."[35] In addition, both men and women express their grief by shaving their head. While women disfigure their face, men grow their beard and keep a disheveled appearance for a while, at least until the *tazikar* (a feast for the dead held on the 40th day). Some, depending on their relationship to the deceased and the intensity of their grief, keep their unkempt appearance for a year, or even more.

Any person who wears the *shamma*, which roughly measures three yards in length and two to four yards in width, covers his or her head. However, whenever one encounters another person, be it a stranger or a friend, the head is uncovered and the person nods to the passerby as a mark of respect or friendliness. Not doing this is considered mean and quarrelsome behavior. For example, if two neighbors or friends meet and one of them pass without uncovering his head and greeting the other, then something must have gone wrong between the two. In addition, as a rule, every subordinate shall not cover his or her head in front of, and in the presence of, a superior, or a master. If the person is on a horse, he or she has to dismount from the horse and uncover the head in the presence of a superior.[36] Covering one's mouth or partially covering one side of the face during conversation, says Norden, "signifies weariness, displeasure, or disgust. The meaning of the action is, 'you and your breath are offensive to me.'"[37]

Diversity in climate also influences the nature of clothing Ethiopians have. Thus, wearing clothes is not common throughout the country. Salt, for instance, described the attire of Ethiopians who live in the hottest lowlands of the northeast in the following manners. "The inhabitants, who came in crowds to look at us, did not seem to be overburdened with clothing: the men wore a short pair of drawers and a loose cloth over their shoulders; and the women had a tanned skin, ornamented with shells, tied round their waists; while the children, both boys and girls, went entirely naked."[38] Ways of life also seem to affect the style of dressing. Rey, who visited Arusi, one of the most fertile lands found in south-central Ethiopia and where cattle raising was the mainstay of the Oromo people, noted that "their clothing is of the scantiest. . . . Men wear, in addition to a . . . loin-cloth, either a half-tanned skin over their shoulders or a piece of cotton sheeting wrapped around them. . . . The women generally wear skins; one as a sort of petticoat and another thrown over the shoulders. But they make up for the inelegance and inadequacy of this part of their raiment by a very large number of rings, bracelets, and necklace of brass and copper, more rarely of ivory, with which they literally cover themselves."[39]

CONCLUSION: WESTERN INFLUENCE, THE ETHIOPIAN CUISINE, AND DRESS

The influx of Europeans into Ethiopia since the turn of the 20th century, the brief Italian occupation of 1936–1941, and the growing number of Ethiopians who were educated abroad and were thus exposed to Western cuisine and attire introduced foreign elements into Ethiopian cuisine such as *salata* (derived from the name salad) and *basta/pasta* (spaghetti), lasagna, *bani* or *furno* (derived from the Italian *panni,* bread), into Ethiopian culinary tradition.

Ethiopian salad, *salata,* which is usually a combination of chopped romaine lettuce, tomatoes (*komidaro,* one of the few borrowed Portuguese words), red onions, green pepper, oil, lemon juice, and sometimes garlic, has become one of the favorite side dishes, which is usually consumed during the longest fasting season, Lent. Spaghetti, however, is a main dish, which is consumed outside of the fasting season as well. The difference between *ytsom-pasta,* (the fasting spaghetti) and *yafisk-pasta* (nonfasting spaghetti) is that while the *ytsom-pasta* uses diced tomatoes as a sauce, the *fisk-pasta* has ground beef as its sauce. Usually people use fork and knife to consume these European dishes. But it is not also uncommon to see people using their hands instead of the fork to eat salad when especially they are using *injera* instead of bread to eat spaghetti. Ethiopian Somalis sometimes use *injera* to eat spaghetti. Nevertheless, like all other European influences, these foods are limited to the urban centers. Even if it is known, in some parts of the country, people associate spaghetti with ascaris (*Ascaris lumbricoides*) and tapeworm, intestinal parasites very common in Ethiopia, and, thus, are averse to eating spaghetti.

The Ethiopian word for bread is *dabo,* and Ethiopians have an old tradition of baking various types of *dabo* such as *difo-dabo* (also referred as *yabesh-dabo*), which is made from wheat dough. The *difo-dabo,* however, is done only for special occasions like *mahiber/zikr,* a feast and a social gathering commemorating one of the many saint days of the Ethiopian Orthodox Church, or when someone has given birth or got married. In the latter instance, the bread is a special kind, *doro-dabo,* bread with chicken and hard-boiled eggs stuck in it.[40] The *doro-dabo* has also a significant symbolic value in that if the bride is found not a virgin, the groom will send the girl to her parents with a broken (split) *doro-dabo,* to demonstrate her infidelity. If the girl is a virgin, guests and family members consume the bread, as a public testimony to her chastity and honoring her parents.

What then makes the *bani* and *furno* different from the Ethiopian *dabo* is that they are mass produced in a bakery, they are small in size, and they are often made of non-wheat flours. What is more, they are not available outside of urban centers. In the same vein, *kek* (cake) and cookies are alien additions to the Ethiopian cuisine. Ethiopians do not have dessert as such. So much so children of Ethiopian immigrants in America mockingly refer to raw meat, which is usually served after meal as "Ethiopian dessert." What is more, eating sweets and less spicy and hot things is synonymous with being less manly, hence the adage *ywand-alicha* (a man without guts). These days, however, cake and cookies have become the favorite of the urban youth. Indeed, as Okello Oculi sums up, either as the result of the colonial legacy or through indirect encounter with the Europeans, Africans have become an enthusiastic consumers of bread, while "the wheat invasion and promotion of African stomachs into colonised silos for bread made from American wheat" has become a common phenomenon.[41]

The European arrival in Ethiopia also initiated a new phenomenon, *hotel mebilat* dining in restaurants. As it could be inferred from the Ethiopian word for hotel, *hotel*, the Ethiopians even adopted the term into their language. Until 1908, the opening of Taitu Hotel, named after the wife of Atse Menelik II, who was also the founder and owner of the hotel, eating outside was unknown in Ethiopia. Bars and tearooms, too, are results of European stimulus. The opening of such premises was solely meant for the Europeans and a handful of foreign-educated Ethiopians.

Until after the Italian occupation, such establishments were unheard of outside of the capital, Addis Ababa. Both Ethiopian and foreign travelers and government messengers had to have their *sinq*, which usually consisted of *dabo qolo* (wheat flour, sugar, salt, cooking oil mix rolled into round thin strips, cut into tiny pieces with scissors and deep-fried in oil or roasted on a big clay pan), *quanta* (lean-meat cut into long and thin strips, mixed with salt and red pepper and dried), *qolo* (any roasted cereals such as barley, wheat, beans, and chickpeas), *basso* (medium-roasted barley flour, mixed with spiced butter, red pepper powder, salt, and false cardamom powder), *chiko* (a lightly roasted barley flour mixed with spiced butter, cardamom, cloves, and red pepper powder), *qore* (roasted wheat or barley mixed with butter), and *bu-naqalla* (dried green coffee beans roasted and then mixed with spiced butter).[42]

The aforementioned varieties of food are more or less dry and spicy and thus last for days, or even months. Except for *basso* that requires water, they are consumed as is. Besides travelers, pre-20th-century Ethiopian soldiers, a ragtag peasant army, also used these food items as military rations. In fact, the origin of these foods could be related to the endless military campaigns of pre-20th-century monarchs of Ethiopia and the Ethiopian tradition of roving capitals. After the decline of the Zagwe dynasty in the 13th century and the rise of Gondar as a permanent seat of the kingdom at the beginning of the 17th century, Ethiopian monarchs had no permanent capital. They ruled the empire by moving from one place to another, residing in tents. Such a lifestyle, no doubt, required a coping mechanism, foods that can be consumed without the niceties of cooking utensils that are cumbersome in such circumstances.

A closer look at some of the previously mentioned food items further reveals their origin and the relationship between the lifestyle and ethnic acculturation. Foods like *chico, qori,* and *bu-naqalla* are some of the contribution of the Oromo to Ethiopian culinary art. The southern part of Ethiopia, where coffee grows wild, is the home of the Oromo. The Oromo, until their assimilation into the rest of Ethiopia, used to have a social system known as the *Gada*. *Gada* is an age-grade system in which the young, after a certain age, must leave their parents' abode to colonize new territories for themselves.[43] During such operations, in addition to other things, they must have developed *chico* and *qore* for food, while *bu-naqalla* was used as a substitute to quench their desire for coffee.

Travelers, depending upon their resources, have *tella* (Ethiopian homemade beer) and *taji* (Ethiopian honey wine), or one of the two, or simply water. Meanwhile, as a custom, every Ethiopian village through which travelers pass was expected to provide shelter and *dirgo,* sometimes referred to as *mitin,* for travelers. The local notable will coordinate provisions for travelers. The provisions include all or some of the following: slaughtering a goat/ship, providing *injara,* beer, *araqi* (locally distilled alcoholic beverage, like vodka), milk, and so on, depending upon the availability of resources. Not providing a traveler with provisions is viewed by Ethiopians as an affront and hence unacceptable. In such circumstances, the traveler leaves the locality as a demonstration of his or her displeasure. Such news, if it reaches other villages, shows the village, or the individual who refused to entertain the travelers, in a negative light. The traveler can also report the incident to the local authorities who admonish the villagers or even exact a punishment.[44]

Like all other aspects of Ethiopian culture, Western influence is also exhibited in coffee ceremony. Though boiling coffee on a hearth—which is usually found in the center of the tukul—or on a locally made clay stove is still customary in rural households, in the urban areas coffee is boiled on *fernello* (a corrupted Italian word to mean furnace). The *fernello* is a portable stove made from scrap metal by the local artisans. These days, Chinese or locally made portable electric stoves are replacing the *fernello.*

Imported powdered coffee and electric coffee grinders are also available in local stores. These coupled with the widespread use of espresso machines, hotels, and cafes that sell coffee endanger the coffee ceremony, and the associated socialization, especially in areas like Addis Ababa where we find a highly urbanized community and where Western influence and presence are much greater.

These days, in addition to the coffee house (*buna-bet*) and tea house (*shai-bet*) where coffee and tea are sold, respectively, there are cybercafés where both are served. In the previously mentioned places, coffee or tea mixed with sugar is consumed—a departure from the common practice in pre-20th-century Ethiopia. In the latter instance, coffee without sugar is drunk, or with a spiced butter (depending upon the means of the household), or laced with salt. Cappuccinos and lattes are also varieties that are associated with the European influence in Ethiopia and very much abound in most urban centers. During "coffee" or "lunch" breaks, employees of various institutions who cannot go home in that short period of time will go to *shai-bets, buna-bets,* or one of the nearby cybercafés for coffee, latte, tea, or cappuccino. They go in groups or alone. If they go in groups, one person might cover the bill, or each pays his or her own bill. The common practice, however, is one person covers the bill but the next day another, and so forth.

The recurrent draught in Ethiopia since the 1970s has compelled Ethiopians in general and victims of famine in particular to reconsider their dietary habits. While the majority of Ethiopians are accustomed to eating *teff,* the international community that generously responded to the plight of Ethiopians donated maize and rice as famine relief. Initially, the Ethiopian government tried to exchange these items in the market for *teff* or wheat, something that Ethiopians were accustomed to. The recipients, too, either tried to sell the rice and maize in the local market, or used the maize for brewing *tella,* or distilling *araqi.* However, as time went on, Ethiopians also began mixing *teff* with maize or even rice to make their daily bread, *injara.*

The migration of Ethiopians in thousands to foreign lands, including the United States, while introducing Ethiopian culinary tradition into the West, also required certain modifications. For instance, until the beginning of the 1980s, *teff* and *injara* were unknown in America and the rest of the world. But, with the migration of Ethiopians to the United States, *teff* was farmed in the United States and Canada in a limited quantity. Yet, with the increasing number of Ethiopians in both the United States and Canada, the *teff* produced was not enough. To alleviate the situation and with the mushrooming of Ethiopian restaurants in the major American and Canadian cities, Ethiopians began importing *teff* from Ethiopia. Ethiopians found out that this too was not enough to satisfy the growing demand, for Americans and Canadians also began to enjoy Ethiopian cuisine. Importing is also expensive. Thus Ethiopians began looking for other ingredients that shorten the time to make *teff injara.* In Ethiopia, it takes a minimum of three days to make *teff injara.* So, in addition to wheat and other flours, Ethiopians use self-raising flour to hasten fermentations. Thus, *teff injara* is no more *teff* in America. The *wot,* too, has changed. It is no more hot and spicy, though it might appear as such for the American palate.

The migration of Ethiopians has brought a new culture in the culinary tradition of Ethiopians, at least for those who are residing abroad. Despite the existence of an indigenous literate culture that thrived for centuries, Ethiopians, like the rest of Africans, do not cook using written recipes. In Ethiopia, the mother teaches her daughter the art of cooking. But, with migration, the preparation of menu and recipes has become the norm, at least abroad, while television shows in Ethiopia have begun to include master chefs teaching cooking lessons. This concept was unknown in Ethiopia, for each and every mother is a master chef.

In terms of attire, too, Ethiopians are changing fast. Looking at the 18th- and 19th-century European comments concerning Ethiopian view of Western clothes and attire would provide a better understanding of the matter. Henry Salt said that "as to the common European costume, I had formerly observed that it tended to excite a species of contempt and ridicule that occasionally became very unpleasant in its effects."[45] After more than a century, Rey had a similar observation concerning Ethiopians toward European costumes: "The nation as a whole has not adopted European dress, although it is worn to some extent in Addis Ababa, and by individuals who have been to Europe. They are proud of their traditional dress and the Emperor still encourages its use at court functions and receptions at the palace."[46] These days, however, urban dweller Ethiopians, especially the younger generation, seem to prefer European attire rather than theirs. A three-piece suit with a necktie or a two-piece is common among professionals. Wearing jackets with jeans or khaki pants is also widespread. Overall, the youth, especially those who have the means, wear Western brands and designer clothes. They get the information on the latest brand jeans, sneakers, and designer clothes from relatives living abroad, or television shows and Hollywood movies. They wear traditional dress only during holidays and special occasions. Even then, not all of them do. In the rural areas, too, the style of dressing is changing, especially among male population. A jacket, a pair of pants, or shorts are the common attire. What is left of the past is the *shamma* that they put on top of their jacket. Most women of the rural households still wear the traditional clothes, though factory-produced cotton and polyester is taking over.

In pre-20th-century Ethiopia, except for kings and queens and for those who were abroad, shoes were uncommon. Plowden observed that "the Abyssinians, generally, may be said to go barefoot, but the military more particularly so, and it is a great thing for the soldier to have hard feet."[47] The soldier was the model that every Ethiopian tries to emulate. Thus, no wonder shoes are desired.

As indicated earlier, pre-20th-century Ethiopian women were noted for using *insosilla* to color their hands and feet. As Salt noted, " [T]he Abyssinians, on the contrary, made the light color of our hair and the pale complexion of our features an occasional subject of ridicule."[48] However, the younger generation, urban-dwelling Ethiopians and especially those who are directly or indirectly exposed to Western makeup are more than willing to lighten their complexion, iron their hair instead of plaiting it, and use cosmetics to adorn themselves.

NOTES

1. David W. Phillipson, "The Antiquity of Cultivation and Herding in Ethiopia," in *The Archaeology of Africa: Food, Metals and Towns,* ed. Thurstan Shaw et al. (New York: Routledge, 1993), pp. 344–57; James McCann, "Maize and Grace: History, Corn, and Africa's New Landscapes, 1500–1999," *Comparative Studies in Society and History* 43, no. 2 (April, 2001): 246–72.

2. For understanding the role of cuisine as identity marker, see for instance Abbebe Kifleyesus, "Muslims and Meals: The Social and Symbolic Function of Foods in Changing Socio-Economic Environments," *Africa: Journal of the International African Institute* 72, no. 2 (2002): 245–76; V. W. Turner, *The Forest of Symbols: Aspects of Ndembu Ritual* (Ithaca, NY: Cornell University Press. 1967); P. Caplan, *Feasts, Fasts, Famine: Food for Thought* (Providence, RI: Berg, 1994); M. Douglas, "Deciphering a Meal" in *Myth, Symbol and Culture,* ed. C. Geertz (New York: Norton, 1971), pp. 61–82.

3. Henry Salt, *A Voyage to Abyssinia and Travels into the Interior of That Country: Executed under the Orders of the British Government in the Years 1809 and 1810* (London: Frank Cass & J. Rivington, 1814), p. 229.

4. C. F. Rey, *The Real Abyssinia,* pp. 65–66.

5. Daniel J. Mesfin, *Exotic Ethiopian Cooking: Society, Culture, Hospitality, and Traditions. Revised Extended Edition.178 Tested Recipes with Food Composition Tables* (Falls Church, VA: Ethiopian Cookbook Enterprises, 1990), pp. xxiii–iv.

6. Salt, *A Voyage to Abyssinia,* p. 402.

7. Hagar Salamon, *The Hyena People: Ethiopian Jews in Christian Ethiopia* (Berkeley: University of California Press, 1999).

8. Osseo-Asare, *Food Culture,* p. xv.

9. Salt, *A Voyage to Abyssinia,* pp. 252, 367.

10. For a detailed Ethiopian traditional recipes, see Girma Bekele, *Ethiopian & Foreign Cook Guide Book* (Addis Ababa, Ethiopia: Team Work, 1992); Webayehu Tsegaye, *Taste of Ethiopia: A Collection of Delicious Vegetarian and Traditional Recipes and Products. Revised and Extended Edition Including Most Popular Food and Spices* (Washington, DC: Merkato Publications International, 1991); Ethiopian Nutrition Institute, *Traditional Recipes* (Addis Ababa, 1969) (Mimeographed).

11. Walter C. Plowden, *Travels in Abyssinia & the Galla Country with an Account of Mission to Ras Ali in 1848* (London: Longmans, Green, and CO., 1868), pp. 91–93.

12. Fran Osseo-Asare, *Food Culture in Sub-Saharan Africa* (Westport, CT: Greenwood Press, 2005), pp. 110–14. See also Tizita Ayele, *Ethiopian Cooking in the American Kitchen* (New York: Vantage Press, 1998).

13. Osseo-Asare, *Food Culture,* p. 123; On the consumption of chat, see L. V. Cassanelli, "Qat: Changes in the Production and Consumption of a Quasi-legal Commodity in North-East Africa," in *The Social Life of Things: Commodities in Cultural Perspective,* ed. A. Appadurai (New York: Cambridge University Press, 1986), pp. 236–57.

14. Daniel, *Exotic Ethiopian*, pp. xxvii–xxx; Fran-Asare, *Food Culture*, pp. 124–25.

15. Fran-Asare, *Food Culture*, pp. 124–25; Daniel, *Exotic Ethiopian*, p. xxx.

16. Igor Cusack, "African Cuisines: Recipes for Nation-Building?" *Journal of African Cultural Studies* 13, no. 2 (December 2000): 209, 207–225).

17. Daniel, *Exotic Ethiopian*, pp. xxxv, 146; Tizita, *Ethiopian Cooking*, p. 17.

18. Daniel, *Exotic Ethiopian*, pp. liii–liv.

19. Frederick J. Simoons, *Northwest Ethiopia: Peoples and Economy* (Madison: The University of Wisconsin Press, 1960), pp. 189–90; Daniel, *Exotic Ethiopian*, pp. xxxv–xxxvi.

20. Hermann Norden, *Africa's Last Empire: Through Abyssinia to Lake Tana and the Country of the Falasha* (London: H. F. & G. Witherby, 1930), p. 16.

21. Rey, *Real Abyssinia*, p. 67.

22. Plowden, *Travels in Abyssinia*, p. 140.

23. See, Salt, *A Voyage to Abyssinia*, pp. 262, 368.

24. Ibid., p. 296.

25. Plowden, *Travels in Abyssinia*, p. 58.

26. Salt, *A Voyage to Abyssinia*, pp. 295–97.

27. C. F. Rey, *The Real Abyssinia* (Philadelphia: J. B. Lippincott Company, 1935), pp. 61, 62–66.

28. For the Gurage history, culture, and the significance of the *Masiqa* holy day, see William A. Shack, *The Gurage: A People of the Ensete Culture* (London: Oxford University Press, 1966); William Shack, "The Masqal-Pole: Religious Conflict and Social Change in Gurageland," *Africa: Journal of the International African Institute* 38, no. 4 (October 1968): 457–68.

29. Osseo-Asare, *Food Culture*, p. 122.

30. Frederick J. Simmons, *Northwest Ethiopia: Peoples and Economy* (Madison: The University of Wisconsin Press, 1960), pp. 186–87.

31. Plowden, *Travels in Abyssinia*, p. 456.

32. Rey, *Real Abyssinia*, pp. 72–75; Plowden, *Travels in Abyssinia*, pp. 49–50, 146–48.

33. Plowden, *Travels in Abyssinia*, pp. 63, 147–48; Rey, *Real Abyssinia*, pp. 72–75.

34. Rey, *Real Abyssinia*, p. 73.

35. Norden, *Africa's Last Empire*, p. 36; see also Plowden, *Travels in Abyssinia*, pp. 147–48; Salt, *A Voyage to Abyssinia*, pp. 201, 252, 422.

36. Rey, *Real Abyssinia*, pp. 72–73; Salt, *A Voyage to Abyssinia*, p. 261.

37. Norden, *Africa's Last Empire*, p. 42.

38. Salt, *A Voyage to Abyssinia*, p. 241.

39. Rey, *The Real Abyssinia*, pp. 48–49.

40. For various types of traditional bread, see Daniel, *Exotic Ethiopian*, pp. 83–100; Tizita, *Ethiopian Cooking*, pp. 42–45.

41. Okello Oculi, *Discourses on African Affairs* (New Jersey and Asmara: Trenton, Eritrea: African World Press, 2000), p. 60.

42. For a detailed preparation of these items, see Daniel, *Exotic Ethiopian*, pp. 25–45.

43. For the Gada system of the Oromo, see Asmarom Legesse, *Oromo Democracy: An Indigenous African Political System* (Lawrenceville, NJ: Red Sea Press, 2000).

44. See for instance, Salt, *A Voyage to Abyssinia*, pp. 239, 242–45, 255, 257, 259–60, 274–76, 283, 284, 402.

45. Salt, *A Voyage*, p. 260.

46. Rey, *The Real Abyssinia*, p. 71.

47. Plowden, *Travels in Abyssinia*, p. 61.

48. Salt, *A Voyage to Abyssinia*, p. 370.

6

Gender Roles, Marriage, and Family

Ethiopia is a diverse country in every aspect. It has different customs, religions, traditions, languages, topographies, and economies. Such divergence is also observed in matrimonial issues and the socioeconomic status of women. In the northern half of Ethiopia, as well as the central part, Semitic speakers are primarily followers of the Ethiopian Orthodox faith, and to some degree, followers of Islam and Judaism are found. Cushitic speakers and adherents of Sunni Islam populate, roughly speaking, the southern half. Followers of the Ethiopian Orthodox Christian faith and recent converts of the Protestant sect are found in southern and western Ethiopia. Nilotic and Omotic speakers, who primarily practice traditional religions, occupy the western and southern borderlands of the country. People residing in southeastern and the eastern part of the country are followers of Islam. Depending on the topography and climate, the lifestyle of these diverse groups of people also varies. While the Nilots and a segment of the Omotic people subsist as fishermen and pastoralists in the lowlands, the highlanders (Semitic speakers and some of the Cushites) practice farming.[1]

The differences in ways of life and religion among the various ethnic groups and nationalities in Ethiopia have a bearing on marital practices. However, because of the dearth of materials on the issue and due to the enormity of the subject, it is difficult to discuss marriage practices, gender relations, and lineage systems observed throughout Ethiopia. Therefore, this chapter primarily deals with marital practices, gender roles, and lineage systems followed by Ethiopians who are highlanders, farmers, and adherents of the Ethiopian Orthodox Church. This chapter also tries to highlight some very common practices of marriages prevalent throughout the country regardless of ethnic and religious dissimilarities.

Types of Marriages

Marriage and the Role of Religion

One such common denominator in marriages, be it municipal or traditional, which can be discerned across ethnic and geographic areas, is the role religion plays in this institution. Religions, such as Christianity, Judaism, and Islam, and traditional beliefs have strong bearings on the material and spiritual lives of these people. Most often, no marriage takes place without the prior knowledge and consent of the local religious leaders and elders of the community. As a result, marriage is consummated (especially in rural areas) not because the bride and bridegroom love each other but because it is a spiritual obligation to be fulfilled and a cultural tradition to adhere to.

In what are called religious marriages, priests of the Ethiopian Orthodox Church officiate the ceremony at church. This religious marriage has two

Ethiopian newlyweds engage in the custom of sharing food during their wedding party in the capital, Addis Ababa, May 21, 2000. (AP Photo/Pier Paolo Cito)

versions, *Takilil* and *Qurban.* The latter is very different from the former in that the bride and groom will take the Holy Communion together. Such marriages are for life. The couple cannot annul their marriage except by a special dispensation by the patriarch. While the laity is encouraged to enter into such marital vow, the Orthodox Church does not strictly enforce such marriages except on priests. In order to be ordained a priest, aside from other criteria and obligations, one has to follow the *Qurban* type of marriage. If his wife dies, he will never remarry. He becomes a monk. But, if he remarries, he no longer serves as a priest and administers priestly function. He becomes a *Debtra* often with a title of a *Merigeta,* especially if the priest had been deemed highly educated by the standards of the Ethiopian Orthodox Church. The same applies to his wife. Upon the death of her husband, she becomes a nun. In extreme cases, the widowed becomes a hermit and joins one of the many monastic centers in the country.

Civil/Municipal Marriages

In addition to religious marriages, there are, though not widespread, municipal marriages in Ethiopia. In municipal marriages, the parties enter into marital vow by themselves, or with the involvement and blessing of parents and relatives, or with some participation of religious figures, or all. In all instances, a government official, be it a magistrate or a municipal official, administers the matrimonial ceremony in the presence of witnesses.[2]

Civil/municipal marriages are a late 19th-century phenomenon that came into effect with the Westernization of the state bureaucracy, which Atse Menelik II (r. 1889–1913) initiated at the turn of the 20th century. However, until after the 1974 revolution, much of rural Ethiopia was relatively unaffected by the transformation of the bureaucracy. Thus, civil/municipal marriages are confined to urban areas and among the educated Ethiopians.

Political Marriages

Political marriage, in this context, primarily refers to marriage held between two dynasties, as it was a custom in Western Europe and parts of Africa. A look at prerevolution marriages within the ruling elites of Ethiopia reveals this fact. The hereditary rulers of Tigray (northern Ethiopia), Keffa (southern Ethiopia), and Wollega (western Ethiopia) were married to the hereditary rulers of Shoa (central Ethiopia), who also became the supreme rulers of the Ethiopian state since 1889. Such dynastic marriage not only cemented allegiances and continuity of the Ethiopian state but also guaranteed the endurance of the ruling dynasty. The Ethiopian monarchy, which traced its origin to King Solomon and the Queen of Sheba and hence referred to itself as the Solomonic dynasty, also encouraged marriages between its offspring and the emergent elite, the Western-educated Ethiopians, especially the high-ranking military officers, thereby securing their obedience and loyalty.[3] In addition, according to Jack Goody, who studied class and marriage in Africa and Eurasia, upper class marriages that also included dynastic marriages were not only meant to bolster class allegiances between equals but were also de-signed to prevent outsiders, lower class elements, from infringing upon class boundaries and sociocultural differences. Upper class or dynastic marriages, therefore, were designed to maintain and guarantee the continuity of the social distance between classes.[4]

Some historians of pre-20th-century Ethiopian history indicated that the royal house and the nobility, like all other monarchies and nobility in the world, were engaged in polygamous relationships despite the strict rules of the Ethiopian Orthodox Church. The polygamous relationship, however, could arise simply because they were monarchs or due to other reasons. When and if the marriage was not blessed with children, the king or king of kings often sought children by other women. Sometimes, even if the marriage was blessed with children, seeking a male heir, the king or king of kings would have been involved in extramarital affairs.

Yet, all the time the Orthodox Church, like all other churches, strongly believed in the sanctity and indissolubility of marriage. It also tried to enforce exogamy on its laity. The church implemented this code of conduct through the institution of father confessor, which every family was obligated to have. Despite this, the monarchy and nobility were noted for breaking this law for politico-military reasons. Until the 1920s, Ethiopia never had a standing army and its soldiers were composed of feudal levies commanded by regional lords. The history of pre-20th-century Ethiopia is a history of war—a war that was fought either against foreign invaders or among the various regional lords. So much so the Ethiopian society was, and still is, dominated by the warrior ethos.[5]

OTHER FORMS OF MARRIAGE

The "Servant of the Thigh," *Yechin Gered*

Due to the continuous military campaigns, marital relationships were unstable. Though oftentimes soldiers and commanders accompanied by ser-vants and wives left for military campaign, which gave pre-20th-century mili-tary campaigns and camps the appearance of massive population movement and a tent city, respectively,[6] others (both nobles and commoners) chose to leave their wives behind, at home. Instead, they took their *yechin gered,* which literally means the "servant of the thigh," who played both the role of a wife and a servant. Children born from the *yechin gered* had rights to inheritance, while the *yechin gered* had similar rights to a legally wedded wife. In most instances, the wife and the community were aware of the existence of the *yechin gered.* The practice was therefore protected under customary laws.

In addition to the constant military campaigns that created the situation for the *yechin gered* and challenged the sanctity of marriage, political ambition was another reason why the Ethiopian nobility and monarchy were averse toward the Ethiopian Orthodox Church's strictest rules of marriage. In order to cement dynastic alliances or guarantee their bloodline, as mentioned earlier, they were engaged in polygamous relationships and divorces.

Marriage by Elopement/Abduction, *"Yteleffa Gabicha"*

In prerevolution Ethiopia where love played less or no role in marriage and in a society where attempts were made to keep class and caste differences intact, imposing one's wish by force became a necessity. *Telefa* was one such practice. The abduction was usually done behind the backs of both parents. Sometimes it was done with the consent and cooperation of one of the parents. Though abduction clearly implies coercion, there were circumstances in which the girl/woman agreed to be abducted.[7]

In general, abduction occurred due to one or all of the following circumstances. When the family of a boy realized that the girl's family was not willing to give their daughter for marriage because of class differences, or when the boy's family was incapable of paying a dowry, or when the boy's family was unable to afford the desired wedding feast, then the boy's family encouraged and supported the abduction of the girl.

Abduction was also done with the consent of the girl. When the latter would find out that her parents were going to wed her to someone other than the person she loved, she would conspire with her lover to be abducted.

The meeting place for the lovers ("abductor" and "abductee") was usually a river, a spring, or a waterhole where women and girls fetch water. The abduction could also occur during a market day as a girl who was of a marriageable age was not allowed to go out except to bring water or go to the market, both of which were often located far away from home and hence opportune moments for abductions.

Abduction could also occur after the girl's family rejected the marriage proposal of the boy's family. At that moment, the boy would decide, with or without the approval of his family, to abduct the girl even if it was against the girl's wish. After the boy decided to abduct her, he would first assign a person or persons to spy on the girl. Based on the information he gathered from the spy, the boy would kidnap the girl. when the girl was returning from the market place, or while she was fetching water, collecting firewood, or doing some other chores. However, if someone from the girl's family happened to witness the kidnapping, a fist fight or a stick fight could break between the boys' and girl's family. The conflict could grow into a gunfight between the two families. In this circumstance, whoever wins the fight would take the girl. To avoid such unpleasantness and revenge from the girl's family, the abduction was carried out to the outmost secrecy, and the young man would leave his parents' residence for a distant place where he would never be identified. The abductor would only return to his village following the restoration of peace through the intervention of elders. All practices related to abduction have continued to this day, though the government tries to strongly discourage such a custom.

Marriage through elopement is practiced among all ethnic groups and nationalities of Ethiopia. The difference is in name. While the Amharas refer to it as *Telefa,* the Oromos call it *Assena* and the Hadyyas call it *Gossima/Gosano.*

Arranged Marriage and Social Control

Marriage in traditional Ethiopia was also used for social control and stability. If, for instance, there occurred a clash between families, villagers, and ethnic groups, and a person or persons died as a result of the conflict, one of the means by which the community brings peace and stability within the feuding families or groups is through marriage. In this context, the community uses marriage as a peacemaker.

In traditional Ethiopia, the presence of young but unmarried women in a community is a source of consternation. If a girl is not married when she is of age, she and her family become targets of gossip. The unmarried woman could be a widow or divorcee. As long as the woman lives in that village, she cannot marry one of the villagers, for it would be considered a slight against the ex-husband and his family. If she remarries a person from the same village, it can result in animosity and even fighting between the ex-husband and her new spouse or between woman's family and her new spouse. To have an unmarried daughter who is old enough to wed is also a sign of loss. The girl/woman is considered a burden and a source of vulnerability to rape and abduction. Besides, the older she gets, the lesser her chance of marriage is. Meanwhile, the community increasingly becomes suspicious of her chastity.

To avoid a problematic situation and to ensure a daughter's virginity, arranged marriages are very common among Ethiopian highlanders. The process of arranged marriage is intricate with slight variations from one province to another and between ethnic groups and nationalities. However, some of its most common elements include sending three elders, *shimagile*. The groom's family send elders to the bride's family. The elders often constitute a priest, a mutual and dear friend of the bride and groom's family, and a person noted for his oratory, bravery, and a higher social standing in the community. On a mutually agreed day, the three elders go to the bride's house. The elders inform the parents of the bride the purpose of their visit in very general and vague terms: "We will come to discuss a very important business." On the scheduled day, after the usual greetings, the father of the bride invites his visitors to come in and be seated. But the elders will refuse to sit before he, the father, agrees to their request. Then the father will ask what their request is. The priest, after citing the sanctity of marriage and what the Lord said to Adam and Eve and the social significance of marriage when it is done with the consent and blessing of the parents as well as elders, will request the father of the girl to wed his daughter with the son of family he represents. The other elders mention the good standing of the parents of the boy, and the various accomplishments the boy has achieved as a trader, soldier/warrior, hunter, or farmer. Meanwhile, in the middle of the conversation, the father will discuss with his wife to help him decide, or she might just join the conversation while preparing *buna* (coffee) or bringing them *tella* (homemade beer).

The parents of the girl, after assessing the gravity of the matter and taking into consideration of the elders (it is unbecoming of a good man to refuse the request of the elders), agrees to the proposal. In a rare occasion, the parents of the girl might ask the elders to give them time to ponder on the matter and promise to let them know after discussing the issue with their kin. If, however, the parents of the bride agree, the elders will agree to be seated and entertained with coffee, beer, and so on. While seated and entertained, the two sides will trace each other's genealogy up to seven generations to make sure there had not been any marriage (marital relationships) between the two families in the past seven generations and thus there is no incest. If incest is found, the proposed marriage will be terminated.

If everything goes well, they fix the date to bring the *tilosh* (dowry) and decide on the date of the marriage. Usually, the wedding day is set between December and March, the harvest season. It is during this time of the year the harvest is collected and hence the silos are full and the cattle are fat. It is also this time of the year that farmers, who make up more than 85 percent of the population, are relatively free to engage in a daunting task such as wedding celebration. Both sides, however, make sure that the wedding happens before the beginning of Lent or the Ramadan, the Christian and Muslim fasting seasons. No wedding, be it Christian or Muslim, is held in the fasting season.

Marriage at Early Age, *Yemadego Gabicha*

Arranged marriages can happen anytime. Sometimes parents ask some-one's child, a boy or a girl, for a marriage. Such proposal, called *yemadego gabicha*, could be forwarded to expectant parents or to the parents of a little boy or girl. *Yemadego gabicha* was very common among Ethiopian highland-ers. Early marriages were contracted among families verbally before or any time after the two children's birth. A wedding celebration where relatives of both families, who reside near and afar, come together to celebrate the bond they have created usually follows this verbal agreement. The wedded little girl usually stays with her parents until she reaches the age of 15. Sometimes, however, the little girl is sent to her in-laws, to grow up with her would-be husband and to learn the qualities of a good woman under the guidance of her mother-in-law. Until the time of her honeymoon, the girl is not allowed to sleep with her would be husband. On the day of her honeymoon, everyone expects the girl to be a Virgin; she is taken to her bridal chambers where a piece of white cloth is used to find if a girl is virgin. A girl is found a virgin if the cloth contains bloodstain (due to consummation). If, however, the girl is not found a virgin, she is beaten until she confesses the truth and why she tried to cover it. The girl is considered unfit for family life and the marriage is dissolved automatically—a norm that is found in all types of marriages, across all ethnic groups and nationalities. The exception, however, is the Suri (Omotic people) who rather encourage premarital sex and extramarital affair. To avoid undesired pregnancy, more experienced and older women who are experts in the art of avoiding pregnancy instruct the Suri girls.[8]

Among the Hadiyya ethnic group of central Ethiopia early marriage, *Il-gana* (in the Hadiyya language), is also common. It involves the agreement of parents on both sides. Parents of young boys and girls arrange the marriage relationship regardless of the consent of the couple, especially the girl. Pres-tige and economic interests play a big part in this regard.

Levirate Marriage/Wife Inheritance

The Hadiyya are also noted for practicing levirate marriage, *Lago* (in Hadi-yya language). Wife inheritance can occur when a brother or a close relative dies. Children also can inherit the wife (usually the youngest one) of their fathers when the latter dies. The Hadiyya society—a polygamous society—was, and still is, though now a rare practice. When the male heads of a family die, their sons (often the eldest) would inherit the lastly married (youngest) wife of their fathers. The adherence to monogamy is attributed to the widespread influence of Christianity, economic consideration, and the increasing awareness of HIV/AIDS.[9]

Either because of the problems associated with early marriage or due to the negative connotation associated with being single women (they were referred to as *galemota, melekon, fet,* which have negative undertones), many girls/women leave their villages for urban centers where nobody knows them. In order to survive in the urban centers, they engage in professions such as prostitution or become domestic servants—in Ethiopia almost all domestic servants are females.[10]

MARRIAGE, COMMUNITY, AND GENDERED DIVISION OF LABOR

Another common ingredient of marriage among the many ethnicities and nationalities of Ethiopia is that, like most of the developing countries, it is more than an affair between two individuals. It is a unity of two families or kinship groups for economic, political, and social purposes.

Once married, the bride leaves her parents and settles in her husband's home (the virilocal pattern). In pre-industrial or semi-industrial societies where labor was badly needed, the addition of a person to a family was appreciated, for it brought another working hand. While women and girls primarily labor at home, men and boys toil in the field. Though underage girls may be observed tending to cattle, this usually happens in the absence of males in the family. In prerevolution Ethiopia, a female farmer was unheard of. Cultural norms did not allow a woman to farm land. If she was single, her brothers or her father farmed the land. If she had neither, then she had to hire a farmhand to till her land. Men and boys, on their part, were not allowed to enter the kitchen. The kitchen was the realm of women and girls. If a husband and wife had an argument and the woman took refuge in her kitchen, no matter what she said and no matter how much she angered him, the husband would not enter the kitchen. Thus, labor and one's behavior were dictated by gender in much of prerevolution Ethiopia, and are dictated still today especially in rural areas.

The consummation of marriage guarantees children. Children in Africa in general, and in Ethiopia in particular, are considered assets. They help in farms and look after cattle. When parents get older, it is the responsibility of the child to take care of them. This is especially true for females than males. The latter could always remarry a younger wife who can take care of him, while it is difficult for an aged woman to marry a younger male.

Children look on as a woman sorts peppers and grain at her house in Checheho, Ethiopia, January 19, 2012. (David Snyder/Zuma Press/Corbis)

Thus, more than men, women depend more on their children at old age. Through marriage, children also bring more family bonding, thereby enhancing parents' position in society. It is through children that the community/village remembers the parents. Thus, a man without children is like a tree without roots. Due to the socioeconomic significance associated with children, a woman who is unable to bear children is divorced, though the source of infertility might have been the husband. In a country like Ethiopia where medical facilities are scarce and the technology to determine fertility is unavailable or even unknown, the woman is always at the receiving end.[11] On the other hand, a woman who gives birth to as many children as possible is highly regarded in the community.

MARRIAGE, MATCH MAKING, AND DOWRY

In prerevolution Ethiopia, while dynastic marriages revealed class affinity as a prerequisite in determining who should marry whom, for matrimonial decision making, families considered essential criteria in match making such as the spouse's education, age, employment, ethnic and regional origin, and household skills. However, not all of these match-making conditions are equally important. While schooling and levels of education in general are important in the urban setting, land and livestock are more vital in the rural areas.

Accordingly, in farming and pastoral communities of Ethiopia, marriage occasions the transfer of assets from parents to children. The assets transferred include land, weapons (rifles and pistols), livestock, jewelry, grains, household goods, and clothing. Asset distribution between spouses at the time of the wedding determines one's bargaining power within the marriage. Because of their privileged position, men have jobs that also make them the sole bread-winners and decision makers of the family, while women are relegated to secondary roles, with little or no voice in decision making. At times of divorce, assets transferred during marriage do not necessarily decide the distribution of property upon divorce.[12]

A closer look at the match-making rules and the transfer of assets (often known as bride price or dowry) at marriage brings to light the prevalence of gender disparity. In traditional marriages, though the bride brings assets at the time of marriage, the groom contributes the most because historically African men have greater access to resources. They have been the beneficiaries of a value system that provided them with greater access to education and prosperity while relegating women to roles of domesticity.[13] The introduction of Western education, which was supposed to be open to all, had not made that much difference in narrowing the gender gap. Under colonialism, education was less available to the masses, while the sons and daughters of African chiefs and kings had relatively easy access. This difference between sovereign and subject was further accentuated in the postcolonial period where education became the sole requirement for employment and social mobility.

In Ethiopia, too, this gender inequality, in terms of access to opportunities, was very common. Though Western education was introduced at the turn of the 20th century, by the time of the 1974 revolution only 1 percent of the school-age population attended secondary schools and universities in Ethiopia. Of these, the number of educated women was very few for various reasons. Traditional values prefer and favor boys than girls; thus, more boys than girls were sent to school. Of those young women who were allowed to attend schools, quite a number of them were pulled out of school for marriage, while the boys were allowed to continue their education. Among the very few female students who made it to high school and higher education, the success rate is very low vis-à-vis their male counterparts.[14] By 2000, though the situation had improved, the gender gap still remained. The enrolment rate of girls in schools is far below that of boys. Some 40 percent of girls across the country are enrolled in primary schools compared to an average for boys of 57 percent. The disparity widens in rural areas. For every 100 boys in school in rural areas, there are only 76 girls.[15]

Therefore, like most African women, Ethiopian women have limited access to education and hence little or no access to jobs and money. Consequently, women in Ethiopia remain dependent on their husbands throughout their life.[16] As Claire Robertson indicated, "The provision of formal education, then, has not so far remedied the economic inequalities between men and women, because that education has been provided unequally."[17]

As mentioned earlier, in Africa, marriage is more than a union of a man and a woman. It involves the whole village and kin group. Thus, divorce, too, is the concern of families and kin.[18] It is the elders, religious figures, and communal norms that decide who should get what. Unlike the legal system, the former considers cultural issues before passing a verdict. It is also these same actors that serve as deterrents against divorce. Hence, compared to the Western world, it is difficult to annul marriages in Africa.

MARRIAGE, GENDER ROLES, AND LINEAGE

All types of marriages and belief systems have a common element: Ethiopians believe that women shall remain subordinate to their husbands. The inferior position of women is also mirrored in the day-to-day life of Ethiopian society. Schoenberger noted, "[Ethiopia is a society] where the status of sexes is of male being superior, and the female, inferior. A woman is expected to carry out only menial tasks and she is not credited with an opinion on anything . . . all she is required to do is to fulfill her obligations either to her father, or to her husband."[19]

The relative difference between rural and urban marriages is that oftentimes woman may be educated and have a job that might give her a certain degree of equality. Yet, even here, the gendered division of labor is apparent. Despite her education and job, the wife is expected to do all of the house chores. If they have children, they are responsible for child care. She can be relatively free from all these domestic responsibilities if the household has a domestic servant. Also, being in an urban area, she has relatively better legal protection from an abusive husband than her rural counterparts do. Women in rural areas do not have such protection due to the limited government control in these areas.

Unlike the Western world where patrilineal descent prevails, in Ethiopia both parents are recognized. Inheritance also depends on one's ability in tracing his or her lineage, which includes and equally recognizes relatives of both the mother and the father. Thus, theoretically speaking, both men and women have equal rights to inheritance, though in some areas such as Tigray, the northern province of Ethiopia, men are favored over women.[20]

Knowing one's lineage is important for marriage as well. For instance, during match making, both families (especially families of the followers of the Ethiopian Orthodox faith) are required to trace and make sure that there are no marital relationships between the bride and the groom's family in the past seven generations. If the matchmakers find marital interactions, then the matrimony will be regarded as incest and will be terminated.

Despite such equality in tracing one's lineage on both sides of the family, children take their father's name. Unlike the practices of the Western world, Ethiopians do not have a last name or family name. The child is identified by his or her given name, which is followed by his or her father's given name.

Grandfathers' names are required in rare cases when a person has similar first and second names, that is, with similar given name and father's name.

WEDDING CELEBRATIONS

Because of the dearth of materials on the issue and due to the enormity of the subject, it is difficult to discuss wedding celebrations in Ethiopia. The practice varies from religion to religion, region to region, from one ethnic group or nationality to another. While urban and rural differences in wedding ceremonies and celebrations are apparent, there still is a marked variation between urban centers depending on the degree of urbanity. Class difference is another variable that further complicates the subject at hand. Thus, this section deals only with wedding celebrations practiced in the capital, Addis Ababa, in very general terms. The city is a fashion setter that every other Ethiopian town tries to emulate. Addis Ababa is also a place where more than 5 million people of diverse ethnic origin and religious affiliation reside.

Almost all marriages such as religious, municipal, or arranged, depending on the wealth of the couple or their parents, involve wedding dresses. The wedding dress could be the locally made traditional cotton cloth *shama qemis* (for the bride) with the finest embroidery and a *kabba,* cloak, which is usually black and embroidered. The groom is dressed in the traditional attire that includes *eje-tebab* (a long white shirt with openings on the side starting from the waist down), *teferi suri* (a pant that is narrower and tightly fitting from the knee down, while bulging and loose from the waist down to the knee) and an embroidered *kabba.* The cloak is worn on top, like an overcoat. If the wedding is religious and the wedded have taken the Holy Communion, the couple will have a traditional headgear, *tekilil* (crown). The *kabba* and

Religious (*Qurban*) marriage of the Ethiopian Orthodox Tewahido Church. (Godong/Universal Images Group via Getty Images)

the *tekilil* can be rented, or the church often provides one. However, those with adequate means have it custom-made.

These days, it is also common to see a wedding celebration with a Western-style tuxedo or a three-piece dark suit with a bow tie for the groom and a wedding gown, *vello* (most probably a name of Italian origin) for the bride. These dresses, too, are available for rent or could be custom-made for the occasion, depending on one's means.

In the rural areas, the wedding dress is a locally made traditional cotton cloth *shama qemis* (for the bride) with or without embroidery and a *kabba,* cloak, which is usually black and embroidered. The groom is dressed with in the traditional attire that includes *eje-tebab, teferi suri,* and an embroidered *kabba.* In the rural areas, more often than not the embroidery and the *kabba* are the symbol of upper-class status. Sometimes, a new dress or even an old but clean dress would suffice. It all depends upon the bride and groom's resources.

On the wedding day, a feast is prepared at the bride's and the groom's parents' house. In fact, festivities usually commence almost a week before the actual wedding day in both places. The festivities are communal events where neighbors and relatives participate by contributing material as well as labor in the preparation of the feast that includes preparing *tella* and *teji* for drinks and *injera* and various types of *wot.* The preparation of *teji* and the number of *frida* (fattened oxen or cow), *mukit* (fattened sheep or goat) reflects the wealth of parents. The slaughtered cattle will be used for *brindo* (raw meat) and the various spicy stew (*wot*) that is consumed on the wedding day and after. *Doro wot* (chicken stew) is, of course, a mandatory component of the feast. Usually, the wedding feast lasts for one week, or eight days.

On the day of the wedding, the groom with his best men comes to the bride's house, usually around noon. Upon arrival at the bride's place, the groom and his men are not allowed to enter the house by the bride's relatives who taunt the groom and his men as weak, nothing to offer and lousy men who do not even know how to sing. The groom and his best men try to prove them wrong. The symbolic "fight" that involves shoving, jostling, singing, and spraying perfumes on the crowed finally ends with the groom's men "overpowering" their opponents and entering the house.[21]

The bride and groom stay at the bride's place almost all afternoon. During this time, invited guests, relatives, and neighbors dine, drink, sing, and dance to the tunes of traditional wedding folk songs. In traditional Ethiopian singing and dancing, *esiksta* (it involves the rhythmic movement of the body, the shaking of the shoulders and neck) is participatory. While there could be a singer or two, the dance is held in groups of unisex or mixed, and hence, everyone is expected to partake.[22] To encourage participation, the singer(s) will say, "Where is the brother," "where is the sister," "where is the mother," "where is the father," "where is the relative," and so on. To each question, every one of the parents, brothers, sisters, and others respond by joining the dancing and singing. While some of the wedding songs alludes how the bride is beautiful, well mannered, and chaste, others console the bride that she is not the only one who gets married and leaves the comforts of her parents' house and that she should not be scared, for it is the fate of every female to be wedded and leave her parents' house to settle in her husband's home'. An *azmari* might be hired to enliven the folk music and dance. However, these days, the *azmari* has been increasingly replaced by "*yemuziqa-band*" (music band). The "band," too, depends on the resources of the couple. A one-man band employs electronic synthesizers combined with vocal wedding songs. The well-to-do, however, employ a complete musical troupe.

These days, it is not uncommon to witness "cocktail" weddings, which the populace of Addis Ababa sarcastically refer to as "*yedigaf-self*" (a parade of support)—a legacy of the *Derg* era. The populace viewed the slaughtering of cattle a feudal norm and an extravaganza in socialist Ethiopia where such resource could be used for outcomes that are more productive. Thus, "cocktail" weddings are held in a rented hall or are held in hotels where the guests are served Pepsi, Coca Cola, or other soft drinks with potato chips and popcorn. The populace of Addis Ababa mockingly refer to such weddings as "*yedigaf self*," an inference to and derived from the many public demonstrations that the military junta calls upon the public. The public has to attend these public gatherings as a testimony of its support and affirmation of loyalty to the junta. The *Derg* viewed reluctance or refusal to partake in such mass rallies or absence from such events a manifestation of counter-revolutionary intent and behavior. Thus, the poor masses trudge in file on a sunny day to the Revolution Square and listen to the lengthy and, often more than boring, speeches of *Derg* officials or their cadres. Compared to the customary wedding, the cocktail wedding is therefore equally boring but the guests have to attend in order to not offend the wedded and to show their support to the bride and groom.

Depending on their means, the couple might go for picnic sometime in the late afternoon. The picnic can be at nearby park such as Bihere Tsege, *Hamile 27*, or the *Ambassador* or an out-of-town place such as Debre Zeit where more convenient and comfortable resort areas are found. There, in addition to the music and dancing, the bride and groom take wedding pictures. After the excursion, the bride and groom accompanied by their entourage, which includes their best men, relatives, neighbors, and invited guests, head for the groom's place. Owning a car automatically makes someone eligible for an invitation to every wedding in the neighborhood even if the person is not related or is a new addition to the neighborhood. If there is no such person, then the bride and groom rent at least one car, preferably a Mercedes. Otherwise, a Fiat 127 would do the job. Relatives and friends rent cars and even cabs to escort the newly wed. To this day, the best wedding is measured not solely by the number of cattle slaughtered or guests attended to but also by the number and variety of cars (taxicabs are excluded) that accompany the bride and groom.

As in the bride's house, the singing, dancing, and eating continue at the groom's house. At the behest of the groom's best man or the father, the bride and groom leave for their *chagula* bet, bridal chamber. What transpires in the bridal chamber will decide the bride's fate and the marriage. In Ethiopia, women are expected to be a virgin at the time of wedding. If the bride is found a virgin, a bloodstained piece of white cloth is brought to the congregation and parents who, on seeing the bloodstain, ululate and sing in the middle of the night. One of the most common wedding songs for the occasion is *bir-ambar sebereliwo jegnaw lijiwo* (it literally means "your chivalrous son has broken the silver bracelet"). The groom's best men then gives the bloodstained piece of cloth to the bride's parents. The groom's family will be rewarded for bringing good tidings. If, however, the girl is found not a virgin at the time of "consummation," it is an outrage and a disgrace for both families. The girl is beaten for not being virgin and sent to her parent's house with a broken bread, which signifies that she is not a virgin and thus not fit for family life.[23]

The deflowering of the bride was the climax of the wedding ceremony. Thereafter, the wedding feast continues for one week at the boy's place. This was followed by *meles,* return invitation by the girl's parents where the newly wed stayed one more week feasting.

These days, however, the significance of virginity and defloration associated with it has declined, at least in the urban centers and among the educated. The institutions that enforced such marriage are in decline. The Orthodox Church's hold on the society has tremendously weakened since the days of the *Derg* that nationalized church property and disavowed the Orthodox Church—as an institution has no role in a secular state. Marriage is increasingly consummated not because parents desire or it is a religious obligation but because the boy and girl love each other. The progress made in empowering women through education is another reason. Unlike earlier times, women have access for education and they are breadwinners who no longer depend on their husband's income. Consequently, virginity and defloration has lost its significance. If need be, however, during their wedding night, the bride and groom often arrange for a bloodstained piece of cloth for public showing.

Social Change and Gender Relation in Post-Revolution Ethiopia

Despite the unfavorable socioeconomic conditions women had in prerevolution Ethiopia, women have contributed no less than their male counterparts for the betterment of their country. Ethiopian history is abundant with the heroic deeds of women such as the ninth-century Youdit (Judith), who rallied the Felasha-Agaw people against Aksumite kingdom's oppression and brought the kingdom to its knees. In the 16th century, during the wars of Ahmad Gragn (1527–1543), the Queen Mother, Helana, continued resisting Gragn and served as a symbol of resistance despite the loss of her husband and the collapse of the Christian Highland Empire. Queen Mintwab, the wife of Atse Bekafa (r. 1713–1723), was another powerful Queen Mother who reigned over Ethiopia after her husband's death. Using Machiavellian tactics, she ruled the empire with absolute authority until her assassination in 1761.

The history of late 19th- and early 20th-century Ethiopia would not make sense without citing women like Etege Taitu (1852–1918), the wife of Atse Menelik II. In addition to her disarming charm and beauty, Taitu was a skilled diplomat who vehemently resisted Italian colonial machinations. When she found out about the infamous Wuchale Treaty that was signed between Italy and Ethiopia and in which Menelik was duped, she instructed the royal court that no treaty be signed without her knowledge. When all initiatives failed to convince Italians to amend the treaty, Taitu marshaled some 10,000 troops and joined the battle against the Italians. She also mobilized women to treat the wounded and to supply water and food to the needy. Taitu was also credited for establishing the present-day capital of Ethiopia, Addis Ababa, and for founding the first modern hotel in Ethiopia. Until this time, dining in hotels was unknown and considered a taboo.[24] No doubt behind these powerful empresses and queens, there were millions of Ethiopian women who partook in such activities. We dwell on the empresses and queens because until very recently, as was the custom in pre-modern Europe and the rest of the world, the history of Ethiopia was a history of kings and monarchs.

Sometime in 1935, for the first time in the history of Ethiopia, women organized themselves and established Ethiopian Women's Philanthropic Association. The chairwoman of the association was Princess Tshai, one of the daughters of Atse Haile Selassie I (r. 1930–1974). Aside from establishing the women's organization, the association was also noted for mobilizing women on the eve of the Italian–Ethiopian war, 1936–1941. During the war, many joined the patriotic resistance against Italy and distinguished themselves at battle. After the war, in November 1943, the Ethiopian Women's Association was officially reestablished as a chartered organization. One of its objectives was to help orphans and the widowed and jobless women, to improve childcare, and so on. Despite these lofty ideals, the association was constrained due to lack of funds. It did not even have its own office. Besides, like the late 19th- and early 20th-century American women organizations, members of the Ethiopian Women's Association were drawn from upper- and middle-class women. Thus, the scope and membership of the association was very limited. It did not have any meaningful operation outside of the capital, Addis Ababa. Gender equality and other rights of women were unknown to the organization. The Imperial Ethiopian Constitution, for its part, treated women as second-class citizens. Thus, women's rights and related things had to wait until the 1974 revolution.[25]

The 1974 revolution in Ethiopia dramatically transformed women in particular and the Ethiopian society in general. One of the major achievements of the revolution was the March 1975 land reform proclamation. It abolished the private ownership of land and redistributed rural and urban land regardless of gender. The Provisional Military Administrative Council (PMAC), otherwise known as the *Derg*, which supplanted Haile Selassie's government, also established the People's Organizing Provisional Office (POPO). The mission of POPO was to implement objectives of the revolution and to build a revolutionary political movement throughout the country. To empower and safeguard the gains of the revolution, the POPO also organized the populace into rural and urban dweller's associations, youth and women's associations, and peasant associations. Various political parties that included women were established. The nationalization of rural land and the limits imposed on the acres of land a person held could have ended the desire to acquire more land through marriages. It also removed the rich peasant class that primarily sustained the traditions of early marriage.[26]

In prerevolution Ethiopia, schools were primarily concentrated in the urban centers, which, more often than not, were provincial capitals. Even then, most of the schools, both primary and secondary, were found concentrated in Shoa, Eritrea, and, to a lesser degree, Wollega. In addition to regional inequality in terms of education, gender disparity was a common theme in Ethiopia's education.[27]

To improve the rate of literacy and propagate the revolution, the *Derg* mobilized university, 11th, and 12th-grade students into what it called Development through Cooperation Campaign. The *Derg* sent students to rural areas, including the remote parts of the country where government control was hitherto unknown. The literacy campaign, as it became to be known, opened schools, launched adult literacy, and taught ideas of equality and freedom to peasants and the rural poor. What is more, for the peasant to witness female students who wore trousers and overalls and who tirelessly worked beside their male counterparts was initially a shock that soon turned into admiration. Female students served as a role model for the peasant women. It was the beginning of a cultural liberation for the rural population where only men wore pants and where trousers were considered as signs of manhood.

However, the recurrent draught and famine that hit the country hard and the endless military campaigns that the *Derg* waged against secessionist forces in Eritrea and national liberation movements in the rest of the country consumed the limited resources that the country had. As a result, despite the establishment of women's organization at local and national levels, the associations were short of funds to implement programs that empowered women, especially rural women. Consequently, harmful traditional practices such as early marriage, marriage by abduction, and female circumcision continued. The gender gap in education and employment, too, persisted.

The downfall of the *Derg* in 1991 brought in a relative peace and prosperity to the country. The new government, Ethiopian People's Revolutionary Democratic Front (EPRDF), promulgated a new constitution that incorporated the United Nations Human Rights principles. The new constitution has two articles, Articles 34 and 35, which specifically deal with marriage and women's rights, respectively. As indicated in Article 34.1 of the constitution: "All men and women attaining the legal age of marriage, shall have, without any distinction as to race, nation, nationality or religion, the right to marry and found a family. They shall have equal rights in the process of contracting the marriage, its duration and dissolution." Article 34.2 of the new constitution also made it clear that "marriage shall be based on the free and full consent of the intending spouses." Thus, these articles effectively prohibit any form of marriages that directly or indirectly forces girls and women into matrimony. Realizing that such law would not stand the test without empowering women through education and employment, the government also introduced an affirmative action program that was intended to narrow the gender gap in education and employment. This, too, was enshrined in the new constitution. Article 35:3 states, "Considering that women have traditionally been viewed with inferiority and are discriminated against, they have the right to the benefit of *affirmative actions* [emphasis added] undertaken for the purpose of introducing corrective changes to such heritage. The aim of such measures is to ensure that special attention is given to enabling women to participate and compete equally with men in the political, economic and social fields both within public and private organizations."[28]

However, the new constitution was also sensitive to religious and cultural practices regarding marriage. Accordingly, while Article 34: 4 indicated, "Particulars relating to the recognition of religious and customary marriages may be determined by law." Article 34:5 stated, "[T[his Constitution shall not preclude the right of parties to voluntarily submit their dispute for adjudication in accordance with religious or customary laws. Particulars shall be determined by law,"[29] thereby opening a backdoor for those who were against women's rights. Thus, either due to this loophole in the constitution or due to the persistence of tradition and limited resources to translate the constitution into a reality, the media and women's organizations air the continued practice of marriage by abduction, and harmful traditional practices, though less frequent compared to previous times.

Generally speaking, though gender gap in education and employment opportunities continues to exist, the inequality is narrowing down. Men's attitude toward their female counterparts is changing. Unlike earlier times, in today's Ethiopia there is no profession where women are not represented. Women are no more confined to domesticity, while men are increasingly involved in domestic work, including child care, which previously was designated as women's domain. Women have professional and gender-based associations that specifically cater for the betterment of women's welfare and women's rights.

NOTES

1. Marcel Fafchamps and Agnes R. Quisumbing, "Marriage, Bequest, and Assortative Matching in Rural Ethiopia," *Economic Development and Cultural Change* 53, no. 2 (January 2005): 347–80.

2. Tesfu Baraki, supervised and edited by Seyoum Gebre Selassie, *Culture, Society and Women in Ethiopia* (Addis Ababa, Ethiopia: Ethiopian Women Lawyers Association, 1997), pp. 11–12, 35.

3. Heran Sereke-Brhan, "Building Bridges, Drying Blood: Elite Marriages, Politics and Ethnicity in 19th and 20th Century Imperial Ethiopia," Ph.D. Dissertation, Michigan State University, 2002.

4. Jack Goody, "Class and Marriage in Africa and Eurasia," *The American Journal of Sociology* 76, no. 4 (January, 1971): 585–603.

5. Donald Crummey, "Family and Property amongst the Amhara Nobility," *The Journal of African History* 24, no. 2, The History of the Family in Africa. (1983): 207–20; "Abyssinian Feudalism," *Past and Present* no. 89 (November, 1980): 115–38; Gene Ellis, "The Feudal Paradigm as a Hindrance to Understanding Ethiopia," *The Journal of Modern African Studies* 14, no. 2 (June 1976): 275–95.

6. Frederick C. Gamst, "Peasantries and Elites without Urbanism: The Civilization of Ethiopia," *Comparative Studies in Society and History* 12, no. 4 (October, 1970): 373–92.

7. Tesfu, *Culture, Society and Women*, pp. 26–27.

8. Ibid., pp. 19–20, 27–28.

9. Gedeon Addise, "A Socio-Economic and Cultural History of the Hadiyya to 1991," M.A. Thesis, History, Addis Ababa University, pp. 77–82.

10. Haile Gabriel Dagne, "Early Marriage in Northern Ethiopia," *Reproductive Health Matters* 2, no. 4, Motherhood, Fatherhood and Fertility: For Women Who Do and Women Who Don't Have Children (November 1994): 35–38.

11. For childbirth, child rearing, and parent–child relation, See Steven Kaplan, "Seen but Not Heard: Children and Childhood in Medieval Ethiopian Hagiographies," *The International Journal of African Historical Studies* 30, no. 3 (1997): 539–53; Dennis P. Hogan, Betemariam Berhanu, and Assefa Hailemariam, "Household Organization, Women's Autonomy, and Contraceptive Behavior in Southern Ethiopia," *Studies in Family Planning* 30, no. 4 (December 1999): 302–14.

12. Fafchamps and Agnes, "Marriage, Bequest, and Assortative Matching," pp. 348–49; see also Jack Goody and S. J. Tambiah, *Bride Wealth and Dowry* (Cambridge: Cambridge University Press, 1973).

13. Eileen Hadley Berry, "The African Family-Household: A Behavioral Model," Ph.D. Dissertation, Clark University, Worcester, Massachusetts, 1981; Barbara A. Arrighi and David J. Maume, Jr., "Workplace Subordination and Men's Avoidance of Housework," *Journal of Family Issues* 21, no. 4 (May 2000): 464–87.

14. Tsigie Haile, "Academic Performance of Female Students in Institutes of Higher Education, the Case of Addis Ababa University," in *Women and Development in Eastern Africa: An Agenda for the Research,* ed. Zeinab El-Bakri and Ruth M.

Besha (Addis Ababa, Ethiopia: Organization for Social Science Research in Eastern Africa, 1989), pp. 106–107; Aster G. M. Mengesha, "Gender and Democracy in Africa," *Ethiopian Register* (March 1999), p. 24; Peter H. Koehn, *Refugee from Revolution: U.S. Policy and Third-World Migration* (Boulder, CO: Westview Press, 1991), p. 279.

15. UN Office for the Coordination of Humanitarian Affairs, *UNIRN News*, "Ethiopia: Women's Empowerment Vital for Development–Government" (June 24, 2002); UNICEF, Girl-Education and Gender Parity (III) (January 24, 2006).

16. Zenebework Bissrat, "Research Priorities on Women Education and Employment in Ethiopia," in *Women and Development in Eastern Africa: An Agenda for the Research*, ed. Zeinab El-Bakri and Ruth M Besha (Addis Ababa, Ethiopia: Organization for Social Science Research in Eastern Africa, 1989), pp. 96–97.

17. Claire Robertson, "Women in the Urban Economy," in *African Women South of the Sahara*, 2nd edition, ed. Margaret Jean Hay and Sharon Stichter (London: Longman Group Limited, 1995), p. 60.

18. Robertson, *African Women South of the Sahara*; Betty Potash, "Women in the Changing African Family," in *African Women South of the Sahara*, 2nd edition, ed. Margaret Jean Hay and Sharon Stichter (London: Longman Group Limited, 1995), pp. 69–92.

19. Quoted in Marion Eva Leitman, "Ethiopian Immigrant Women: Transition to a New Israeli Identity? (Volume I and II)," Ph.D. Dissertation, Ohio State University, 1993, p. 6.

20. Crummey, "Family and Property," pp. 207–20.

21. See Ronald A. Reminick, "The Symbolic Significance of Ceremonial Defloration among the Amhara of Ethiopia," *American Ethnologist* 3, no. 4 (November 1976): 751–63, especially, pp. 753–54.

22. There are a variety of wedding songs and dances in Ethiopia, a country of more than 75 ethnic groups and nationalities. According to a 1960s research, there are more than 150 varieties of dances in Ethiopia. See György Martin, "Dance Types in Ethiopia," *Journal of the International Folk Music Council* 19 (1967): 23–27.

23. See Reminick, "The Symbolic Significance of Ceremonial Defloration," p. 756.

24. Minale Adugna, *Women and Warfare in Ethiopia: A Case Study of Their Role during the Campaign of Adwa, 1895/96, and the Italo-Ethiopian War, 1935–41* (Addis Ababa, Ethiopia: Organization for Social Science Research in Eastern and Southern Africa, 2001).

25. For women's movement in Ethiopia, see, *Kiwanena Raey: Ye-Ethyopiya Setoch Inqisiqase Ba-20gnaw Kifle-Zaman* [Objectives and Accomplishments of Ethiopian Women's Movement in the 20th Century] (Addis Ababa, Ethiopia: Prime Minister' Office Women's Affairs Subdivision, 2000).

26. John W. Harbeson, "Socialism, Traditions, and Revolutionary Politics in Contemporary Ethiopia," *Canadian Journal of African Studies* 11, no. 2 (1977): 217–34; see also Andargachew Tiruneh, *The Ethiopian Revolution, 1974–1987: A Transformation From an Aristocratic to a Totalitarian Autocracy* (Cambridge:

Cambridge University Press, 1993); Teferra Haile-Selassie, *The Ethiopian Revolution 1974–1991: From a Monarchial Autocracy to a Military Oligarchy* (London: Kegan Paul International, 1997).

27. John Markakis, *Ethiopia: Anatomy of a Traditional Polity* (Oxford: Clarendon Press, 1974), pp. 149–50; Gebeyehu Ejigu, "Educational Planning and Educational Development in Ethiopia: 1957–1973" Ph.D. Dissertation, University of Wisconsin-Madison, 1980, pp. 210–33; for number of university students and dropouts by department and year, see Teshome G. Wagaw, *The Development of Higher Education and Social Change: An Ethiopian Experience* (East Lansing: Michigan State University, 1990), pp. 98–106.

28. See Negarit Gazeta (Negarit Gazeta of the Federal Democratic Republic of Ethiopia), August 21, 1995.

29. Ibid.

7

Social Customs and Lifestyles

National Holidays and Festivals

Few holidays and festivals exist that do not have the mark of the Ethiopian Orthodox Tewahedo Church, one of the oldest churches in the world, and Islam.[1] Ethiopia was the first country in the world to peacefully accept Islam. To save some of his followers from persecution in Mecca, prophet Moham-mad sent them to Ethiopia. The Ethiopians accepted the refugees, among whom were the Prophet's closest relatives. As a result of the good deed of Ethiopians, the Prophet spared Ethiopia from Jihad and instructed his fol-lowers not to attack Ethiopia unless they attacked. Some of the consequences of this reciprocity between the prophet Mohammed (Islam) and Ethiopia are that Islam became an integral part of Ethiopian way of life, but the country was not Arabized and the Muslims of Ethiopia rarely have an Arabized name. Above all, however, Muslims and Christians coexisted peacefully. Therefore, it is not an exaggeration to say that Ethiopia's Judeo-Christian and Islamic religious traditions decidedly influenced festivals, holidays, and the lifestyles of Ethiopians.

In order to know holidays and festivals of Ethiopia, one has to understand the Ethiopian calendar, which is very unique. It was created by the Ethio-pian Orthodox Church. This calendar starts counting with the creation of the world, which, according to the Ethiopian Orthodox Tewahedo Church, is 5,550 years before the birth of Christ. These years are called *Zemene-fida* or

Zemene Kunene (Years of the Law of Consciousness and Years of the Old Testament), while the years after the birth of Christ are referred to as *Amete Mihiret,* (Year of Mercy or the Era of the New Testament). According to the Ethiopian calendar, 7,500 years have passed since the earth was created and it has been 2,005 years since Jesus was born. This means the Ethiopian calendar is seven years behind the Western/Gregorian calendar. The Gregorian and Ethiopian calendar vary by 6 days in *Nehase* (August), 10/11 days in *Meskrem* (September) and 7 years from *Meskrem* (September) to *Tahisas* (December) and 8 years from *Tir* (January) to *Nehase* (August). The discrepancy between the Western and Ethiopian calendar is attributed to the fact that different countries used various ways to trace the year Christ was born and the year Rome was established. The Gregorian calendar believes that the fall of Jerusalem happened 77 years after the birth of Christ, while the Ethiopian Orthodox Tewahedo Church indicates it happened 70 years after Christ's birth. Similarly, while the Ethiopian calendar indicates that Jesus was born approximately 745 years after the establishment of Rome, the Gregorian calendar asserts that Jesus was born 753 years after the establishment of Rome. The discrepancy between the two calendars is also partly due to Pope Gregory, who abandoned the rules for calculating Easter while formulating new rules in 1582.

The Ethiopian calendar divides the year into 13 months. While the 12 months are equally divided into 30 days, the 13th month, *Pagume,* however, has only five or six days depending on whether the year is a leap year or not. The name of the 13th month was derived from the Greek word *Hepagumen,* which means "extra" or "inserted." The names of these 12 months are *Meskrem, Tiqimt, Hidar, Tahisas, Tir, Yekatit, Megabit, Meyazia, Ginbot, Sene, Hamile,* and *Nehase.* Like the names of the seven days of the week, the name of each month has meaning related to biblical or other events. The Ethiopian months roughly correspond with the months of September, October, November, December, January, February, March, April, May, June, July, and August. The Ethiopian Orthodox Tewahedo Church also uses a four-year cycle to name each New Year after one of the four evangelists in the following order: *Matewos* (Mathew), *Marqos* (Mark), *Luqas* (Luke), and *Yohannis* (John). The church divides each year into four seasons, while each week is divided into seven days in line with the days of creation mentioned in the Bible. Each day of the week is divided into 12 hours of daylight and 12 hours of night. While the Ethiopian midday and midnight fall at the Western 12 A.M. and 12 P.M., respectively, the day starts at dawn and the night begins at dusk. The church justifies its hour-counting system by referring to the Bible. For instance, in the New Testament the time sequence when Christ was flogged, crucified, and the time of his resurrection corresponds with the Ethiopian time keeping.

Enqutatash (New Year)

The Orthodox Tewahedo Church, in addition to creating the Ethiopian calendar, has pointed out when and how holidays occur and are celebrated. Accordingly, one of the major national holidays is *Kidus Yohannis* (St. John). This holiday is Ethiopia's New Year (*Addsi Amet*), also known as *Enqutatash*. This holiday falls on the first day of the first Ethiopian month, *Meskrem* 1 (September 11 or 12).

The choice of *Meskrem* 1 as the New Year was influenced partly by biblical events and stories and partly was a consequence of natural proceedings. Accordingly, the beheading of St. John the Baptist marks the beginning of the New Year. This is because according to the tradition of the Ethiopian Orthodox Tewahedo Church, St. John is regarded as a transitional prophet between the Old and the New Testament prophets, and hence, his death marks the beginning of a new era. Thus, the first day of the first month is named after St. John, *Kidus Yohannis*. The celebration of the New Year on September 1 is also related to stories in Genesis 8:1. There, it informs us that the storm that happened during Noah's time receded in the "first year in the first day of the month." The Ethiopian New Year also marks the end of the Ethiopian rainy season, *Kiremt* (winter), which falls roughly between May and September.

On the eve of New Year's Day, the priests of the Ethiopian Orthodox Tewahedo Church pass the night, chanting about the arrival of the New Year and praying that the Lord may protect the country from manmade and natural disasters in the New Year. In the morning, children gather fresh *Adey Abeba,* or *Mesiqel Abeba* (*Coreopsis negriana*)—a deep yellow-colored flower that blooms only once a year, at the end of the rainy season, between late August and early September—and give them to neighbors, relatives, and friends. Those who receive these flowers in return offer the children money, clothes, cattle, homemade bread, or simply promise to give them something. While the gift of money and clothes is common in urban centers, gifts of a goat, a sheep, or a calf are common in the rural areas. These days, children give or distribute drawings of flowers or angels instead of the customary *Adey Abeba*.

The exchange of gifts, more or less, happens in the following manner: The child will say *Enqutatash* to the person he or she is giving the flowers to. The receiver will reply, *Beyametu Yamitash,* meaning, "May He bring you forth every year, *sitedar kuta,* or I will present you a *Kuta* (a finely made cotton cloth that resembles a Roman Toga) when you get married. The exchange of gifts or well wishes usually happens before noon. When children are presenting these gifts, they also say *Enkuwan kezemene Matewos wede zemene Marqos beselam ashegagerot* (May He peacefully transition you from the year of Mathew to Mark).

People can also simply say *Enqutatash,* or *Enquwan aderseh,* to mark and honor the arrival of the New Year. Though the circumstances for the use of the word *Enqutatash* is known, the exact meaning is not. The word *Enqutatash* is a corrupted term that used to mean *Enqu Letatish* (Diamonds for your fingers) or *Enqu Letatash* (Diamonds for your troubles or expenses). Both instances, however, are related to the Queen of Sheba and her travel to Israel and hence her affair with King Solomon. The story has it that when the Queen arrived in Israel, she presented King Solomon with various gifts. Solomon reciprocated by giving Sheba diamonds. Upon her return to Ethiopia, children and the populace at large welcomed the Queen by saying *Enqu letatash*—a reference to Solomon's gift to the Queen to cover her travel expenses. Since then, children celebrate the New Year by saying *Enqutatash.* Others, however, claim that the gift was a diamond ring, and thus upon her arrival in Ethiopia, the children welcomed her by saying *Enqu Letatish*—meaning Solomon gave you a diamond for your finger. Despite such differences regarding the interpretation of *Enqutatash,* Ethiopians continue celebrating the New Year by saying *Enqutatash.*

The Ethiopian Orthodox Tewahedo Church has a different account of *Enqutatash.* The Amharic language was not developed at Queen of Sheba's time. Therefore, *Enqu letatish* or *Enqu letatash* could not possibly have been derived from the Amharic word. Instead, the bouquet of *Adey Abeba* given during the New Year is a symbolic reminder of what happened once the flood ebbed during Noah's time. Sticking to its religious interpretation of the New Year celebration, the church declares that the flowers represent *ketema* (a green reed that grows on soggy land) or the olive branch that the dove brought to Noah (Genesis 8:11–13). Therefore, the church asserts, the flowers signify the end of the rainy season in Ethiopia and the beginning of brighter and sunny days.

On that day, children, especially girls, sing the following song in groups of two. One group says *abebaye-hoy* (have you seen flowers?), the other group responds with *lemilem* (blooming, lush, green), and then the first group continues saying *qumumubetera* (stand in a row), while the second group responds *lemilem,* and *inchet sebire* (until I collect [dry] wood) . . . *lemilem, bet iskisera* (until I build a house). Apparently, like many Ethiopian song lyrics, the song has double meaning, which is roughly known as *samina wariq* (wax and gold.) The direct or apparent meaning is referred to as *sem* (wax), while the hidden or subtle meaning or message is referred to as *wariq* (gold). Accordingly, *abebaye-hoy* could mean "my flower" as well as "have you seen a flower?" The other group's response, *lemilem* too has a double meaning: Lemilem can be a person's name. So when one combines both stanzas, it means, "Lemilem, have you seen flowers?" Or, it can also mean "have you seen blooming flowers for "lemilem" can also be interpreted to mean "blooming," "fresh," "green," and so on. Also, when one combines the words "stand in a row . . . until I build a house" signifies the troubles of finding dry wood during the rainy season (winter) but now the summer is here, it will be easier to find dry wood and build a house. All, however, reflect the change of season, from winter to the Ethiopian summer, as well as the coming of better and brighter days.

Mesiqel Beal (Commemorating the Finding of the True Cross)

Another important holiday that is celebrated in *Meskrem* is the commemoration of the finding of the True Cross (Mesiqal), observed on *Meskrem* 16 and 17 (September 26 and 27). Around 4 A.M., on the 16th of *Meskrem,* a bonfire (*demera*) is lit in each and every Christian household throughout Ethiopia. Each and every adult and child lights the *demera* with *chibo* (a torch). After the *demera* is lit, the lit *chibo* is used to bless each family's house: the front and back doors of the house, furniture, cattle. and so on. While sanctifying, adults and children say, *yegomen tofa wuta-wuta, yedinich tofaa giba-giba* (the cooking pot used for *Gomen* [collard greens] be replaced with the cooking pot for potatoes). The saying heralds the coming of nutritious foods other than collard greens. It should be remembered that the *Mesiqal* holiday is held in September, which is immediately after the end of the rainy season and the beginning of harvesting time. More often than not, during the winter season, the majority of the peasant household suffers from a lack of food until the harvesting season comes. As a consequence, most rural households depend on *Gomen* (collard greens) for survival. Thus, the wish for the end of the collard greens and the coming of potatoes is a declaration of the approaching better days. In fact, when people meet, they greet one another by saying *engoro-gobash,* an abridged version of *enkuwan guwaro gebesh* and the other person responds with *yiterkus-abash,* which means "welcome to my table" or "welcome the new harvest." Children and adults also sing, *Eyoha Abebaye Meskrem Tebeya; Meskrem siteba wedadis Ababa,* which roughly translates to "September is here (the rainy season is over). Let us now travel (for there are no rains, storms, rivers, fords, etc that can hinder our journey)."

The next day, around 10 A.M., there is another and a much bigger bonfire that is lit at a central location of each and every village, town, and city in Ethiopia. This bonfire has a special name, *Ate Demera,* which literally means the "bonfire of all bonfires." It also means the king of kings of the *Demeras* as *Ate* is the other name for king of kings. The public square in Addis Ababa, Ethiopia's capital, is even known as *Mesiqel Adebababy* (Meskel Square). There, the Ethiopian head of state accompanied by the patriarch of the Ethiopian Orthodox Tewahedo Church lights the *Mesiqel Demera.* The patriarch blesses the *demera* before it is lit. In the old days, especially during Gondarian times (1600s–1890s), no one could light the *Atse Demera* other than the person who held the office of the *Demera Lequwash,* bonfire lighter. The *Demera Lequwash* position was hereditary. It was passed from father to son. For his service, the *Demera Lequwash* was paid five Maria Theresa Thalers (MTT)[2] or its equivalent in kind annually. The last *Demera Lequwash,* a man named Birassw Melese, died in Gondar in the early 1990s. Therefore, during monarchial Ethiopia, the tradition was the *Demera Lequwash would* light the bonfire, and then the king of kings, the king, or other dignitaries would continue lighting the *demera.*

The direction toward which the central pole falls is very important. On the pole, a cross is affixed on its top end, and logs of wood and the Mesiqel daisies are piled surrounding it. The populace believes that it is a good omen for the provinces (states), villages, and towns toward which the pole falls. These provinces or regions will have a bumper crop and thus a prosperous year.

The lighting ceremony is accompanied by the Orthodox Church's chant, followed by traditional folk music and dance. In bigger and multiethnic cities like Addis Ababa, one catches a glimpse of the music and dance of the many ethnic groups of the country such as the Oromo, the Amhara, the Tigrians, the Gurage, and the Dorze.

People who are returning from the festivity mark their forehead with a cross using the ash from the *demera.* Almost everyone who attends the event tries to get access to the ash or charcoal to mark his or her forehead with a cross.

While it is the head of state or governors and administrators of respective areas who light the bonfire, in villages and households it is the head of the household or the village elder who does it. After the bonfire is burned, the head of the family or the elder of the village kills a sheep or bull, depending on the means of the household or the village, in the morning, and with that the festivity commences and will last for weeks among ethnic groups such as the Gurage.

Like *Enqutatash,* the *Mesiqel* holiday has religious roots. It is associated with Queen Elleni, otherwise known as Hellena, mother of King Constantine the Great of the Eastern Roman Empire, finder of the True Cross. According to the traditions of the Ethiopian Orthodox Church, the Queen was on a quest to uncover the whereabouts of the True Cross on which Jesus was crucified. After years of futile, and often frustrating, efforts, she finally succeeded with the help of a holy man. The holy man advised the Queen to build a *demera* and follow the smoke from the bonfire. The smoke directed her to where the cross was buried. Building a *demera* and the good omen associated with the direction where the pole, on which the *demera* is placed, falls symbolizes this story of the finding of the True Cross.

The Ethiopian Orthodox Tewahedo Church claims it has a fragment of the True Cross. The details of the arrival of a fragment of the True Cross are documented in a religious book called *Tefut*, which was written during the reign of *Atse* Zera Yacob (r. 1434–1468). The custodian of the religious object is the Gishen Mariam monastery, located in one of the most inaccessible parts of Wollo Province, northeastern Ethiopia. The faithful pays a visit every year on Meskrem 21 (October 1) to celebrate the deposition of the right arm of the True Cross in that monastery.

The *Genna* (Ethiopian Christmas) Celebration

The Ethiopian Christmas is celebrated on *Tahisas 29* (January 7). Like the rest of the Christian world, Ethiopians celebrate *genna* to commemorate the birth of Jesus at Bethlehem. On this day, in addition to attending mass, children and adults alike commemorate the event by playing the game of *genna* (hockey). The game is a reenactment of what the sheepherders were doing on the day Jesus was born. The game is played between two contending parties either on foot or on horseback. During the game, mistakenly hitting a person, even if that person is a king or a lord, does not warrant a grudge or punishment against the person (a commoner) who did the hitting. Hence, the traditional adage goes like this, *begena chewata ayqotum getta* (in a game of *genna* the master will not get angry if [mistakenly] hit by his servant).

The *Timqet* (Epiphany) Celebration

Timqet is a holiday that celibrates the baptism of Jesus by John the Baptist in the River Jordan. The holiday is honored on *Tir* 11 (January 19). According to the traditions of the Orthodox Tewahedo Church, the holiday includes three events: *Ketera, Timqet,* and *Qaana.* On the day of *ketera* (to dam), which happens on the eve of *Timqet,* churches come out with their *tabots* (the Ark of the Covenant),[3] accompanied by the townsfolk, with a colorful pageantry and pomp, going to a river or a place where a sizable body of water is available. Throughout the night, the church holds its mass while the people pass the night playing their *trunba* (a traditional trumpet made out of a horn), singing and dancing. On the early morning of the 12th of *Tir,* a priest sprinkles water over the silently waiting congregation. The sprinkling of water at this time of the day is a symbolic reenactment of the baptism of Jesus. Once the church has blessed and sprinkled the water, children, adults, and elders of all genders jump into the water. In the city of Gondar, where there is the swimming pool of King Fasiledes (r. 1622–1632), commonly known as Fasiledes Bath, people jump into the pool. This is followed by singing a variety of traditional songs and dancing. Around 10 A.M., the *Tabot* (the Ark of the Covenant) start marching back to their

Timqet festival, Lalibela, Ethiopia. (Carolyne Pehora/Dreamstime.com)

respective churches. The return journey is as colorful as the coming of the Ark to the *Timiqete-Bahir* (the Sea of Baptism). The priests, dressed in their dazzling ceremonial clothes and decorated umbrellas, chant while returning to the church. Their chanting is accompanied by *kebero* (drums) and the rhythmic clink of *sinasil* (cestrums). The return procession is very slow, often marked by intermittent breaks so that the priests carrying the *tabot* can catch their breath. The populace continues the festivity even after the Arks have been returned to their respective churches.

Qaana, which is observed on the 12th of *Tir* (January 20), is celebrated to commemorate the changing of water into wine by Jesus. On this day, while all the *tabots* are returned to their respective churches, the *tabot* of the Archangel Michael stays at the *Timqete-Bahir*. The *tabot* of the Archangel returns on the 20th of January, the day after *Timqet*.

Aside from the religious significance *Timqet* has, the occasion is noted as one of the most favored events for young adults to choose or meet their potential lovers and soul mates. However, in urban centers, this practice is waning, for there are other ways of meeting their lovers.

The *Timqet* holiday is also noted as one of the most glamorous holidays in Ethiopia. Whoever is attending the *Timqet* holiday is expected to be dressed in his or her best cloth. Due to this, it is said that people often keep their best dress for this occasion. In fact, there is even a saying that befits this custom: *letimqet yalihne qemis yibetates* (a good dress that is not worn on *Timqet* is useless).

Like many of the aforementioned holidays, the name *Timqet* has a meaning. According to the tradition of the Orthodox Tewahedo Church, *Timqet* is an Amharic word taken from the Geez word *Asterio,* which means "to reveal"—the revelation of the Holy Trinity during the baptism of Christ. It is also worth to note that the word *Timqet* means "immersion," which clearly describes the baptism of Jesus—his immersion in the River Jordan.

The *Fasika/Tinsae* (Easter) Celebration

The Easter celebration always happens on Sunday. It is celebrated to remember the Resurrection of Jesus Christ. The Holy Mass is held until midnight—coinciding with the time Jesus was resurrected. After the mass is over, some people who brought food and drink serve the priest, the laity, the homeless, and the poor. The people light *tuwaf* (handmade candles from bees' wax and cotton threads) and candles symbolizing the end of darkness.

On this day, christen Ethiopians who have been fasting for Lent break the fast. Until *Tinsae,* according to the rules of the Orthodox Tewahedo Church, Ethiopians are not allowed to eat meat, poultry, and dairy products in addition to the keep fasting until past 3:00 P.M. Only children, the sick, and the very old are spared of this stringent law. As a result, during the fasting season, no Christian butchery house is open in any part of Ethiopia.

On the morning of *Tinsae,* people break the fast by first eating *enjera* with *wot* (stew) made from flaxseed. A flaxseed stew is believed to reduce the stress on body that has been fasting for 50 or so days without eating meat and dairy products. During the fasting season, Christians only eat stew made of legumes and vegetables. Of course, in addition to killing sheep and chicken on Easter Day, there will be the usual coffee ceremony and homemade beer (*tella*) to mark the occasion.

Eid al-Adha (Feast of the Sacrifice)

In addition to the aforementioned national holidays, there are holidays that pertain to Islam. Due to the universality of Islam, however, the Islamic holidays follow the Muslim calendar, also known as the Lunar calendar. Until the 1974 revolution, though the country's Muslims celebrated all the holidays that pertained to Islam, they were never part of the national holidays. The country's leaders, policymakers, and academics portrayed Ethiopia as a Christian land, while in reality Muslim's accounted for almost half of the nation's population.

Eid al-Adha is one of the Muslim festivals that became a national holiday after the 1974 revolution. *Eid al-Adha* is celebrated on the 10th day of the last month, *Dhu al-Hijra,* of the Islamic calendar. The celebration lasts for four days. The holiday commemorates Abraham's (Ibrahim in Arabic) willingness to sacrifice his eldest and only son, Ismael (Ishmael in Arabic), in an act of devotion to *Allah*'s (God's) command. The holiday also recognizes Ismael's willingness to be sacrificed. *Allah,* however, intervened. He gave Abraham a sheep to sacrifice instead.

Eid al-Fitr (Breaking the Fast of Ramadan)

Ramadan occurs at the end of the Muslim fasting month and holy season. It is a one-day festival. Like their Muslim brethren in other parts of the world, Ethiopian Muslims celebrate by breaking the fast in the morning. While Muslims in the Arab world break the fast by eating sweets such as dates, Ethiopian Muslims prepare a special sweet that is made from *abish*. The *abish* is soaked in water a few days, until it germinates. Then it is sun-dried and grounded into a fine powder. The powder is mixed with water and sugar and is left until the mixture settles. The water is slowly drained into another container, thus becoming a sweet drink. Those who live in urban centers can supplement the sweetened *abish* with dates as per the requirement of breaking the fast by

Ethiopian Muslims attend prayers during *Eid al-Fitr* in Addis Ababa, August 8, 2013. (Reuters/Corbis)

eating sweets. Honey mixed with water, known as *birth,* is another sweet drink. *Bubugn,* a locally made drink, is specially made for the occasion in rural and semi-urban areas. The way it is prepared is similar to that of *tella,* the locally made beer. However, the difference between *tella* and *bubugn* is that the latter does not have *gesho,* thus making it an alcohol-free beverage. Here, one has to note that Muslims do not drink alcoholic beverages. *Sambussa, beqlava,* and other sweet cookies complete the fast-breaking dish.

During the fasting season, Ethiopian Muslims do not eat, drink, and even swallow their saliva all day, between 6:00 A.M. and 6:00 P.M., or between sunrise and sundown. However, those who are sick and feeble may fast at another time. Fasting the Ramadan is one of the five pillars of Islam and thus obligatory. On this holiday, Muslims of Ethiopia greet one another by saying *Ed Mubarek* (Have a blessed *Eid* or Happy *Eid*). They also extend help to those in need. The help, in addition to buying a lamb, chicken, or other animals, can include buying clothes for the children of a needy family.

Mawlid (The Birthday of the Prophet, Mohammed)

Mawlid is celebrated to commemorate the birth of the Prophet. The holiday occurs on the 12th day of the third month of the Muslim calendar, Rabi I. Rabi I is also the day the Prophet died. Some sects of Islam consider *Mawlid* as un-Islamic and thus equate it with idolatry. However, the major and dominant sect of Islam, Sunni, honors the birth of the Prophet. More than 99 percent of Ethiopian Muslims are Sunni.

Aside from Islamic rituals that every Muslim performs, the manner in which Ethiopian Muslims celebrate the holidays is not that different from their Christian Ethiopians. In addition to the usual coffee ceremony, the killing of chickens, lamb, goat, or a bull is part of the celebrations. During such holidays, it is often customary to invite neighbors irrespective of their religion to honor the occasion. During this time, the Muslim provide, depending on his means, a sheep, a chicken, or a bull to his Christian neighbor so that he can kill the animal according to his Christian faith and feed the invited guests on behalf of his Muslim neighbor or friend. If the Muslim is poor, he will offer his Christian friends and neighbors *nifro* (boiled beans and wheat), or *qolo* (roasted chickpeas, barley, wheat, etc.) accompanied with, of course, coffee. The same holds true for Christian Ethiopians during the Christian holidays.

In addition to the abovementioned holidays, there are holidays that both Christians and Muslims celebrate irrespective of their religious beliefs. These holidays are, however, confined to certain places. For instance, *Sheh* Abadir (a *waliy* who died and was buried in Wollo Province, northern

Ethiopia) is venerated throughout the country, especially in the northern parts of Ethiopia. As the name might imply, it is celebrated to honor a local saint, as per the tradition of the Sufi order. During this event, both Muslim and Christians honor the Muslim saint. Similarly, the celebration of Qulubi Gabriel (St. Gabriel's Day) in Harar Province, southeastern Ethiopia, on the 19th day of *Tahisas,* is honored by both Christians and Muslims.

These days, however, with the rise of Islamic fundamentalism and its spread among the younger generation Ethiopian Muslims, such tolerance and camaraderie among young generation Muslims and their Christian counterparts is becoming a rarity. Equally significant is that the spread of Pentecostalism in Ethiopia since the late 1980s, usually at the expense of Muslims and Orthodox Christians, and Orthodox Christian revivalism, the other side of Islamic fundamentalism, is threatening the peaceful co-existence that existed for millennia between Muslims and Christians of Ethiopia.

Qulubi Church, where Ethiopian Orthodox Tewahido Christians celebrate the feast of Saint Gabriel, December 29, 2004. (Reuters/Corbis)

IMPACT OF WESTERNIZATION AND URBANIZATION

The impact of Westernization on the festivals and holidays is immense. As mentioned earlier, the New Year celebration, which is usually associated with the giving of *Adey Ababa,* is now being replaced with giving handmade paintings of flowers and angels drawn on paper. Though the use of paper can be attributed partly to environmental change and land degradation that made *Adey Ababa* less and less available, fast-paced urban development that claimed those lands on which *Adey Ababa* used to grow is another culprit. Also, for the urbanites going out and collecting these flowers from increasingly distant places has become a costly endeavor, as public transport is unavailable and, even if there is, it is expensive and thus discouraging. This is very true, given the commercialization of holidays. A child might get a few dimes for the *Adey Ababa* he or she presents.

The Ethiopian *genna* is another victim of Westernization. The game of *genna,* which is associated with the Ethiopian Christmas celebration, is no longer held in all urban centers and in most rural areas. Western-style schools, often known as *Askula,* through which basketball, soccer, volleyball, and other sports were introduced, and where these and other Euro-American games are taught and held, do not include *genna* and other indigenous sporting events. The so-called sport teacher, be it Ethiopian or expatriate, does not instruct students to play traditional Ethiopian games and sports.

The use of a Christmas tree during *genna* was unknown except among the expatriate community and among the very few Western-educated Ethiopians who tried to mimic the Euro-American lifestyle. However, after the 1974 Ethiopian revolution that pushed tens of thousands of Ethiopians out of their country, things began changing. The relatively easier access to television and other forms of media such as movies increased the exposure of Ethiopians to Western-style celebration of *genna,* including the use of Christmas trees. The Ethiopian refugees and immigrants who began returning to their country in large numbers after 1991 further accelerated the invasion of Westernization on Ethiopian lifestyles and holidays. Today most Ethiopians who reside in urban centers celebrate *genna* with Christmas trees. Those who cannot afford to have a real tree buy an artificial tree that they can use every year. In addition to Christmas lights, Ethiopians use cotton balls for snow—an interesting development in a country where there is no snow and snowy winter season.

Timqet festival, too, is not immune from Western influence. With the development of "religious" tourism, the event is more geared toward attracting tourists than for religious purposes. The celebration of *genna* in Gondar is now used to exhibit the so-called Ethiopian cultural heritage to the expatriate community. Today one finds fake tkuls, grass-thatched and mud-plastered houses adjacent to the entrance of the *Timekete-Bahir*. They were meant to depict the rural life style of Ethiopians and the rural household. Today the tkuls are in shambles. After the event, no one, including the municipality and the tourist office, tries to maintain them. These days *timqet* celebration is accompanied with the buzz of helicopters and planes that try to capture the event and broadcast it live to the whole nation.

Economic hardship that often accompanies development in third world countries has also impacted holiday celebrations. These days the majority of urban-dwelling Ethiopians are finding it increasingly difficult to buy sheep or goats or to partner with someone to slaughter a bull and share it, due to the ever-growing inflation and declining income. The people no longer share meals with their neighbors—not because they have become greedy, but because they cannot afford the extra cost. Coffee drinking, which is a communal event, has also become difficult. This is partly due to the ever-increasing price of coffee and partly as a consequence of the emergence of a new middle class that desires to reside away from the poor in enclosed suburbs such as Bole, Gerje, and Laftoo.

The EPRDF government's effort to address the shortage of urban housing is another reason for the disruption of the traditional way of life in Ethiopia's urban centers such as Addis Ababa. The houses the government is building are "condominiums." These are apartment houses that are built in newly developed areas or areas that the government considers "slums." The problem with the government endeavor is that those who are given the condominiums are non-natives of the "slums," or simply people who do not know one another. They get the "condos" because they have the money to afford them or simply because they won the "lottery." To be fair and to avoid corruption and nepotism in the distribution of "condos," the government introduced a "lottery" system by which the person whose name is randomly picked gets the "condo." While the government's effort is commendable in addressing housing problems and in restraining the unnecessary horizontal growth of cities, it, however, totally decimates the social fabric of the community and its cultural safety-net programs such as *eder, equb,* and *senbete.* These traditional institutions are established after years of acquaintance and mutual trust, which can only happen after living together in the same neighborhood for so long and through thick and thin.

One major consequence, in addition to the aforementioned drawbacks, is an increase in crime in the newly established "condo" neighborhoods and suburbs. Because the residents of these "condo" neighborhoods and suburbs are an amalgam of people who do not know one another and often come from other cities and provinces, they are easy targets for criminals. The old neighborhoods of Addis Ababa and other cities like Gondar, which are traditionally known as *sefers* and *menders,* respectively, came into existence either as the result of profession/occupation. Such *sefers* in Addis Ababa include *Gola* (pot makers), Qes/Kahin (priests), *Dorze* (weavers), and Congo and Korea *sefers* (residential areas of Ethiopian soldiers who returned serving in the UN-led missions in Congo and Korea). Other neighborhoods reflect the provincial origin of residents such as Wollo and Sidamo *sefers*. Residents of such neighborhoods more or less knew one another and thus were able to identify intruders and new comers, which in turn made it easier to keep the safety of the neighbored from thieves and brigands. Today, suburbs like Bole, Old Airport, Gerji, and the many newly sprouted "condo" neighborhoods have to depend on the police or employ guards to protect their property and neighborhoods. The same is true with the newly emerging suburbs of Gondar such as *Addisu* Gondar (the New Gondar) and the former Samuna Ber, the now America *Mender* (American Village). In these areas, especially in the latter case, one can see villas with barbed wire fences and armed guards—a new phenomenon in Gondar.

NOTES

1. I am greatly indebted to *Ato* Bantalem Tadesse, a lecturer at the University of Gondar, who unlocked some of the mysteries of the Ethiopian calendar and its founder, the Ethiopian Orthodox Tewahido Church. Almost all the pertinent information for this chapter is gleaned from his book: *Bantalem Tadese, A Guide to the Intangible Treasures of Ethiopian Orthodox Tewahido Church: Historic Perspectives and Symbolic Interpretations of the Festivals* (Addis Ababa, Ethiopia: Kalu Printing Press, 2010).

2. Ethiopia used to mint its coins, mostly made of gold, during Aksumite times (between 500 BC and AD 900). However, after the downfall of Aksum, the country used all sorts of things such as bars of copper, iron, salt, and gold, cartridges. Since the reign of Iyasu II (1730–1755), however, MTT began circulating widely in Ethiopia as a currency as well as source of silver. The Thaler, which was first minted in Austria in 1741 and which is more than 90 percent pure silver and weighted more than 28 grams, remained as one of the most favorite currency in Ethiopia until around the 1940s. So much so colonial powers that had overt and covert interest over Ethiopia used MTT instead of their own currencies while dealing with Ethiopia. Even one of the most powerful and resourceful kings of Ethiopia, Menelik II (1889–1913), had to imitate the MTT while introducing his own silver dollar, the *Alad*. Alas, the Ethiopians remained reluctant to use his *Alad* in favor of the MTT. In addition to Ethiopia, the MTT was the favorite currency in the Middle East, the Red Sea, the Indian Ocean, and beyond in addition to, of course, the wider Europe. It remained an international medium of exchange for a long while. See for instance, Adrian E. Tschoegl, "Maria Theresa's Thaler: A Case of International Money," *Eastern Economic Journal* 27, no. 4 (Fall, 2001): 443–62; Raymond A. Silverman and

Neal W. Sobania, "Gold and Silver at the Crossroads in Highland Ethiopia," *International Journal of Ethiopian Studies* 1, no. 2 (Winter/Spring 2004): 82–109; Jan Warren Duggar, "The Development of Money Supply in Ethiopia," *Middle East Journal* 21, no. 2 (Spring, 1967): 255–61; Shepard Pond, "The Maria Theresa Thaler: A Famous Trade Coin," *Bulletin of the Business Historical Society* 15, no. 2 (April, 1941): 26–31.

3. According to the *Kibre-Negest* (Glory of the Kings), on which the history of Ethiopian kings who reigned over Ethiopia since its creation is recorded, Menelik I, the son of Queen of Sheba and King Solomon, brought the Ark of the Covenant to Ethiopia. Upon its arrival, the church fathers made replicas of the Ark to prevent theft. While the original Ark is believed to have been deposited at St. Marry Zion Church of Aksum, each and every church in the country also has one.

8

Music and Dance

INTRODUCTION

Before delving into musical genres, dance, and external influence on Ethiopian music, it is imperative to put Ethiopian music into historical perspective. Understanding Ethiopian secular music requires exploring the history of the Ethiopian Orthodox Church, which, until the late 19th century, remained the sole author and custodian of anything and everything Ethiopian. Ethiopian music is rooted in religious ceremonies and services, especially that of the Ethiopian Orthodox Church, which was established in the fourth century. As noted by the Ethiopian composer, conductor, and ethnomusicologist Professor Ashenafi Kebede, "Chanting was intended and used as the sole expression of the belief in one God. It is almost entirely sung; it is the human voice, not a musical instrument, that is considered important."[1] Ashenafi also indicated that the introduction of monastic practices into the Ethiopian Orthodox Church in the fifth century encouraged the creation and preservation of culture, and "gave birth to a system of formal church education that integrated music, poetry, gesture, and personality development. A system of notation was introduced as part of the Church's objectives to preserve its large repertory of sacred chants."

The person credited with the creation of Ethiopian church musical notations was Saint Yared who lived during the reign of Atse Gebra Meskel (476–571). The Ethiopian notations employ *milikitoch*, pneumatic signs, such as dots, dashes, and curves, and letter notations (*siraye*). The *siraye* notation, which is written in small letters and in red ink, is placed above the lines of text, while the *milikit* notations, which are written in black and are recognizable by their distinct shapes, are placed below the line of text. The neumatic signs also dictate performance approaches such as special ornamental inflections, dynamics, and tempo.

Ethiopian church music has 10 different neumatic signs. These are *yizat* (*staccato*), *deret* (singing in law deep voice, humming), *qinaat* (upward *glissando*), *chirat* (downward *glissando*), *difat* (drop the voice), *qurit* (singing to a cadential formula, equivalent to *coda*), *rut* (equivalent to *vibrato*), *rikirik* (equivalent to *tremolo*), *hidat* (equivalent to *accelerando, crescendo,* and *portamento* at the same time), and *serez* (slight pause).

Each religious chant has tempo or speed indicators at its beginning. These are *mergd* (equivalent to *largo and grave*), *nuis-meregd* (equivalent to *adagio*), *abiy-tsefat* (equivalent to *allegretto*), *tsefat* (equivalent to *allegro*), and *arwaSi* (equivalent to *prestissimo*).

The Ethiopian notations also employ three technical terms, which Westerners refer to as "modes," while Ethiopians call them *selt* (order), or *zema* (chant). The *zema* (chant) determines the tonal range and principles of performance. The technical terms are *ge'ez, izil,* and *araray* that roughly correspond to three octave ranges—low, middle, and high. *Ge'ez, izil,* and *araray* also entail the emotional and psychological state that the chant is performed. Accordingly, *ge'ez* is sung in a relaxed, sad, and soft tonal range, and expresses a feeling of sorrow, disappointment, and despair. The church often uses *ge'ez* during funerals and fasting days. *Izil,* on the other hand, is sung in a medium, ordinary, and comfortable vocal range. It reflects an emotionally neutral state, and due to this fact the Ethiopian church prefers using the *izil* style. *Izil* is also used for hymns of the ordinary days. *Araray,* however, expresses joy, elation, animation, and satisfaction.[2]

The presence of the Ethiopian Orthodox Church and its clergy in the many facets of life has empowered it to affect virtually every aspect of life. One of the areas where the church exhibited its influence is in secular folk music. Some studies indicated that the *debtra,* one among the most learned individuals of the Ethiopian Orthodox clergy, greatly influence secular music. Almost all secular music teachers who taught in Haile Selassie I University (now Addis Ababa University) and the Yared School of Music were, and, to some degree, still are either clergymen or Western-educated Ethiopians with strong church background. In fact, when Western education was introduced into Ethiopia at the turn of the 20th century, the first to attend or to teach were also clergymen, or advanced students of the church.

The instruments used in this Western-style school of music, in addition to the Western musical instruments, were Ethiopian traditional musical instruments such as *washint* (flute), *kirar* (bow-lyre), *bagana* (sacred box-lyre), *masinqo* (a single bowed spike lute or fiddle), *sinasil* (sistrum), and *melekt* (long trumpet). Of these, the *bagana* and *sinasil* are sacred church musical instruments.[3]

Equally important but less known and studied is the traditional Muslim song, *Manzuma*. The circumstance of its origin and when *Menzuma* became one of the Ethiopian Muslim songs is unknown. For that matter, much of the history of Ethiopian Muslims, though they account for almost half of the Ethiopian population, is not adequately studied or given due attention. *Menzuma,* however, is associated with northeastern Ethiopia, with the Muslims of Wallo Province. From there, *Menzuma* is believed to have spread to the rest of Ethiopia especially Harar (eastern Ethiopia) and Jimma (southern Ethiopia). In both places, it is sung in Amharic, the official language of the country, and Afan Oromo, the language of the Oromo.[4] Its impact on contemporary Ethiopian music needs to be explored.

Ethiopian boy plays the *masinqo*. (Zaramira/Dreamstime.com)

TRADITIONAL MUSICIANS AND PERFORMERS, THE *LALIBELA* AND THE *ALQASH,* IN PREREVOLUTION ETHIOPIA

Prior to the 20th century, the Ethiopian monarchy and the nobility were the sole benefactors of the Ethiopian Orthodox Church and its clergy. The church, on its part, remained the fountain of wisdom, the sole custodian of Ethiopian history and culture, including music. Hence, the monarchy and the nobility provided protection and means of sustenance for the clergy and musicians.[5] Among the latter two, the musician had more categories and was vulnerable to periodic changes in Ethiopian society. The *amina,* sometimes also referred to as *lalibella,* the *azimare,* and the *alqash,* also known as *musho awarag,* are some of the singers who serve or perform at different circumstances and for different occasions and thus fall under the musician category.

The *amina,* or *lalibela,* usually a husband and wife, are people who sang once a year and during the wee hours of the night, before sundown. They had nice voice. They did not use any musical instruments and they did not reveal themselves, so nobody knew who they were. One of the reasons for such mysticism surrounding the *amina* was that they were believed to be lepers, and thus, unless they sung once a year, their sickness would afflict them terribly; the other reason was the social scorn that Ethiopians had for the musical profession and professionals. One can also ascribe the secrecy that surrounds the *amina* to their character. An *amina* praised the person who gave him or her money. But, if the person failed to give money, the *amina,* who were usually very well informed about the people for whom they were singing, would completely tarnish the person's image and reputation. Some of the badmouthing included character assassination or exposure of the bad deeds of the individual. The problem with this is that because *amina* sang in the early morning hours, every villager and neighbor could hear what they said about the person. The next day, the humiliated individual and his family would be the center of gossip. Thus, no *amina* dared to reveal herself or himself unless he or she had a death wish.

The *alqash,* or *musho awrag,* on the other hand, did his or her profession in the open. They were professionals whose skills were sought after every time someone died—someone who was important and could afford to pay. Usually, the *alqash* were residents of the town, or they could have been neighbors. Sometimes, however, they could have been people from other villages or towns. In the latter instance, the relatives of the deceased would provide the necessary information (e.g., name, age, marital status, occupation) of the deceased to the *alqash.* The *alqash* would sing with the stanza eulogizing the deceased: how he was a courageous soldier, if he had been one, or how he had been an expert hunter, and so on. If the deceased was a woman, a mother, the verses would have included how she was kind, generous, a beautiful wife, pretty, and skillful.

After the 1974 revolution, both the *amina* and the *alqash* lost their significance, especially the former. The military junta that espoused Marxism and Leninism denounced *amina* and the practice surrounding it as a backward feudal culture that was incompatible with the objectives of the Ethiopian revolution, social equality, and respect for the professions. The *alqash*, however, continued until the spread of the HIV/AIDS in Ethiopia. Due to the scores of individuals who were dying each day, people found it impossible to have *alqash* for each and every one of the deceased. Moreover, because the majority of Ethiopians associate HIV/AIDS with sexual infidelity, it is difficult to eulogize such a person. Finally, the Orthodox Church entreated the populace not to do such extravagant things since life and death is natural and God's will. Consequently, these days the role of *alqash* in public funerals has declined.[6]

TRADITIONAL MUSICIANS AND PERFORMERS, THE *AZIMARE*, IN PREREVOLUTION ETHIOPIA

In pre-20th-century Ethiopia, every royal court had an *azimare*, who accompanied the monarch wherever he or she went. Sylvia Pankhurst compared the *azimare* with "the bygone minstrels of England, the Celtic bards, the troubadours and rapsodes of ancient Greece." One might as well add that the *azimare* in Ethiopia was, more or less, an equivalent of the *griot* in West Africa. He sang songs praising the king and his accomplishments especially his fits in battle, his magnanimity, his kindness, and his courage. The *azimare* told the story, through his music, about the greatness of the king and his forefathers. The *azimare* brought forth the rumors and gossips in the royal court as well as the bitterness, grievances, and joy of the masses in the realm.

The best *azimare* was a person noted for his ambiguity and the use of words with double meanings, *samina-wariq* (lit. wax and gold). One of the reasons for such development was that despite the existence of an Ethiopic script to record music and its notations, secular folk music was never preserved in writing. The folk singers, the *azimare*, kept it memorized and it has been always open for modification. Also, in the tradition of the Ethiopian music, ambiguity "is considered an art form to make statements having multiple meanings—obvious and hidden. Ambiguity has been used in songs to say what one would never say or could not say in ordinary speech. Ambiguity is one of the building blocks that helps create tension and climactic points in musical composition. And in ordinary discourse, ambiguity is also a means of protection and for 'saving face.'"[7] Thus, using such skills, the *azimare* was not averse from admonishing the king or queen whenever he saw fit and for which he was often tolerated and even rewarded. A 19th-century French traveler who visited Ethiopia observed that the *azimare* were "in the service of the princes and nobility, . . . armed with their viols (*masenqo*), improvident friends of pleasure, living on their caustic or gay sprits, as children of the household—but sometimes as 'enfants terribles'. Their pointed tongues do not always spare the great lords of the manor who feeds them."[8] Pankhurst, on her part, noted that like the kings and emperors of Medieval Europe, Ethiopian "Emperor[s] and the nobles maintained their Azmaris. Though the mission of these retainers was to produce songs of praise and eulogy, they were allowed great license; their humorous sallies were often pointed with irony. . . . Their ballads embody chronicles of past and present Ethiopian history, extolling victory and honor, appealing to patriotic sentiment, reflecting Ethiopian public opinion."[9] Modeled after the royal court, regional lords and notables also had their own *azimare.*

While the general public and the notables had a disdain for the musician, *azimare,* the *azimare,* however, had a tremendous respect for his profession. The Ethiopian *azimare* claimed to be the direct descendants of Izra. According to the biblical story, when St. Mary was passing, it was Izra who played the *masinqo* while David played the *bagana* in order to ease the pain of death. Thus, the Ethiopian *azimare* ascertained that not only was their profession holy but that they were also the sole guardians of the *masinqo.* True to their claim, Burbox (a small village south of and a few kilometers away from the city of Gondar) was, and still is, the home of the majority of the *azimares* in Ethiopia. These *azimares* did not marry with other Ethiopians who were not *azimares.* They, girls and boys of Brobux, practiced to make and play the *masinqo* at a very early age. When they realized that they were good enough to play the *masinqo,* they left their village to go to a nearby rural town and thence to bigger cities like Gondar, Bahir Dar, Addis Ababa, the capital of Ethiopia.

While passing through these villages and towns, they would append to one of the local notables as a musician. The notable provided protection, food, and shelter while the musician was referred by the populace of the locality as so and so's *azimare.*

Like all African music, Ethiopian music was (and still is) participatory.[10] Hence, the audience also provided the *azimare* with verses, befitting the occasion such as eulogizing the royal court or congratulating the bride and bridegroom, the successful or unsuccessful hunter or the individual for whom the occasion was held. The verses often had double-meanings, which might have elicited a response in kind from the opposite quarter. The *azimare* would then modify the next stanza to fit the melody and then sing it. The person who provided the verse or the individual for whom the occasion was held rewarded the *azimare* with a rifle, a pistol, a cow, a calf, a dollar, or a drink. In prerevolution Ethiopia, the lord could offer the *azimare* a drink from his glass. The audience considered such a gesture as the utmost respect for the *azimare,* while the *azimare* viewed this act as an honor. The melody for most folk music was the same. What differed is the stanza and the skillfulness of the *azimare* in modifying and improvising the song.

ETHIOPIAN FOLK MUSIC AND DANCE

In traditional Ethiopia, everyone is expected to participate in singing and dancing, *esiksta,* which involves the rhythmic movement of the shoulder and neck, and the occasional shuffling of the legs. While there could be a singer or two, the dance is held in unisex groups and hence everyone is expected to partake.[11] To encourage participation, for instance during weddings, the singer/s will say, "Where is the brother," "where is the sister," "where is the mother," "where is the father," "where is the relative," and so on. To each question, the aforementioned family members will respond by joining the dancing and singing. While some of the songs allude to the bride's beauty, manner, and chaste, others console the bride. Some serve to remind the bride that she is not the only one who is getting married and leaving the comforts of her parents' home and that she should not be scared, for it is the fate of every female to be wedded and leave her parents to settle in her husband's home. Depending on the resources of the bride and groom, an *azimare* might be hired to enliven the singing and dance.

However, these days, the *azimare* are increasingly being replaced by "*yamuzeqa-band*" (music band). The "band," too, depends on the resources of the couple. A one-man band employs electronic synthesizers combined with vocal wedding songs. The well-to-do, however, employ a complete musical troupe.

On Ethiopian holidays such as *Inqutatash* (New Year), *Mesqael* (the Finding of the True Cross), and *Timqet* (Epiphany), Ethiopians of all ethnic groups and from all walks of life celebrate and dance. During such times, both men and women wear their traditional clothes. Women braid their hair in a variety of styles, while men often have theirs in afros. The New Year is celebrated on Meskerem 1 (September 11), which marks the end of the rainy season (winter) in Ethiopia. On that day, children collect a bunch of *Adey Ababa,* a deep-yellow colored flower which blooms only once a year, and go door-to-door giving them to the head of the household saying *inqutatash.* The person who receives the flowers replies "*beyametu yamitash*" (may the Lord bring you every year) and gives the children a blessing, food, or various gifts, including money. While roaming the neighborhood or village, they sing a group song called *Abebaye-hoy* (have you seen the flowers?).

However, the best dances are witnessed on *Mesqael* and during *Timqet*. While the Amhara and Tigre share a somewhat similar dance, the dance of the Oromo, Gurage, and Hadiyya greatly differs from that of the Amharas and Tigres as well as from each other. There is also dissimilarity within the ethnic groups. For instance, the Shoa Oromo dance style involves jumping high and imitating the movements of a man on a galloping horse. One of the Oromo dances from Wolloga (western Ethiopia) is done standing in two rows, one male and one female, facing each other. The men and women have each of their arms on the waist of the next person other. This formation involves the slight forward and backward movement of the upper body, and the shaking of the neck as well as shuffling of the legs. At the same time, the men utter synchronized guttural sounds that are in unison with the rhythm of the song. Sometimes, depending upon the occasion, the Wolloga Oromo also dance in circles that include a mix of both genders. This style is most common in wedding celebrations.

The dances of the Arusi (south central Ethiopia) and Harar (eastern Ethiopia) Oromo also differ from that of the Wolloga, and from each other.

The Arusi Oromo dance in two rows, one male and one female, standing face to face. The male dancer intertwines his chin with the female and moves his head in tandem with hers while humming. There is also a part of the dance in which the female kneels down and spins her head, both clockwise and counterclockwise.

There is a slight difference between the dance of the Harar and Arusi Oromo. The setup of the dance is the same as the Arusi. The only difference with the Harar is seen when the females bend forward in front of their

Hamer tribesmen performing jump dance, Omo Valley, Ethiopia, January 28, 2012. (Matej Hudovernik)

partners and move each of their arms back and forth alternatively. This is coupled with a rhythmic downward movement of the shoulders. While the women are dancing in this manner, the men hover above them and each man waves his hands above the head of his female partner. This difference arose between the Arusi and Harar Oromo dances primarily because of the Harar Oromos' interaction with the Somali and Muslim Arabs.

The Hadiyya and Walaetta dance resembles that of West Africa's. Much of the dance is done below the waist, with the periodic shaking of the waist coupled with a slight shuffling of the feet. This gives the female dancer a wave-like movement similar to the belly dancing move called shimming. The male dancer follows the female with rhythmic jumping and moving in tandem with her.

EXTERNAL INFLUENCE ON ETHIOPIAN MUSIC

However, by the 1920s, "Westernization" began taking its toll on Ethiopian music. While visiting the Holy Land, the then crown prince, Tefere Mekonen, met a group of Armenian refugees in Jerusalem. Seeing their circumstances and impressed by their musical skills, he offered them refuge in Ethiopia. These Armenians, who were also known as the Armenian Boys and Arba lijoch (the forty boys) interchangeably, became the first Ethiopian Brass Band. In the meantime, the Ethiopian government introduced Western education where schools employed English or French as mediums of instructions and where one of the subjects taught was European music. The Ethiopian government also accelerated the training of Ethiopians in Western Europe and the United States. Western-educated and oriented Ethiopians, foreign diplomats, and travelers provided the audience for Western-style music in Ethiopia. The army, which was the most modern institution in 20th-century Ethiopia, also organized marching brass bands styled after European armies. Soon, schools in Ethiopia followed suit.

During the Italian occupation, 1936–1941, Benito Mussolini instructed his generals to exterminate all *azimare* in Ethiopia. The *azimare,* with their music, were accused of extolling the gallantry of the forefathers against foreign invaders and encouraging people to join the patriotic resistance. As a result, a large majority of them were killed.[12]

The aforementioned circumstances and the desire of the Ethiopian elite to portray itself as "modern" slowly but surely began denting the influence of the clergy and its hold on traditional music and musicians, the *azimare,* on Ethiopian secular music. As Professor Ashenafi Kebede sums it,

> The artistic interaction between performers and audiences through spontaneous improvisation has been discontinued in contemporary musical practice. The traditional private and church schools are considered "archaic" and "old

fashioned"; the number of singers versed in poetry and melody (*kine-zema*) has fast diminished. . . . Those few performers of the traditional schools who survive are hired to play in the urban "orchestras" and dance bands; those who are dedicated to practicing the hereditary crafts do not find appreciative and knowledgeable audience to interact artistically with them.[13]

In addition, European musical concepts, institutions, sound structures, and practices such as the employment of salaried "artists," construction of theaters, charging fees of audiences, establishing musical bands and orchestras, employing salaried administrators, stage performance, and many more were introduced. Despite the establishment of *yebahil orkestra,* traditional or folklore ensemble, which was composed of *azimaeis,* traditional musical instruments such as *kirar* (bow-lyre), *bagana* (sacred box-lyre), and *masinqo* (fiddle), their purpose was to accompany single vocal melodies than as part of an ensemble. With this, and the development and introduction of the recording industry, radio and television, the significance and role of the *azimare* as entertainer and performer almost ended. In addition, the symbolic and historical significance of some of the traditional musical instruments of the Ethiopian Orthodox Church were manipulated and used for secular dance music.[14]

WESTERN INFLUENCE AND MUSIC TODAY

The forays of Western music on Ethiopian musical traditions were challenged with the emergence of independent African nations in the 1960s. All of a sudden, Ethiopians found themselves amid the new Africa where authentic Africanness was sought and celebrated. Because music is part of identity, the newly independent African countries looked to their traditional African musical roots rather than immediately following Western music.

As a contribution to pan-African ideas, the late Atse Haile Selassie gave scholarship to students of the newly independent African nations. The presence of African students in Ethiopia, who shunned colonial domination and anything associated with it, including Western music, gave Ethiopians a chance to rethink their musical test and heritage.

The 1960s was also a period of upheaval in America where the civil rights movement was challenging the status quo; and it should be noted that by then America had become a major destination for Ethiopian students, and American culture had become the fashion setter.

It may have been due to the aforementioned international and national encounters that Ethiopians decided to strengthen their "authentic" musical heritage. While the university sponsored and opened the Creative Arts Center in

1960, the Ministry of Education and Fine Arts established the Yared School of Music in 1967. At these schools, "required courses in Ethiopian sacred music, chant, liturgy, versification, and dance were offered by highly qualified masters. Renowned *azmare* artist-teachers were officially hired to give performance instruction on Ethiopian traditional instruments of music."[15]

However, the greatest revival of Ethiopian folk music occurred after the 1974 Socialist revolution in Ethiopia. The military junta (*Derg*), as part of its socialist principles and cultural revolution, encouraged the revival of Ethiopian traditional music, including war songs, *fukera-shilella,* which traditionally were used to motivate the warrior spirit. The profession of the *azimare,* which was relatively shunned and thus considered the occupation of the lower class during the imperial regime, was appreciated and sought after. The *Derg* organized the country into urban and rural associations; each association had a local, *kabale,* organization and each had a musical troupe, *yakabale kinat,* where every member of the *kabale* association was expected to participate regardless of gender or socioeconomic and age difference. These *kabale kinet* again were organized into higher, *kafitagna,* association and then into provincial musical troupe. Above all, the *Derg* tried to redress the prevalent national and ethnic inequality among the 80 or so ethnic groups of the country. By encouraging the establishment of ethnic musical groups, the *Derg* brought to the public's attention that Ethiopia is a multiethnic and multicultural society and that all are equal in the new Ethiopia.

Among the revived and highly sought professions, especially in light of many *kinat* (musical troupe) that badly needed professional performers and musicians as trainers, was the *azimare,* the traditional folk singer and performer. Thus, today we still have many *azimare* both in Ethiopia and abroad such as the United States. The observable change among the present-day *azimare* is that more and more the profession has become a one-man band, as opposed to the traditional where usually a man and a woman used to sing and perform. The one-man band, sometimes also one-woman, is usually accompanied by synthesizers and other electronic equipments. The audience, too, seems to have changed. In the old days, it was customary for the audience to provide stanza to the *azimare.* But these days either due to lack of knowledge and skill or because of the staged arrangement of the musical performance, there is little audience participation in music. The only thing that has visibly continued from the past is the participation of the audience in the traditional dance. This, too, is modified. The audience dances away from the stage and hence away from the *azimare,* or the band.

In addition to the audience–performer divide and the staged performance that we witness today as a result of Western influences on Ethiopian musical traditions, contemporary Ethiopian singers and performers began copying

Renowned Ethiopian composer and musicologist, Mulatu Astatiqe. (Jessica Rinaldi/ Reuters/Corbis)

some of the musical genre of the Western world, including Caribbean styles as early as the 1960s. Vocalists like Telahun Gessesse, Mehamud Ahmed, Muluqen Melese, Ali Birra, Alemeyhu Eshete, and Bizunesh Bekele were noted for infusing jazz in their singing style. Often people likened Alemayhu to James Brown while they called Bizunesh, Ethiopia's Aretha Franklin. Both singers were working for the Police Orchestra, while Telahun, who is famed as the king of Ethiopian music of the 1950–1970s, played for the Imperial Body Guard Orchestra. In the same period, Mulatu Astatiqe, a musicologist and composer, created what is now known as Ethio-Jazz. Outside of the various orchestras that were affiliated to one or the other sections of the Imperial Armed Forces (Air Force, Navy, Police, Body Guard, and Army), there were no musical bands in Ethiopia until the 1974 revolution, though nightclubs were common.[16] However, the emperor was noted to forbid the aforementioned singers from performing in night clubs. Hence, live music and entertainment was a privilege reserved for the few, the well-to-do Ethiopians.

A contemporary Ethiopian singer and performer who greatly influenced Ethiopian music is Aster Aweke. She began her musical career at an early age. Before her stardom in the 1980s, Aster performed in hotels and various local bands, including the Ibex (later named Roha after the 12th-century Ethiopian capital) in the Ethiopian capital. Her musical style resembles and incorporates some elements of jazz, soul, and R&B. Jeff Tamarkin, a historian of music and popular culture, who has also written songs for famous American singers such as the Beach Boys, Dean Martin, and many more, describes Aster's songs in the following way: "with their Memphis-style horn section, soulful keyboards and crackling drums," and it's immediately apparent why she's sometimes been dubbed the "African Aretha Franklin." Tamarkin also indicated that in addition to traditional Ethiopian musical style, Aster's songs exhibit the influences from "Lady Soul, along with the Godfather, James Brown, and vocally versatile jazz singers such as Ella Fitzgerald and Sarah Vaughan, loom largely in her roots, her deep R&B/funk groove a reminder that bridges are meant to be crossed."[17] One of her albums, *Kabu*, remained at the top of the College Music Journal's (CMJ) New Music Chart and stayed for 10 weeks as one of the top 10 albums on Billboard's World Music Charts in 1990.

Due to the repressive political climate in Ethiopia, Aster left for the United States in 1979 where her musical style matured and where she became an icon of modern Ethiopian music in Ethiopia and its Diaspora. Her concerts attract many fans from all over the world, both Ethiopians and non-Ethiopians. Aster has been a resident of Washington, D.C, since the late 1970s. She currently owns and runs an establishment in one of the blooming and most expensive quarters of Addis Ababa.

Tewodros Kassahun, otherwise known as Teddy Afro, is a young and rising star of contemporary music in Ethiopia. He is a singer and songwriter often equated with Bob Marley, "in part because of his ability to bring a political, spiritual, and rhythmic presence to his listeners,"[18] and in part because of the Reggae beat that his songs possess. While the 2001 album *Abugida*, named after the Ethiopian alphabet, brought him attention in Ethiopia and its Diaspora, the 2005 *Jah Yasteseryal* album strengthened his position as one of the rising stars whose songs have crossed boundaries between Ethiopian and Reggae musical genera. He is most admired by the younger generation of Ethiopians at home and abroad.

NOTES

1. Ashenafi Kebede, "The Sacred Chant of Ethiopian Monotheistic Churches: Music in Black Jewish and Christian Communities," *The Black Perspective in Music* 8, no. 1 (Spring, 1980): 25.

2. For a detailed history, use of notations and modes of the Ethiopian liturgical music, See Ashenafi, "The Sacred Chant," pp. 20–34; Michael Powne, *Ethiopian Music: An Introduction* (London: Oxford University Press, 1968), pp. 84–101;

Habita Mariam Assefa, *Ye-Etyopiya Tarik Tiyaqewochna Bahiloch* [Ethiopian History, Questions and Cultures], (Addis Ababa, 1986), pp. 539–42; Kay Kaufman Shelemay, Peter Jeffery, and Ingrid Monson, "Oral and Written Transmission in Ethiopian Christian Chant," *Early Music History* 12 (1993): 55–117; Abba Tito Lepisa, "The Three Modes and the Signs of the Songs in the Ethiopian Liturgy," *Proceedings of the Third International Conference of Ethiopian Studies*, Vol. II (Addis Ababa, Ethiopia: Institute of Ethiopian Studies, Haile Selassie I University, 1966), pp. 162–87.

3. Kay Kaufman Shelemay, "The Musician and Transmission of Religious Tradition: The Multiple Roles of the Ethiopian Dabtara," *Journal of Religion in Africa*, 22, Fasc. 3 (August, 1992): 242–60; Sylvia Pankhurst, *Ethiopia: A Cultural History* (Essex, England: Lalibella House, 1955), pp. 409–40.

4. See "Netsite for the Music in the Horn of Africa,"http://www.uni-mainz.de/Organisationen/ETHIOPIA/music/index.html (accessed January 7, 2008).

5. Shelemay, Jeffery, and Monson, "Oral and Written Transmission," p. 116.

6. For a detailed account of the different categories of singers and performers such as *lalibella* and *mush-awarag* see Kay Kaufman Shelemay, *A Song of Longing: An Ethiopian Journey* (Urbana: The University Press, 1991), p. 133; Michael Powne, *Ethiopian Music: An Introduction* (London: Oxford University Press, 1968), pp. 68–81.

7. Cynthia Tse Kimberlin, "The Scholarship and Art of Ashenafi Kebede (1938–1998)," *Ethnomusicology* 43, no. 2 (Spring–Summer, 1999): 321–32; See also Shelemay, *A Song*, pp. 14–15.

8. Quoted in Powne, *Ethiopian Music*, p. 61.

9. Pankhurst, *Ethiopia*, pp. 422–23.

10. Powne, *Ethiopian Music*, p. xxii.

11. There are a variety of wedding songs and dances in Ethiopia, a country of more than 75 ethnic groups and nationalities. According to a 1960s research there are more than 150 varieties of dances in Ethiopia. See György Martin, "Dance Types in Ethiopia," *Journal of the International Folk Music Council* 19 (1967): 23–27.

12. Pankhurst, *Ethiopia*, p. 423.

13. Ashenafi Kebede, "Zemenawi Muzika: Modern Trends in Traditional Secular Music of Ethiopia," *The Black Perspective in Music* 4, no. 3 (Autumn, 1976): 289–301.

14. Ashenafi, "Zemenawi Muzika," pp. 291–94.

15. Ashenafi, "Secular Music," p. 295.

16. Francis Falceto, *Abyssinie Swing: A Pictorial History of Modern Ethiopian Music* (Addis Ababa, Ethiopia: Shama Books, 2001); see also "Alemayhu Eshete's Biography," http://www.last.fm/music/Alemayehu+Eshete/+wiki (accessed February 6, 2008).

17. "African Legends: Aster Aweke," posted November 9, 2006,http://www.globalrhythm.net/AfricanLegends/AsterAweke.cfm (accessed February 5, 2008); see also African Musician Profiles, "Aster Aweke," http://www.africanmusiciansprofiles.com/asteraweke.htm (accessed February 5, 2008).

18. "Teddy Afro: Ethiopian Pop Music Artist," http://issues-in-focus.blogspot.com/2008/01/teddy-afro-ethiopian-pop-music-artist.html(accessed February 6, 2008).

Glossary

Abba	Father, title of a priest or a monk
Arba tsome	Lent season
Atakilt wot	Vegetarian dish
Atse	Niguse Negst (relatively similar to emperor)
Awash	An Ethiopian river that flows toward east, Djibouti
Azimare	Traditional musician, minstrel
Balg (belg)	Autumn
Bajirond	Treasurer
Bagana (begena)	Sacred box-lyre
Barbare (berbere)	Spiced chili, pepper powder
Brindo	Raw meat
Bu-naqalla	Roasted coffee beans mixed with spiced butter
Chagula bet	Bridal chamber
Dabo	Bread
Debtera	A learned man of the church, cleric
Dega	Highland (colder climatic zone)
Dejazimach	Commander of the center
Demera	Ash Wednesday
Derg (Darg)	Military junta

Doro wot	Chicken stew
Due'a	Ethiopian Muslim prayer
Esiksta	Ethiopian traditional dance
Finjal or sine	Coffee cups
Fitawrare	Commander of the front
Fukera-shilella	Ethiopian war song
Gada	An age-grade system practiced among the Oromo
Genna or Lidet	Christmas
Gered	Domestic servant
Gragn	The left handed, also known as Ahmad Ibn Ibrahim Al-ghazi or Gragn Ahmad
Grazimach	Commander of the left
Id-al-fatir	The end of the Fasting of Ramadan, the Muslim fasting month
Inqutatash	New Year
Itan-machesha	Incense burner, often made of clay
Jebenna	Small clay pot, usually used for making coffee
Kebele	Urban neighborhood (local) association
Kebero	Drum
Kefitegna	Higher (an amalgam of many locals) urban dweller's association
Kegnazimach	Commander of the right
Kentiba	Mayor
Kinet	Musical troupe
Kirar	Bow-lyre
Liul	Prince
Lielt	Princess
Masinqo	A single bowed spike lute or fiddle
Mawiled	The birth of the prophet Mohammad
Mekir Bet	Parliament
Melekt	Long trumpet
Menzuma	Ethiopian Muslim chant
Mesqael	The Finding of the True Cross
Milikit	Notations
Mitad	A round clay pan used for backing *injera*

Mugecha	Mortar, usually made of wood
Nech Shinkurt	Garlic
Nigeste Negestat	Queen of queens (relatively to empress)
Nigst	Queen
Nigus	King
Niguse Negsit	King of kings (relatively similar to emperor)
Qay shinkurt	Red onions
Qimama-qimam	Various spices
Qolla	Lowland (hotter climatic zone)
Qollo	Roasted wheat or barley mixed with spiced butter
Qurban	Holy Communion
Qutti	Coffee made from roasted coffee leaves
Ramadan	The Muslim fasting season
Ras	Head of the army
Ras Dajen (Ras Dashan)	The highest mountain in Ethiopia
Rekebot	Coffee table, often made of wood or grass
Sanbat	Sabbath
Sefer (mender)	Neighborhood
Shema	A locally made cotton cloth
Simt Sheleqo	Rift Valley
Sinasil	Sistrum
Tabot (Silat)	A replica of the Ark of the Covenant
Tadjoura	Gulf of Djibouti
Teji	Honey mead
Tejibet	Honey mead house, a place where honey mead is sold
Telefa	Abduction
Tella	Homemade beer
Timqet	Epiphany
Tinsae	Easter
Tsome (Som)	Fasting
Washint	Flute
Wot	Stew
Woyna-dega	Temperate (climatic zone)
Yefedereshn Mekir Bet	Federal Parliament
Ye-shnibra assa	Chickpea fish stew

Yetsom wot	Fasting dish
Zamana Masafent	Era of the Princes
Zar	Cult/possession
Zayit	Cooking oil
Zenezena	Wooden pestle

Bibliography

CHAPTER 1: INTRODUCTION

Abir, Mordechi. *Ethiopia and the Red Sea*. London: Frank Cass, 1980.

Alvarez, F. *The Prester John of the Indies*, II vols, edited by C. F. Beckingham and G. W. B. Huntingford. London: Hakluyt Society, 1961.

Aregay, Merid W. "Land Tenure and Agricultural Productivity, 1500–1850." *Proceedings of the Third Annual Seminar of the Department of History*, Addis Ababa University, Ethiopia, 1986.

Aregay, Merid W. "Population Movements as a Possible Factor in Muslim-Christian Conflict of Medieval Ethiopia." Symposium Leo Frobenius, Munich, 1974.

Aregay, Merid W. "Society and Technology in Ethiopia, 1500–1800." *Journal of Ethiopian Studies* XVII (1984).

Bekele, Shiferaw. "The Evolution of Land Tenure in the Imperial Period." In *An Economic History of Modern Ethiopia, 1941–1974*, edited by Shiferaw Bekele. Dakar, Senegal: CODESRIA, 1995.

Bekele, Shiferaw. "The State in the *Zemena Masafent* (1786–1853): An Essay in Interpretation." In *Kassa and Kassa; Papers on the Lives, Times and Images of Tewodros II and Yohannes IV (1855–1889)*, edited by Taddesse Beyene, R. Pankhurst, and Shiferaw Bekele, 25–68. Addis Ababa, Ethiopia: Institute of Ethiopian Studies, 1990.

Bender, M. I. *Languages of Ethiopia*. London: Oxford University Press, 1976.

Berkley, G. F. H. *The Campaign of Adwa and the Rise of Minilek*. London: 1936.

Besah, Girma, and Merid Wolde Aregay. *The Question of the Union of Churches in Luso-Ethiopian Relations, 1500–1632*. Lisbon, Portugal: Centro de Estudos Historicos Ultramarinos, 1964, 37–52.

Bruce, James. *Travels to Discover the Source of the Nile in the Years 1768, 1769, 1770, 1771, 1772 and 1773*, 5 vols. London: G.G.J. and J. Robinson, 1790.

Caraman, Philip. *The Lost Empire: The Story of the Jesuits in Ethiopia, 1555–1634.* NotreDame: University of Notre Dame Press, 1985.

Caulk, Richard. "Firearms and Princely Power in Nineteenth Century Ethiopia." *Journal of African History* XII (1974): 4.

Caulk, Richard. "Religion and State in Nineteenth Century Ethiopia." *Journal of Ethiopian Studies* XIII (1975): 1.

Crummey, Donald. *Land and Society in the Christian Kingdom of Ethiopia from Thirteenth to the Twentieth Century.* Urbana-Champaign: University of Illinois Press, 2000, 73–93, 144–61.

Donham, D., and W. James, eds. *The Southern Marches of Imperial Ethiopia.* Cambridge: Cambridge University Press, 1986.

Doresse, Jean. *Ethiopia: Ancient Cities and Temples.* London, 1959.

Fisseha, Abebe. "Education and the Formation of the Modern Ethiopian State, 1896–1974." Ph.D. Dissertation, University of Illinois, 2000.

Hassen, Mohammed. *The Oromo of Ethiopia: A History, 1570–1850.* Cambridge: Cambridge University Press, 1990, 1–47, 84–113, 202–9, 214–19.

Huntingford, G. W. B., trans. *The Land Charters of Northern Ethiopia.* Addis Ababa, Ethiopia: IES, 1965.

Kaplan, Steven. *The Monastic Holyman and the Christianization of Early Solomonic Ethiopia.* Wiesbaden, Germany: Franz Steiner Verlag Wiesbaden GMBH, 1984, 103–8, 109–32.

Kobishanov, Youri. *Axum.* University Park: Pennsylvania State University Press, 1966.

Marcus, Harlod. *The Life and Times of Menelik II: Ethiopia, 1844–1913.* Oxford: Clarendon Press, 1975.

Pankhurst, Richard. *An Introduction to the Economic History of Ethiopia from Early Times to 1800.* London: Lalibela House, 1961.

Pankhurst, Richard. *A Social History of Ethiopia.* Addis Ababa, Ethiopia: Institute of Ethiopian Studies, 1990.

Phillipson, David. *Foundations of an African Civilization, Aksum and the Northern Horn, 1000 B.C.–AD 1300.* Croydon, England: James Currey, 2012, 19–69.

Rubenson, Sven. *King of Kings Tewodros of Ethiopia.* Addis Ababa, Ethiopia: Oxford University Press, 1996.

Rubenson, Sven. *The Survival of Ethiopian Independence.* London, 1976.

Rubenson, Sven. *Wichale XVII: An Attempt to Establish A Protectorate over Ethiopia.* Addis Ababa, Ethiopia: Artistic Printing Press, 1964.

Selassie, Sergew Hable. *Ancient and Medieval Ethiopian History to 1270.* Addis Ababa, Ethiopia: Artistic Printers, 1972, 11–18.

Tafla, Bairu. *A Chronicle of Emperor Yohannes IV, 1872–1889.* Wiesbaden, Germany: Franz Steiner Verlag GMBH, 1977.

Tamrat, Taddesse. *Church and State in Ethiopia, 1270–1527.* Oxford: Clarendon Press, 1972.

Tamrat, Taddesse. "Ethiopia, the Red Sea, and the Horn." In *The Cambridge History of Africa from c. 1050–c. 1600*, Vol. III, edited by Roland Oliver. Cambridge: Cambridge University Press, 1977.

Tamrat, Taddesse. "The Horn of Africa: The Solomonids in Ethiopia the States of the Horn of Africa." In *UNESCO General History of Africa: Africa from the Twelfth to the Sixteenth Century*, Vol. IV, edited by D. T. Niane, 423–54. Berkeley, CA: Heinemann, 1984.

Tamrat, Taddesse. "Some Notes on the Fifteenth Century Stephanite 'Heresy' in the EthiopianChurch." *Rasagna di Studi Etiopici*. Roma, 1968.

Trimingham, J. S. *Islam in Ethiopia*. London: Frank Cass & Co. Ltd. 1965.

Wolde-Mariam, Mesfin. *An Introductory Geography of Ethiopia*. Addis Ababa, Ethiopia: Brehanena Selam Printing Press, 1972.

Wolde-Mariam, Tekalign. "Slavery and Slave Tradein the Kingdom of Jimma, ca. 1800–1935." M.A. Thesis, Department of History, Addis Ababa University, 1984.

Zewde, Bahru. "The Concept of Japanization in the Intellectuals History of Modern Ethiopia." *Proceedings of the Fifth Seminar of the Department of History*, Addis Ababa, 1990.

Zewde, Bahru. "Concessions and Concession-Hunters in Post Adwa Ethiopia: The Case of Arnold Holz." *Rivista trimestrale di Studi e Documentazione dell'Instituto Italo-Africano* 45, no. 3 (1990).

Zewde, Bahru. *A History of Modern Ethiopia, 1855–1991*. Addis Ababa, Ethiopia: Addis Ababa University Press, 2002.

Zewde, Bahru. *Pioneers of Change in Ethiopia: The Reformist Intellectuals of the Early Twentieth Century*. Oxford: James Currey, 2002.

CHAPTER 2: RELIGION AND WORLDVIEW

Ahmed, Hussein. "Historiography of Islam in Ethiopia." *Journal of Islamic Studies* III, no. 1 (1992): 15–46.

Ahmed, Hussein. *Islam in Nineteenth-Century Wallo, Ethiopia: Revival, Reform and Reaction*. Leiden, The Netherlands: MacMillan & Co., 1860.

Alvarez, Francisco. *The Prester John of the Indies*, translated and edited by Beckingham and Huntingford. Cambridge: Cambridge University Press, 1961.

Besah, Girma, and Merid Wolde Aregay. *The Question of the Union of Churches in Luso-Ethiopian Relations, 1500–1632*. Lisbon, Portugal: Centro de Estudos Historicos Ultramarinos, 1964, 37–52.

Braukamper, Ulrich. *Islamic History and Culture in Southern Ethiopia, Collected Essays*. Munster, Germany: LIT Verlag, 2002, 12–104.

Federal Democratic Republic of Ethiopia, Office of Population and Housing Census Commission, Central Statistics Authority, The 2007 Census.

Kassu, Wudu Tafete. "The Ethiopian Orthodox Church, The Ethiopian State and the Alexandrian See: Indigenizing the episcopacy and Forging National Identity, 1926–1991." Ph.D. Dissertation, University of Illinois at Urbana-Champaign, 2006.

Selassie, Sergew Hable. *Ancient and Medieval Ethiopian History to 1270.* Addis Ababa, Ethiopia: Artistic Printers, 1972. pp. 11–18.

Tamrat, Taddesse. *Church and State in Ethiopia, 1270–1527.* Oxford: Clarendon Press, 1972.

Tamrat, Taddesse. "Ethiopia, the Red Sea, and the Horn." In *The Cambridge History of Africa from c. 1050–c. 1600,* Vol. III, edited by Roland Oliver. Cambridge: Cambridge University Press, 1977.

Tamrat, Taddesse. "The Horn of Africa: The Solomonids in Ethiopia the States of the Horn of Africa." In *UNESCO General History of Africa: Africa from the Twelfth to the Sixteenth Century,* Vol. IV, edited by D. T. Niane, 423–54. Berkeley, CA: Heinemann, 1984.

Chapter 3: Literature and Media

Caraman, Philip. *The Lost Empire: The Story of the Jesuits in Ethiopia, 1555–1634.* Notre Dame: University of Notre Dame Press, 1985.

Fusella, Luigi, ed. *Yate Tewodros Tarik.* Rome, 1959. (writer unknown).

Gabra-Selassie. *Tarika Zaman Za Dagmawi Minilek Nigusa Nagast Za Ityopiya.* Addis Ababa, Ethiopia: Berhanena Salam Printing Press, 1959 E.C.

Gebre Selassie, Zewde. *Yohannes IV of Ethiopia, A Political Biography.* Oxford: Clarendon Press, 1975.

Haile-Selassie. *Heywotena Ya Ityopiya Ermejja.* Addis Ababa, Ethiopia: Berhanena Salam Printing Press, 1965 E.C.

Kassu, Wudu Tafete. "The Twin Churches of Raguel, 1889 to 1985." B.A. Thesis, Department of History, Addis Ababa University, 1989.

Molvaer, Reidulfk. *Black Lions: The Creative Lives of Modern Ethiopia's Literary Giants and Pioneers.* Lawrenceville, NJ: The Red Sea Press, 1997.

Muche, Bilal. "History of the Ethiopian Electric Light and Power Authority (EELPA),1956–1974." B.A. Thesis, Department of History, Addis Ababa University, 1995.

Pankhurst, Richard. *A Social History of Ethiopia.* Addis Ababa, Ethiopia: Institute of Ethiopian, 1990.

Tafla, Bairu, ed. and trans. *Asma Giyorgis and His Work: History of the Galla* (sic) *and the Kingdom of Sawa.* Stuttgart, Germany: Franz Steiner Verlag Wiesbaden Gambh, 1987.

Tafla, Bairu. *A Chronicle of Emperor Yohannes IV, 1872–1889.* Wiesbaden, Germany: Franz Steiner Verlag GMBH, 1977.

Tamrat, Taddesse. *Church and State in Ethiopia, 1270–1527.* Oxford: Clarendon Press, 1972.

Tarekegn, Ayele. "The History of the Imperial Highway Authority (IHA). 1951–1980." B.A. Thesis, Department of History, Addis Ababa University, 1987.

Temesgen, Mekonnen. "The History of Berhanena Selam Printing Press, 1921–1957." B.A. Thesis, Department of History, Addis Ababa University, 1990.

Tewodros, Assefa. "History of Telecommunications in Ethiopia up to 1974." B.A. Thesis, Department of History, Addis Ababa University, 1985.

Walda-Maryam. *Chronique de Theodros II, Roi Des Rois d'Ethiopie, 1853–1868*, edited and translated by C. Mondon-Vidailhet. Paris: Libraire Orientale & Americaine, 1904.

Zeleke, Hailu. "A History of Ethiopian Television, ETV, 1964–1991." B.A. Thesis, Department of History, Addis Ababa University, 1998.

Zeneb (*Dabtara*). *Ya Tewodros Tarik*, edited by Enno Littmann. Princeton: The University Library, 1902.

Zewde, Bahru. *A History of Modern Ethiopia, 1855–1991*. Addis Ababa, Ethiopia: Addis Ababa University Press, 2002.

Zewde, Bahru. *Pioneers of Change in Ethiopia: The Reformist Intellectuals of the Early Twentieth Century*. Addis Ababa, Ethiopia: Addis Ababa University Press, 2002. Studies, 1990.

CHAPTER 4: ARCHITECTURE AND ART

Alehegn, Tseday. "Maitre Afeworq Tekele's Odyssey." *Tadias: Ethiopian-American Lifestyle Magazine* II, no. II (June–July 2004), http://www.tadias.com/v1n7/coverstory.html.

Amos, Francis J. C. "A Development Plan for Addis Ababa." *Ethiopia Observer* VI, no. 1 (1962).

Bekele, Shiferaw. "A Modernizing State and the Emergence of Modern Art in Ethiopia (1030s–1970s) with Special Reference to Gebre Kristos Desta (1932–1981) and Skunder Boghossian (1937–2003)." *Journal of Ethiopian Studies* XXXVII, no. 2 (December 2004).

Chojnacki, Stanislaw. "Attempts at the Periodization of Ethiopian Painting: A Summary from 1960 to Present." In *Proceedings of the Six International Conference of Ethiopian Art*, edited by Birhanu Teferra and Richard Pankhurst. Addis Ababa, Ethiopia: Institute of Ethiopian Studies, 2003.

Chojnacki, Stanislaw. "Gebre Kristos Desta: Four Years Later." *Ethiopia Observer* XI, no. 3 (1967).

Chojnacki, Stanislaw. "Gebre Kristos Desta: Impressions of His Recent Exhibition." *Ethiopia Observer* XIV, no. 1 (1971).

Chojnacki, Stanislaw. "Gebre Kristos Desta: Some Press Comments from Germany." *Ethiopia Observer* XIV, no. 1 (1970).

Debre Hayq Ethiopian Art Gallery online, accessed February 16, 2008, http://www.ethiopianart.org/articles/index.php.

Deressa, Solomon. "Gebre Kristos Desta: Somber Colors and Incantatory Words." *Ethiopia Observer* XI, no. 3 (1967).

Deressa, Solomon. "Skunder: In Retrospect Precociously." *Ethiopia Observer* X, no. 3 (1966).

Doresse, Jean. *Ethiopia: Ancient Cities and Temples*. London: G.P. Putnam's Sons, 1959.

Fisseha, Girma. "The Ethiopian Avant-Grade in the Thirties and 'Tejbet' Painting." In *Proceedings of the History of Ethiopian Art*, edited by Birhanu Teferra and Richard Pankhurs. Addis Ababa, Ethiopia: Institute of Ethiopian Studies, 2003.

Fisseha, Girma. "Ethiopian Folk Art Painting." In *Proceedings of the First International Conferenceon the History of Ethiopian Art*, edited by Birhanu Teferra and Richard Pankhurs. London: The Pindar Press, 1989.

Fisseha, Girma. "The Hunt in Ethiopian Folk Art." In *Proceedings of the First International Conference on the History of Ethiopian Art*, edited by Birhanu Teferra and Richard Pankhurs. London: The Pindar Press, 1989.

The Fourth Annual Blen Art Show. "Honoring the Painter-Poite Gebre Kristos Desta," http://www.blenartshow.com/fourth/honorary.htm.

The Fourth Annual Blen Art Show. http://www.blenartshow.com/fourth/gallery.htm.

Getahun, Solomon A. *A History of the City of Gondar.* Newark, NJ: Africa World Press, 2006.

Giorgis, Elsabet W. "Modernist Spirits: The Images of Skunder Boghossian." *Journal of Ethiopian Studies* XXXVII, no. 2 (December 2004).

Giorgis, Elsabet W. "Skunder Boghossian: Artist of the Universal and the Specific," http://www.the3rdman.com/ethiopianart/articles/boghossian.html.

Harney, Elizabeth. "The Poetics of Diaspora." In *Ethiopian Passages: Contemporary Art from the Diaspora.* London: Philip Wilson Publishers, 2003.

Head, Sydney W. "A Conversation with Gebre Kristos Desta." *African Arts* 2, no. 4 (Summer 1969).

"Julie Mehretu." White Cube, http://www.whitecube.com/artists/mehretu/paintings one/.Kobishchanov, Yuri M. *Aksum.* University Park: Pennsylvania State University Press, 1979.

Medhin, Esseye G. "Ale Felege Selam: The Modernization of Art." Debre Hayq Ethiopian Art Gallery (May 29, 2007), http://www.ethiopianart.org/articles/articles.php?id=80.

National Museum of African Arts. "Ethiopian Passages: Dialog in the Diaspora," http://africa.si.edu/exhibits/passages/boghossian.html#.

Pankhurst, Richard. "The Battle of Adwa (1896) as Depicted by Traditional Ethiopian Artists." In *Proceedings of the First International Conference on the History of Ethiopian Art*, edited by Birhanu Teferra and Richard Pankhurs. London: The Pindar Press, 1989.

Pankhurst, Richard. *History of Ethiopian Towns from the Middle Ages to the Early Nineteenth Century.* Wiesbaden, Germany: Steiner, 1982.

Pankhurst, Richard. *History of Ethiopian Towns: From the Mid-Nineteenth Century to 1935.* Stuttgart, Germany: Franz Steiner Verlag Wiesbaden GMBH, 1985.

Phillipson, David W. *Ancient Ethiopia, Aksum: Its Antecedents and Successors.* London: British Museum Press, 1998.

Quaranta, Ferdinando. *Ethiopia, An Empire in the Making.* London: P.S. King, 1939.

Ramos, Manuel Joao, and Isabel Boavida, eds. *The Indigenous and the Foreign in Christian Ethiopian Art.* Burlington, VT: Ashgate Pub. Co., 2004.

RKPP. "The Art of Afeworq Tekele." *Ethiopia Observer* IX, no. 3 (1965).

Sellassie, Sergew Hable. *Ancient and Medieval Ethiopian History to 1270.* Addis Ababa, Ethiopia: United Printers, 1972.

"Sir Patrick Abercrombie's Town Plan." *Ethiopia Observer* I, no. 2 (March 1957).

Unknown. "Afework Tekele." *Ethiopia Observer* VI, no. 3 (1962).

Wax, Emily. "Ambitious Plans for Ethiopia's Capital: Mayor Envisions Addis Ababa as Hub for E. Africa." *Washington Post,* June 11, 2004, A14.

CHAPTER 5: CUISINE AND TRADITIONAL DRESS

Ayele, Tizita. *Ethiopian Cooking in the American Kitchen.* New York: Vantage Press, 1998.

Bekele, Girma. *Ethiopian & Foreign Cook Guide Book.* Addis Ababa, Ethiopia: Team Work, 1992.

Caplan, P. *Feasts, Fasts, Famine: Food for Thought.* Providence, RI: Berg, 1994.

Cassanelli, L. V. "QAT: Changes in the Production and Consumption of a Quasilegal Commodity in North-East Africa." In *The Social Life of Things: Commodities in Cultural Perspective,* edited by A. Appadurai. New York: Cambridge University Press, 1986.

Cusack, Igor. "African Cuisines: Recipes for Nation-Building?" *Journal of African Cultural Studies* 13, no. 2 (December 2000).

Douglas, M. "Deciphering a Meal." *Myth, Symbol and Culture,* edited by C. Geertz. New York: Norton, 1971.

Ethiopian Nutrition Institute. *Traditional Recipes* (Mimeographed). Addis Ababa, 1969.

Kifleyesus, Abbebe. "Muslims and Meals: The Social and Symbolic Function of Foods in Changing Socio-Economic Environments." *Africa: Journal of the International African Institute* 72, no. 2 (2002).

Legesse, Asmarom. *Oromo Democracy: An Indigenous African Political System.* Lawrenceville, NJ: Red Sea Press, 2000.

McCann, James. "Maize and Grace: History, Corn, and Africa's New Landscapes, 1500–1999." *Comparative Studies in Society and History* 43, no. 2 (April 2001).

Merkato Market. *Taste of Ethiopia: A Collection of Delicious Vegetarian and Traditional Recipes and Products. Revised and Extended Edition Including Most Popular Food and Spices.* Washington, DC, 1991.

Mesfin, Daniel J. *Exotic Ethiopian Cooking: Society, Culture, Hospitality, and Traditions. Revised Extended Edition. 178 Tested Recipes. With Food Composition Tables.* Falls Church, VA: Ethiopian Cookbook Enterprises, 1990.

Norden, Hermann. *Africa's Last Empire: Through Abyssinia to Lake Tana and the Country of the Falasha.* London: H. F. & G. Witherby, 1930.

Oculi, Okello. *Discourses on African Affairs.* New Jersey and Asmara: Trento, Eritrea: African World Press, 2000.

Osseo-Asare, Fran. *Food Culture in Sub-Saharan Africa.* Westport, CT: Greenwood Press, 2005.

Phillipson, David W. "The Antiquity of Cultivation and Herding in Ethiopia," In *The Archaeology of Africa: Food, Metals and Towns,* edited by Thurstan Shaw, et al. New York: Routledge, 1993.

Plowden, Walter C. *Travels in Abyssinia & the Galla Country with an Account of Mission to Ras Ali in 1848.* London: Longmans, Green, and CO., 1868.

Rey, C. F. *The Real Abyssinia*. Philadelphia: J. B. Lippincott Company, 1935.

Salamon, Hagar. *The Hyena People: Ethiopian Jews in Christian Ethiopia*. Berkeley: University of California Press, 1999.

Salt, Henry. *A Voyage to Abyssinia and Travels into the Interior of That Country: Executed under the Orders of the British Government in the Years 1809 and 1810*. London: Frank Cass & J. Rivington, 1814.

Shack, William A. *The Gurage: A People of the Ensete Culture*. London: Oxford University Press, 1966.

Shack, William A. "The Masqal-Pole: Religious Conflict and Social Change in Gurageland." *Africa: Journal of the International African Institute* 38, no. 4 (October 1968).

Simoons, Frederick J. *Northwest Ethiopia: Peoples and Economy*. Madison: The University of Wisconsin Press, 1960.

Turner, V. W. *The Forest of Symbols: Aspects of Ndembu Ritual*. Ithaca, NY: Cornell University Press, 1967.

CHAPTER 6: GENDER ROLES, MARRIAGE, AND FAMILY

Adugna, Minale. *Women and Warfare in Ethiopia: A Case Study of Their Role during the Campaign of Adwa, 1895/96, and the Italo-Ethiopian War, 1935–41*. Addis Ababa, Ethiopia: Organization for Social Science Research in Eastern and Southern Africa, 2001.

Arrighi, Barbara A., and David J. Maume, Jr. "Workplace Subordination and Men's Avoidance of Housework." *Journal of Family Issues* 21, no. 4 (May 2000).

Baraki, Tesfu. *Culture, Society and Women in Ethiopia*, supervised and edited by Seyoum Gebre Selassie. Addis Ababa, Ethiopia: Ethiopian Women Lawyers Association, 1997.

Berry, Eileen Hadley. "The African Family-Household: A Behavioral Model." Ph.D. Dissertation, Clark University, Worcester, Massachusetts, 1981.

Bissrat, Zenebework. "Research Priorities on Women Education and Employment in Ethiopia." In *Women and Development in Eastern Africa: An Agenda for the Research*, edited by Zeinab El-Bakri and Ruth M Besha. Addis Ababa, Ethiopia: Organization for Social Science Research in Eastern Africa, 1989.

Crummey, Donald. "Abyssinian Feudalism." *Past and Present*, no. 89 (November 1980).

Crummey, Donald. "Family and Property amongst the Amhara Nobility." *The Journal of African History* 24, no. 2.

Crummey, Donald. *The History of the Family in Africa*. (1983).

Dagne, Haile Gabriel. "Early Marriage in Northern Ethiopia: Motherhood, Fatherhood and Fertility: For Women Who Do and Women Who Don't Have Children." *Reproductive Health Matters* 2, no. 4 (November, 1994).

Ejigu, Gebeyehu. "Educational Planning and Educational Development in Ethiopia: 1957–1973." Ph.D. Dissertation, University of Wisconsin-Madison, 1980.

Ellis, Gene. "The Feudal Paradigm as a Hindrance to Understanding Ethiopia." *The Journal of Modern African Studies* 14, no. 2 (June, 1976).

Fafchamps, Marcel, and Agnes R. Quisumbing. "Marriage, Bequest, and Assortative Matching in Rural Ethiopia." *Economic Development and Cultural Change* 53, no. 2 (January 2005).

Fafchamps, Marcel, and Agnes R. "Marriage, Bequest, and Assortative Matching." *Studies in Family Planning* 30, no. 4 (December 1999).

Gamst, Frederick C. "Peasantries and Elites without Urbanism: The Civilization of Ethiopia." *Comparative Studies in Society and History* 12, no. 4 (October 1970).

Goody, Jack. "Class and Marriage in Africa and Eurasia." *The American Journal of Sociology* 76, no. 4 (January 1971).

Goody, Jack, and S. J. Tambiah. *Bride Wealth and Dowry*. Cambridge: Cambridge University Press, 1973.

Haile-Selassie, Teferra. *The Ethiopian Revolution 1974–1991: From A Monarchial Autocracy to a Military Oligarchy*. London: Kegan Paul International, 1997.

Haile, Tsigie. "Academic Performance of Female Students in Institutes of Higher Education: The Case of Addis Ababa University." In *Women and Development in Eastern Africa: An Agenda for the Research*, edited by Zeinab El-Bakri and Ruth M. Besha. Addis Ababa, Ethiopia: Organization for Social Science Research in Eastern Africa, 1989.

Harbeson, John W. "Socialism, Traditions, and Revolutionary Politics in Contemporary Ethiopia." *Canadian Journal of African Studies* 11, no. 2 (1977).

Hogan, Dennis P., Betemariam Berhanu, and Assefa Hailemariam. "Household Organization, Women's Autonomy, and Contraceptive Behavior in Southern Ethiopia." *Studies in Family Planning* 30, no. 4 (December 1999).

Kaplan, Steven. "Seen but Not Heard: Children and Childhood in Medieval Ethiopian Hagiographies." *The International Journal of African Historical Studies* 30, no. 3 (1997).

Kiwanena Raey: Ye-Ethyopiya Setoch Inqisiqase Ba-20gnaw Kifle-Zaman [Objectives and Accomplishments of Ethiopian Women's Movement in the 20th Century]. Addis Ababa, Ethiopia: Prime Minister' Office Women's Affairs Subdivision, 2000.

Koehn, Peter H. *Refugee from Revolution: U.S. Policy and Third-World Migration*. Boulder, CO: Westview Press, 1991.

Leitman, Marion Eva. "Ethiopian Immigrant Women: Transition to a New Israeli Identity? (Volumes I and II)." Ph.D. Dissertation, Ohio State University, 1993.

Markakis, John. *Ethiopia: Anatomy of a Traditional Polity*. Oxford: Clarendon Press, 1974.

Martin, György. "Dance Types in Ethiopia." *Journal of the International Folk Music Council* 19 (1967).

Mengesha, Aster G. M. "Gender and Democracy in Africa." *Ethiopian Register* (March 1999).

Negarit Gazeta. Negarit Gazeta of the Federal Democratic Republic of Ethiopia, August 21, 1995.

Potash, Betty. "Women in the Changing African Family." In *African Women South of the Sahara*, 2nd ed., edited by Margaret Jean Hay and Sharon Stichter. London: Longman Group Limited, 1995.

Reminick, Ronald A. "The Symbolic Significance of Ceremonial Defloration among the Amhara of Ethiopia." *American Ethnologist* 3, no. 4 (November 1976).

Robertson, Claire. "Women in the Urban Economy." In *African Women South of the Sahara*, 2nd ed., edited by Margaret Jean Hay and Sharon Stichter. London: Longman Group Limited, 1995.

Sereke-Brhan, Heran. "Building Bridges, Drying Blood: Elite Marriages, Politics and Ethnicity in 19th and 20th Century Imperial Ethiopia." Ph.D. Dissertation, Michigan State University, 2002.

Tiruneh, Andargachew. *The Ethiopian Revolution, 1974–1987: A Transformation from an Aristocratic to a Totalitarian Autocracy.* Cambridge: Cambridge University Press, 1993.

UN Office for the Coordination of Humanitarian Affairs. *UNIRN News*, "Ethiopia: Women's Empowerment Vital for Development–Government" (June 24, 2002); UNICEF, Girl-Education and Gender Parity (III) (January 24, 2006).

Wagaw, Teshome G. *The Development of Higher Education and Social Change: An Ethiopian Experience.* East Lansing: Michigan State University, 1990.

CHAPTER 7: SOCIAL CUSTOMS AND LIFESTYLES

Andargachew Tiruneh. *The Ethiopian Revolution, 1974–1987: A Transformation from an Aristocratic to a Totalitarian Autocracy.* Cambridge: Cambridge University Press, 1993.

Harbeson, John W. "Socialism, Traditions, and Revolutionary Politics in Contemporary Ethiopia." *Canadian Journal of African Studies* 11, no. 2 (1977).

Martin, György. "Dance Types in Ethiopia." *Journal of the International Folk Music Council* 19 (1967).

Teferra Haile-Selassie. *The Ethiopian Revolution 1974–1991: From A Monarchial Autocracy to a Military Oligarchy.* London: Kegan Paul International, 1997.

CHAPTER 8: MUSIC AND DANCE

"African Legends: Aster Aweke." Posted November 9, 2006, accessed February 5, 2008, http://www.globalrhythm.net/AfricanLegends/AsterAweke.cfm.

African Musician Profiles. "Aster Aweke," accessed February 5, 2008, http://www.africanmusiciansprofiles.com/asteraweke.htm.

"Alemayhu Eshete's Biography," accessed February 6, 2008, http://www.last.fm/music/Alemayehu+Eshete/+wiki.

Assefa, Habita Mariam. *Ye-Etyopiya Tarik Tiyaqewochna Bahiloch.* Addis Ababa, Ethiopia: Ethiopian History, Questions and Cultures, 1986EC.

Falceto, Francis. *Abyssinie Swing: A Pictorial History of Modern Ethiopian Music.* Addis Ababa, Ethiopia: Shama Books, 2001.

Kebede, Ashenafi. "The Sacred Chant of Ethiopian Monotheistic Churches: Music in Black, Jewish and Christian Communities." *The Black Perspective in Music* 8, no. 1 (Spring 1980).

Kebede, Ashenafi. "Zemenawi Muzika: Modern Trends in Traditional Secular Music of Ethiopia." *The Black Perspective in Music* 4, no. 3 (Autumn 1976).

Kimberlin, Cynthia Tse. "The Scholarship and Art of Ashenafi Kebede (1938–1998)." *Ethnomusicology* 43, no. 2 (Spring–Summer, 1999).

Lepisa, Abba Tito. "The Three Modes and the Signs of the Songs in the Ethiopian Liturgy." *Proceedings of the Third International Conference of Ethiopian Studies*, Vol. II. Addis Ababa, 1966.

Martin, György. "Dance Types in Ethiopia." *Journal of the International Folk Music Council* 19 (1967).

"Netsite for the Music in the Horn of Africa," accessed January 7, 2008, http://www.uni-mainz.de/Organisationen/ETHIOPIA/music/index.html.

Pankhurst, Sylvia. *Ethiopia: A Cultural History.* Essex, England: Lalibella House, 1955.

Powne, Michael. *Ethiopian Music: An Introduction.* London: Oxford University Press, 1968.

Shelemay, Kay Kaufman. "The Musician and Transmission of Religious Tradition: The Multiple Roles of the Ethiopian Dabtara." *Journal of Religion in Africa* 22, Fasc. 3 (August 1992).

Shelemay, Kay Kaufman. *A Song of Longing: An Ethiopian Journey.* Urbana: The University Press, 1991.

Shelemay, Kay Kaufman, Peter Jeffery, and Ingrid Monson. "Oral and Written Transmission in Ethiopian Christian Chant." *Early Music History* 12 (1993).

"Teddy Afro: Ethiopian Pop Music Artist," accessed February 6, 2008, http://issues-in-focus.blogspot.com/2008/01/teddy-afro-ethiopian-pop-music-artist.html.

Index

About the Authors

SOLOMON ADDIS GETAHUN was born and raised in Ethiopia. He earned his BA and MA in Ethiopian history from the Addis Ababa University, Addis Ababa, Ethiopia, in 1985 and 1994, respectively. He received his PhD in African history from Michigan State University in 2005. He is currently an associate professor at Central Michigan University. Some of Professor Getahun's publications include "Sedät, Migration, and Refugeeism as Portrayed in Ethiopian Song Lyrics." *Diaspora: A Journal of Transnational Studies* 15 (2011): 341–359 and *The History of Ethiopian Immigrants and Refugees in America, 1900–2000: Patterns of Migration, Settlement, Survival and Adjustment* (New York: LFB Scholarly Publishing LLC, 2007).

WUDU TAFETE KASSU, PhD, is an assistant professor of history at the Addis Ababa University (AAU), Ethiopia. He earned his PhD from the University of Illinois at Urbana-Champaign in 2006. His dissertation, "The Ethiopian Orthodox Church, the Ethiopian State and the Alexandrian See: Indigenizing the Episcopacy and Forging National Identity, 1926–1991," is one of the few studies that examines church and states relation in 20th-century Ethiopia. Dr. Kassu has published half a dozen articles focusing on the various aspects of the Ethiopian Orthodox Tewahedo Church and the resistance movement against the Italian occupation (1936–1941) in Wag, Wollo Province, northeastern Ethiopia.